Treasure hunting is rapidly becoming one of America's most fascinating hobbies. With the development of electronic metal locators such as the Fisher M-Scope, it is now possible to locate metal bodies hidden from view under the surface of the earth.

What the term "treasure" means to the individual varies. To one person it could be only jewels and gold. While this is entirely possible, to others it could mean souvenirs and trinkets of by-gone days. This booklet is designed to help the latter.

The metal locator is being sold by the thousands, and it provides a tool for the search. The big problem to most people is where to look. For the most fruitful searching it is necessary to have permission to search over private property or open ground that is government land.

While it is not possible to dig up the streets of Tombstone, and you will probably be frowned upon for digging in its vicinity, there are still many places in Arizona that beckon the treasure hunter.

The trick of the hunt is to find some spot used long ago that has vanished from the present memory of man. To find the site of a long abandoned ranch house, a dried water hole, or an old mine may take a great deal of patience, and the results are always in doubt until worked.

However, if you are the type of searcher who would thrill at the discovery of an old knife or rusted gun barrel, this hobby is for you and this booklet will be a help. Find the places that "used to be" and they will provide the thrill of the hunt. Not the usual haunts of the ghost town fan or the well-traveled roads, but the out-of-the-way places are the best fields. And remember, you do not have to look in a town site. The bend of a road or the vicinity of a shade tree can also produce good results. Once located, a covered dump site can sometimes provide hours of happy digging.

For the browsing surface scratcher, the folded map at the back of the booklet will provide plenty of leads. Some of these places have not been visited for years, but they are out there somewhere. Others have not been properly searched. You have to be a real enthusiast to brave the desert, survive the heat, and still have energy and enthusiasm left to walk, hunt and dig. The map shows many places that are still active today where treasure hunting would be impossible, but there are many others just waiting for exploration.

Treasure hunters have the thrill of searching an unknown for something of interest or value. For only they can know the exhilarating chill that comes when the "treasure" comes into view. The locator buzzes, you dig and then the find is located. It could be a gun, a pioneer tool, or a bandit's loot. Treasure hunters experience the same excitement of the hunter or fisherman. The treasure is there waiting to be discovered.

The professional will spend a great deal of time on research. Where was the bandit last seen with the loot? Where was the house located when the flash flood hit? What was the size of the treasure? At what bend of the road did the stage coach tip over? How near the surface might it be? What other landmarks will help pin-point the spot?

The vacation-time hunter usually wants plenty of action, good country, and a few simple rewards for his efforts. Any intelligent use of the simple materials at hand will give him all these, and in addition he will be able to tell stories that will rival those of the most ardent fisherman.

The use of an M-Scope narrows the search. It will give you a place to dig, and happily you will not have to go too deep. The hunting is fun, but the digging is hard work and can be boring. Since even the remotest area of the desert seems to have an under-coating of tin cans, you usually do not want to dig too deep. Unless you have a specific important lead on the treasure, it is most fruitful and delightful to have many small excavations rather than one major effort.

Railroad rights-of-way and abandoned road beds may also produce results. Bottles were thrown from windows of trains and from wagons. Work crews left evidence of passing. Sometimes mistakes were made and the wrong item discarded. Today it could be considered treasure.

Treasure hunting may not always be considered easy, but it can be tempered to your own needs. You can hunt long hours or a few minutes at a time. You can walk long distances or practically not at all. It can be great out-of-door family fun for those who do not wish to hunt, fish or collect rocks, or you can combine all of the activities in one effort for greater activity. Except for the real pro, treasure hunting can be great fun and produce its share of interesting trophies.

As in every activity, there are do's and don'ts and a few common sense rules. Be sure to read the page relative to the desert rules of decency and basic safety suggestions. These may appear simple, yet they save lives.

Happy treasure hunting.

THERON FOX

March 1, 1964

ARIZONA

TREASURE HUNTERS GHOST TOWN GUIDE

COMPILED BY THERON FOX

Includes

1881 Fold-In Map of Arizona

with glossary of over 1200 place names

1868 Map of Arizona

Handy reference for locating

Old Mining Camps — Ghost Town Sites

Mountains — Rivers and Creeks

Railroads — Abandoned Roads — Forts

Indian Reservations — Cañons and Passes

Nevada Publications

4135 Badger Circle, Reno,

Nevada 89519

Photos by Nell Murbarger

ARIZONA TERRITORY

Historical and Descriptive.—The Territory of Arizona is situated between latitude 31° and 37° north, and longitude 109° and 114° 40′ west; and is bounded on the north by Utah, on the east by New Mexico, on the south by Mexico, and on the west by California. Its area is 113,916 square miles, or 72,906,240 acres, of which 67,098,366 are unsurveyed. That portion of the Territory lying north of tne Gila river was acquired by the treaty with Mexico, signed at Guadalupe Hidalgo, Feb. 2, 1848, and that south of it was bought from Mexico under the Gadsden treaty of Dec. 30, 1853, it being desired to straighten the southern frontier, and to acquire what were believed to be mineral lands of much value. Arizona was made a Territory by the act of February 24, 1863, prior to which time it had formed a part of New Mexico. It is divided into ten counties.

Arizona was first visited by Spanish exploring parties as early as 1526. They found there indications of mineral wealth, but also warlike and hostile Indians, so that they made but few settlements, and the country was but little better known when it passed into the hands of the Americans than it was 300 years before. The middle and northeastern portions of the Territory consist of plateaus which have an elevaticn of from 3,000 to 8,000 feet above the sea, and are here and there dotted by volcanic cones rising 2,500 feet above the plateaus. The southern portion is a plain with a slight elevation above the sea, amounting to only 200 feet at the mouth of the Gila. The mountain ranges, of which there are many, have generally a northwest and southeast course, with the exception of the Mogollon range, in the east, which runs nearly east and west, joining the Sierra Blanca. The Sierra Prieta, and the Aztec range, in Central Arizona, are flanked by foot-hills, which sink gradually to the level of the table land on the northeast, and of the *mesas* sloping toward the Colorado river in the southwest. The highest mountain is the San Francisco, a volcanic cone, whose summit is 11,000 feet above the sea. The Colorado, which is the largest and the only navigable river, is formed by the junction, in Southern Utah, of the Green and Grand rivers, and flows southerly along the western boundary of Arizona, emptying into the Gulf of California just south of the southern line of the Territory. This river has during the course of centuries cut for itself a deep channel through the rocks, so that for long distances it flows between perpendicular walls 7,000 feet in height. It is navigable for a distance of 612 miles from its mouth; above that point it becomes shallow, except in the rainy season, has a very swift current and is filled with rapids. Its principal tributaries are the Gila, which has its source in New Mexico and flows in a southwesterly course, until it joins the Colorado about 180 miles above the Gulf of California; the Colorado Chiquito, which rises in the northwest; and Bill Williams fork.

The climate is mild and generally healthful, lung and malarious diseases being almost unknown. The summer temperature of the treeless plains in the south is intensely hot, the thermometer often indicating 118° Fahrenheit, and rarely falling in winter below 34°. In the central and more elevated portion of the Territory the temperature is moderate, seldom exceeding 90° in summer. Snow falls on the mountains, but remains only a short time. The rainfall along the Gila averages from four to five inches, while at the base of the range, it rises to twenty-five or thirty. Showers are most frequent in July and August.

There was not a mile of railroad in the Territory in 1877. During 1878, thirty miles were constructed; in 1879, 152; and in 1880, 198, making a total at the present date of 380. The rapid progress made during the last two years is due to the effort to push forward to completion the Southern Pacific railway, which crosses the Territory from west to east. The building of this road has given a great impetus to the mining interest of the Territory.

DIAGRAM SHOWING THE RELATIVE STRENGTH OF RELIGIOUS DENOMINATIONS IN THE TERRITORY OF ARIZONA.

(The small squares or subdivisions represent the number of ministers in the denomination.)

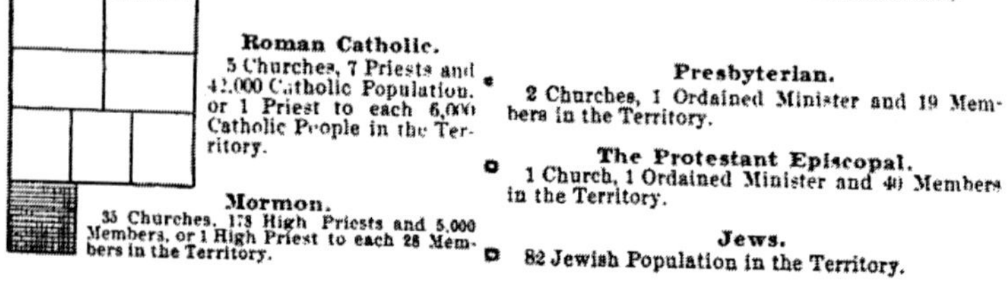

Mines and Minerals.—No part of the United States is more richly endowed by nature with mineral wealth than Arizona, but it is only within a few years that the development of its resources has been commenced. Up to a late period there were no railways in the Territory, and the cost of transporting the products of the mines was so great as to make it impossible to work them profitably. Besides this, the Apaches, one of the most savage and warlike of the Indian tribes, having their homes in the inaccessible fastnesses of the mountains, have often made it unsafe for white men to live outside the towns or the garrisoned forts. But the Indians have now been subdued, the United States and Mexico co-operating against them, and, as one of the continental railways has been completed across the Territory, this will speedily become one of the great mining districts of the West. Nearly all the mountain ranges are mineral-bearing, and contain lodes of gold, silver, copper and lead. The silver ores found are argentiferous galena, native silver and sulphates and sulphurets of silver. The copper ores are usually the sulphurets. Traces of gold are found at numerous points, but the richest mines yet discovered are in Yavapai county, where gold is obtained in the sands of the gulches and also in the quartz, slate and talcose rocks. The production of bullion in 1879 was $1,900,000, and in 1880, $4,500,000. The carbonates and oxides of iron are abundant, and traces of tin and nickel are found. Near Callville are remarkable salt mountains, whose extensive deposits of pure and transparent salt have been worked to some extent. There are indications of coal in this vicinity. Excellent lime is found in large quantities, and there are beds of gypsum in several localities.

Agriculture.—Here, as in New Mexico, agriculture can generally be carried on only where irrigation is practicable, which applies to about five per cent. of the total area. There are desert tracts covered with shifting sands, which are utterly unfit for cultivation, and much of the Territory south of the Gila is an arid waste, where only the cactus will grow. But the soil in the river bottoms and in the mountain valleys of Middle and Eastern Arizona, is of great richness, and often bears two crops a year, corn being planted after wheat or barley has been harvested. All the cereals, potatoes, and grapes, oranges and other fruits, produce abundant harvests wherever water can be obtained. When the Spaniards first visited the country, they found in the valley of the Gila the ruins of numerous Indian dwellings and the remains of irrigating canals, indicating that at one time that now desolate region had been thickly settled and well cultivated. There is much land which, while not suited for agriculture, is yet admirably adapted for stock-raising. The ground is covered with a luxuriant growth of rich gramma and bunch grass, and, owing to the warmth of the climate, no shelter is needed for cattle during the winter season. There were in 1880, 145,000 head of cattle, 1,326,000 sheep, and 9,700 swine.

Pine and cedar grow on the mountains in the central and northern part of the Territory, and walnut, cherry and cottonwood are found along the streams. On the plains south of the Gila only the cactus, artemisia and mesquite can live.

Government, etc.—Like the other Territories, Arizona has a governor and secretary and three supreme court judges, all appointed by the president, and confirmed by the senate. The Territorial legislature of two branches, and a delegate to Congress, are elected by the people. The free schools are supported by a tax of ten cents on each $100 of property, and such other taxes as county supervisors, or boards of trustees of school districts, may see fit to levy. There were by the last report 3,089 children of school age—six to twenty-one—of whom 2,740 were enrolled, the average attendance being 890. There was paid teachers, $14,947; for all school purposes, $21,396. The population of Arizona, according to the census of 1870, was 9,658; and in 1880, 40,441. There were 20,800 Indians, all of whom are peaceful, with the exception of the Apaches. The assessed valuation of property was: Real estate, $2,512,985; personal property, $2,849,918; total, $5,362,903; actual value, $8,043,000. The county indebtedness is $277,136. The expenditures for Territorial purposes are small. Nineteen newspapers are published, six being dailies. There are six banks. The internal revenue collections were in 1879, $24,470. Prescott is the Territorial capital. The laws are in nearly all respects similar to those of California.

ARIZONA--RAILROADS.

1 **Southern Pacific.** Wells, Fargo & Co.'s Express.
Yuma City, A 20, to El Paso, Mexico. leaving the State at San Simon, W 23.

Photos by Nell Murbarger

Counties.

County	Map	Pop. '80.
Apache	T-10	5,283
Maricopa	L-18	5,689
Mohave	D-9	1,190
Pima	Q-23	17,007
Pinal	O-19	3,044
Yavapai	K-10	5,013
Yuma	D-18	3,215
Total Population		40,441
Cachise	U-24	
Gila	Q-17	
Graham	U-18	

Canons.

Arivaypa......R-20
Blue Rock....M-16
Canebreak.....B-19
Canon........V-24
Canon..........R-7
Canon..........D-9
Canon........V-21
Canon de Chelly...........W-6
Canon Diablo .O-11
Clear.........M-13
Crow..........D-12
Deadman's...N-16
Dry Beaver....M-13
Gila...........Q-19
Gold..........P-22
Grand Canon of the Colorado.E-8
Hell...........J 12
Hog............R-19
Horseshoe....W-25
Iceberg........D-7
Lower Paria....M-4
Marble.........K-7
Muddy....... G-11
Queen........N-19
Quirino.......W-10
Rattlesnake...J-12
Salt River.....O-17
San Carlos.....S-18
Turkey.......K-12
Virgin.........C-7
White River..V-25

Mining Districts.

Ajo Mine–Copper.......H-22
Aqua Fria....K-15
Arco Mines...P-18
Arivaca.......W-25
Arnold Mines.D-13
Aubrey.......D-14
Aztec.........P-23
Belcher Mines.P-18
Bigbug.......K-14
Bill Williams Fork......D-15
Black Canon..K-15
Bronco Mine...S-25
Bronco Mines.A-19
Buena Vista Mines.....B 19
Burning Coal Beds.......S-6
Burro Mine...F-13
Castle Dome...C-20
Cedar Valley..D-13
Centennial Mine......F-13
Cerro Colorado Mine......O-25
Champion Mines.....Q-18
Cherry Creek..L-13
Clifton........W-19
Coal Region....S-6
Colorado MineM-25
ColoradoMinesB-18
Congress MineD-12
Copper Mines.D-16
Copper Mines.V-19
Copper Mines.N-23
Cormorant Mines.....B-20
Cumberland Mine......H-16
Cumberland Mines.....H-15
De Frees.....R-19
DiamondBasinR-18
Diamond FieldsT-4
DiscoveryMineT-25
Dos Cabezas...V-22
Empire Mines.P-18
Esperanca Mines.......O-24
Essex Mines..O-18
Eureka.......A-19
General Lee Mines.......Q-18
Gleason MinesQ 18
Globe.........Q-18
Gold and Copper Mines....C-20
Gordon Mine..T-25
Greenwood....F-13
Hanibal MinesQ-17
Harcuvar......D-16
Hartford MinesP-18
Hassa Yampa.J-14
Heintzelman Mines.......M-25
Henry Clay Mines.......Q-18
Hershaw Mine Q-26
Hidden Treasure Mines...O-18
Hope..........D-14
Huachuca.....R-26
Hualapai......C-10
Humbug......J-15
La Paz........C-17
Las Flores Mines.......B-20
Lead Mines....C-19
Los Alamos Mine........N-25
Lynx Creek...J-13
Martinez......H-15
Maynard......D-11
Mine..........V-23
Mineral.......P-19
Mines.........H-23
Mines..........K-5
Mines..........E-6
Mines..........G-7
Mines.........C-20
Montezuma Mine........N-23
Mowry's Mine.Q-26
Mulberry Camp.......D-12
Myers.........H-21
Old Hat.......Q-22
Omega Mines.D-14
Oro Blanco....O-26
Oro Mine......E-15
Ostrich Mine..O-26
Owens........E-14
Patagonia.....Q-26
Patagonia Mine........Q-26
Pima.........O-24
Pima Mines...O-24
Pinal..........P-19
Pine Grove....K-15
Pioneer.......O-18
Planet Mines..D-15
Bandolph.....O-18
Richmond Mines.......G-13
Sa. Catarina...Q-22
Salero Mine...P-25
San Francisco:B 11
San Xavier Mines.......O-24
Silver..........B-19
Silver BillMineP-26
Silver King Mines......O-18
Silver Queen Mines.......O-18
Sky BlueMinesO-18
Stonewall Jackson Mines...Q-17
Surprise Mines O-18
Summit......O-18
Swisshelm....V-25
Tabo Mine....M-25
Tiger..........J-13
Tinaja Mines..O-24
Tombstone....T-25
French Mine..Q-26
Turkey Creek..J-14
Tyndall.......P-25
Vernon Mines.A-18
Vulture Mine.H-16
Walnut Grove.J-14
Weaver........B-18
Weaver No. 2..I-15

Indian Reservations.

Colorado......B-16
Navajoe........V-6
Papago........O-23
Pima..........L-17
Pima and Marigora.......L-19
White Mo'nt'n.S-17

Springs.

Bear Spring...K-11
Coal Oil Spring .I-7
Grapevine Sp'gO-16
Mear's SpringsH-14
Pah-ghun Spr'gD-6
Pine Spring... G-8
Washie-pah-ghun Spring.E-5
Water Spring..L-6
Yellow Rock Spring...... H-4
Jacob's Well..V-11
Tousand Wells P-6

Lakes.

Laguna.......B-16
Laguna.......P-14
Laguna........S-7
Laguna........T-6
Laguna........R-6
Laguna........R-5
Laguna Esperanco....... K-25
Ojo Limita.....S-5
Red............D-9

Passes.

Alison Pass..O-26
Apache Pass..V-23
Chaves Pass...O-12
Dragon Pass..T-24
Eagle Pass....S-20
Ewell's Pass..S-23
Explorers PassB-20
Mule Pass.....T-25
Pinal Pass....Q-19
R. R. Pass....U-22
Sitgreaves PassC-11
Sunset Pass...P-12
Union Pass....B-11
Weaver Pass..B-17

Creeks.

- Aliso.........Q-18
- Aqua Fria.....K-16
- Arivapa.......R-20
- Ash N-14
- Ash S-18
- Babocomari ...S-25
- Badger........M-4
- Bear..........V-23
- Bog...........M-15
- Bonito D-11
- Boulder.......G-13
- Burro.........F-13
- Butler R-16
- Camp.........L-16
- Canon........Q-16
- Canon N-17
- Carrizo U-11
- Carrizo.......R-16
- Castle........O-17
- Cataract I-8
- Cave K-16
- Cedar.........S-16
- Cedar..........J-9
- Charco de Roth J-24
- Cherry P-16
- Cibicu R-16
- Cliff..........F-11
- Coon R-16
- Cottonwood ..R-11
- Cubico........R-15
- Date G-14
- Deer Q-19
- Deer..........Q-15
- Deluge Wash.E-12
- Dragoon K-12
- Dry Wash N-9
- Dry Wash.....F-19
- Dry Wash......I-24
- Dry Wash......N-9
- Eagle V-19
- Fossil M-14
- Gothic........W-4
- Graham M-15
- Granite........J-13
- Granite Wash.D-16
- Grapevine.....E-11
- Greenback N-16
- Grove.........L-15
- Hardscrabble..M-14
- Hassayampa...I-17
- Hassayampa...I-15
- Humbug J-15
- Island.........P-17
- Kirkland......H-13
- Krauss........M-14
- Limestone......M-16
- Lithodondron.U-11
- Locust Q-15
- Main Beaver..M-13
- Mescal........R-19
- Middle Fork....J-9
- Milpa..........T-17
- Mineral P-19
- Mineral.......U-14
- Neutroso.... .W-15
- North Fork or Blue.......W-18
- Oak Q-15
- Oak L-12
- Oak L-14
- Oak N-15
- Parke K-9
- Partridge I-11
- Pinal.........P-17
- Pine O-17
- Pine,.........N-14
- Pinery........V-23
- Pinto.........P-17
- Prospect R-22
- Prospectors....V-24
- Pubelo Colorado T-9
- Red...........M-15
- Rice. M-16
- Rock M-14
- Rock G-13
- Rock Q-19
- Saddle Q-19
- San Francisco.F-12
- Short H-4
- Showlow S-14
- Silver.........S-14
- Skulls.........O-17
- Soap L-4
- Spencer F-13
- Sycamore......M-14
- Sycamore......H-13
- Sycamore......R-17
- Sycamore.....M-17
- Tonto........O-15
- Trout F-11
- Turkey........V-24
- Warm Water...N-4
- Willow........T-24

Valleys.

- Antelope Plains G-5
- Aqua Fria Valley.........K-13
- Aubrey Valley H-10
- Baboquivari Valley K-25
- Big Chino Valley I-12
- Bonito Valley .W-8
- Cactus Plain ..F-15
- Carrizo Valley W-14
- Cedar Valley..E-13
- Chemehuevis Valley C-14
- Colorado Valley B-16
- Cottonwood Valley A-10
- Date Creek Valley H-14
- Detrital Valley.B-8
- Ferguson Valley..........H-13
- Grass Valley ..S-21
- Green Valley .N-14
- Hanecras Plain D-17
- House Rock Valley K-4
- Hualapai Valley D-9
- Kirkland Valley I-14
- Little Colorado Valley O-9
- McMullen's Valley E-16
- Maricopa Pl'ns K-19
- Marshy Valley O-14
- Mint Valley ...I-13
- Mohave Valley A-12
- Nan-co-Weap Valley L-7
- Navajoe Valley U-8
- Nine Mile Valley J-4
- Open Plains...E-21
- Open Plains...L-18
- Open Plains...L-21
- Peeples Valley H-14
- Posas Valley. C-17
- Prospect Valley G-7
- Pueblo Valley.T-19
- Round Valley.G-11
- Sacramento Valley B-10
- Sonoyt Valley.I-24
- Sulphur Spring Valley U-23
- Truxton Valley F-9

Miscellaneous.

- American Flag C-12
- Aztec Mill Q-15
- Beales Road 1857 ....K-10
- Black Forest ...J-9
- Breaks L-7
- Capt. Sitgreave and Lt. Parke 1851.........H-10
- Cascades I-7
- Cedar Forest...G-9
- Cerros de Tecolote K-24
- Cienega..... .V-21
- Cienega W-25
- Coconino Caves O-10
- Coconino Forest K-8
- Colorado Forest H-7
- Deseret Telegraph H-4
- Ft. Defiance...W-9
- Fine Grazing and Timber.L-10
- Forest Dale...R-15
- Forest Lagoons H-8
- Fronteras Road U-25
- General Crook's Road R-14
- Gila and Salt River Base Line L-20
- Gila and Salt River Meridian K-17
- Heavy Pine Timber ... L-11
- Horsehead Crossing ..S-12
- Horse Tank...C-18
- Juniper Basin.F-11
- Lt. Ives' Trail..T-9
- Llanos Del Flores N-25
- Lower Crossing R-23
- Mohave and Prescott Road...H-12
- Monument.... P-26
- Monument S-26
- Moquis Q-8
- Moquis Domes.Q-9
- Morgan's R...Q-25
- Mormon Wagon Road N-6
- Navajoe Forest V-9
- Navajoe Mesa..U-4
- Navajos Trail..N-5
- Ochoas Q-25
- Old C F-11
- Old C.... .H-14
- Old Cal. Road..D-4
- Painted Desert.N-7
- Parker's R.....I-18
- Pass C-8
- Pioacho del Diablo P-25
- Placers O-18
- Placers B-20
- Placers Q-25
- Prieto Park . .U-18
- Proposed Road to Prescott ..J-16
- Pueblos........R-8
- Puerta de los Mulas T-26
- Rain Tanks. ...I-7
- Ruins..........R-7
- Ruins..........Q-6
- Ruins of Indian Villages N-9
- Ruins of Old Pueblo......P-22
- Salt Works....Q-17
- San Bernardino Flat W-26
- San Francisco Forest M-12
- San Simon....V-22
- Sheavwitz' Trail G-5
- Sierrita O-24
- Sink G-4
- Supposed Underground passage of Santa Cruz River M-21
- Tanks S-13
- Tenney's Gulch J-5
- Tonto Basin ..O-15
- Trail.........U-22
- Trail to Prescott C-15
- Trail to St. George..... ..D-5
- Underground passage of Rio de Sanz V-22
- Underground passage of White River U-25
- Water........ .R-7
- Waterhole R-24
- Whitelock's ..V-21
- White River Basin V-25

Mountains, Peaks, Hills, Etc.

Agassiz Peak.M-10
Antelope Peak.I-15
Apache Q-17
Aquarius......F-12
Artillery Peak.E-14
Atasooso O-25
Aubrey Cliffs...G-7
Baboquivari Peak........M-25
Backers Butte.N-13
Back Tank Mt.F-16
Big Horn......G-19
Bill Williams..K-11
Black A-10
Black Butte ..M-12
Black Canon Range........A-7
Black Hills ...K-13
Blue Mesa......I-8
Bold Hill......L-10
Boot Peak B-20
Bradshaw......J-15
Buckskin K-5
Buckskin, or KaibaPlateauK-5
Cababi........M-23
Cabeza Prieto.F-22
Calabasa........R-4
Canon Butte ..T-12
Carizo.........W-4
Castle Dome ..D-20
Castle Dome Rock........C-19
Cathedral Rock........E-19
Cayetan Mt....P-25
Cedar Knoll....H-4
Cherum Peak..C-10
Chevions Butte........Q-13
Chimney Peak.Q-9
Chimneys......J-19
Chiri Cahua..W-23
Chocolate......B-19
Chromo Butte.Q 18
Coronation Peak C-20
Cotto..wood Range.......E-11
Crater.........W-26
Cross G-11
Cygnus Peak..F-12
Date Creek....H-15
Desert Peak...O-21
Devin's Peak..R-15
Diablo Hills...E-22
Diamond Butte.F-5
Divide of Puerco and De Chelly.......W-7
Dome Rock Range.......B-18
Dragoon.......T-24
Eagle Tail.....E-19
Echo Cliffs M-5
El Rincon ....P 23
Emal Pais E-22
Frog Peak N-17
Galiuro R-21
Gemini Peak..G-12
Gila Bend .....H 19
Gila Peak.....S-18
Gila Plateau.W-20
Gila Range....T-19
Gila Range....C 22
Graham Peak.T-21
Granite Peak..I-13
Granite Peak..D-12
Granite Wash.D-16
Gray Peak....V-19
Green's Peak.U-15
Harcuvar E-16
Haroua-Hala ..F-17
Helen's DomeW-23
High Mesa P-8
Hopkins Peak.O-25

Huachuca.....R-26
Hualapai D-12
Humphreys Peak M-10
Hurricane Ledge........F-5
Ives Peak.....F-14
Jarito O-26
Jerked Beef Peak O-15
John Daisy Peak S-17
Juniper.......H-11
Kanab Plateau..I-5
Kelley's Peak.S-16
Kendrick H-14
Lana Negro.. Q-5
Las Quavitas..B-22
Lava Butte N-8
Lava Buttes ..N-10
Limestone S-23
Mal Pais O-25
Maxatzal N-15
Mesa Butte M-6
Mesa Butte L-9
Mesa La Vaca..S-6
Mescal Mountain Range P-19
Mogollon Q-12
Mohawk M....E-21
Mohawk Ra'ge F-21
Mohawk Summit E-21
Mohave Range B-13
Mt. Davis.....A-10
Mt. Floyd I-10
Mt. Hope R'geG-12
Mt. Kendrick . L-10
Mt. Ord..... .N-16
Mt. Sitgreave . L-10
Mt. Tipton.....C-9
Mt. Turnbull..R-19
Mt. Wrights . . P-25
Mule Pass.....T-25
Music.........E-9
Mustang R-25
Natane's ButteS-18
O'Leary'sPeak M-10
Orange Peak . W-21
Ord Peak U-16
Oro Blanco Peak.........O-26
Padricks A-21
Painted Rock . G-19
Paria Plateau . . L-4
Patagonia.......Q-26
Peacock E-10
Pedrogosa V-26
Peloncillo.... W-20
Picacho del Alma Puerto M-24
Picacho Peak.N-21
Picacho Peak. .I-11
Picacho Stat'nN-21
Picket Post Butte O-23
Pinal Summit.P-19
Pinaleno R'ngeT-21
Pinole Peak...O-15
Pinto Hills....E-22
Plateau........S-17
Plateau U-18
Plomas C-17
Pt.of MountainO-22
Pt. of MountainS-22
Poso Butte....C-21
Pottery Hills..Q-10
Powell's Plat'u.J-6
Prieto Plateau V-17
Promontory Peak P-14
Punta de Aqua P-23
Quartz Hill .P-19
Quigotoa L-24
Rabbit Hills..R-11
Red Butte......J-8

Red Mesa......H-9
Rincon R-23
River Mesa O-8
Rose Peak....V-18
Sa. Estrella...K-19
St. Prieta J-14
Salt River N-18
San Carlos Mt.R-17
Sand Dune Plateau........S-4
San Francisco.M-10
Santa CatarinaQ-21
Santa Maria ...I-13
Sanup Peak.....E-7
Sanup Plateau . E-7
Sa. Rita.......Q-24
Sa. Teresa.....S-20
Sentinel Mt...D-19
Sheavwitz F-7
Sheavwitz Plateau G-6
Sierra Colorado H-20
Sierra Colorado Q-23
Sierra de la Cabeza Prieto. F-22
Sierra de la Naril..........J-23
Sierra de la Petahaya W-18
Sierra del Ojo H-23
Sierra NatanesU-19
Sierra Tucson.N-22
Sierra Verde..M-25
Signal Butte...Q-9
Signal Butte...P-19
SilverBall PeakS-16
Solitaire Butte.F-5
Sombrero B'tteQ-16
Sonora Mesa..A-21
Spring Butte ..Q-9
Squash S-7
Squaw Peak...L-14
Stockton's R . M-10
Sugar Loaf Butte N-17
Summit J-19
Superstition ..N-18
Table Mt..... Q-20
The Needles..B-13
Thomas Peak.V-16
Tinajas Atlas..C-22
Tortila........P-20
Tortilita.......O-21
Triplets R-18
Turkey Hill...U-17
Twins Q-16
Verde L-15
Vermillion Cliffs M-4
Virgin Range..D-4
Weaver........I-15
WeaverNeedleN-18
Whetstone ... R-24
White V-16
White Bluffs . . K-7
White Ledge . . M-9
White Mesa....O-5

Rivers.

Beaverdam Wash D-4
Big Sandy F-13
Bill Williams' Fork E-15
Black R-17
Bonita Fork . . U-17
Colorado.......K-7
Diamond G-8
East Fork M-14
Gila E-20
Gila Bonita ...U-19
Grand Wash ...D-6
Headwaters of Little Colorado V-15
Kanab Wash ..I-15
Leroux Fork . . S-11
Little ColoradoQ-11
North Fork....T-16
Pha-ria M-4
Rio Carize.....U-5
Rio Puerco....T-12
Rio Verde M-15
Running WaterQ-4
Sacramento Wash B-12
Santa Cruz....O-25
Salt L-18
Salt U-17
San Carlos R-18
San FranciscoW-19
San Pedro Q-21
Santa Maria...G-14
Sherlou's ForkR-12
Sherlou's ForkQ-12
Virgin D-4
Wake UpWashD-13
White Mo'nt'nT-16
White Mo'nt'nS-17
Zuni U-13

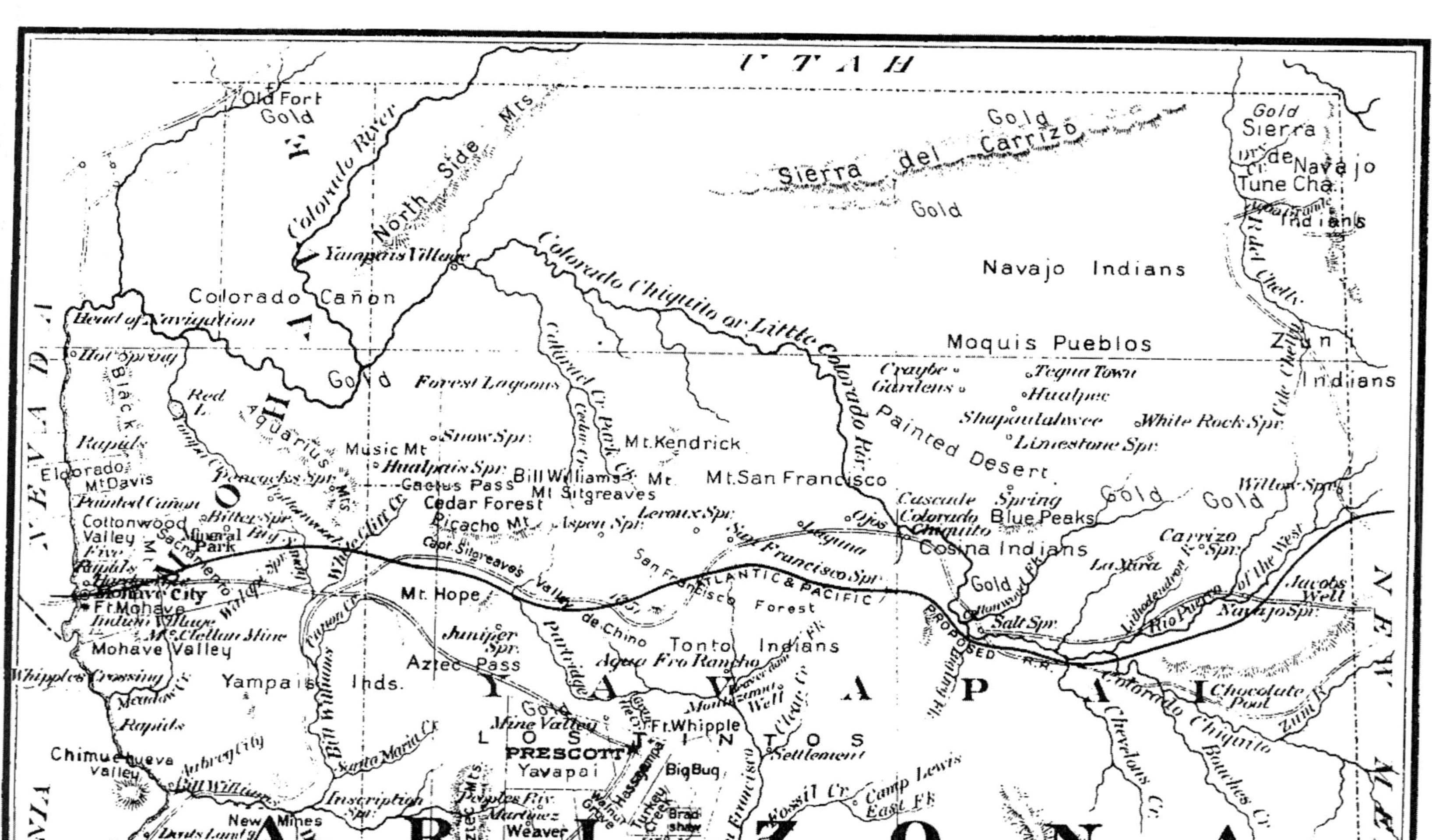

UTAH
NEVADA
NEW MEXICO
ARIZONA
YAVAPAI
Old Fort
Gold
Colorado River
North Side Mts
Yampais Village
Colorado Cañon
Head of Navigation
Hot Spring
Black
Rapids
Eldorado
Mt Davis
Painted Cañon
Cottonwood Valley
Mohave City
Ft Mohave
Indian Village
Mc Clellan Mine
Mohave Valley
Whipples Crossing
Meadow Cr.
Chimuehueva Valley
Aubrey City
Bill Williams
Red L.
Aquarius
Music Mt
Snow Spr.
Hualpais Spr.
Forest Lagoons
Cactus Pass
Bill Williams Mt
Mt Sitgreaves
Cedar Forest
Picacho Mt
Bitter Spr.
Mineral Park
Sacramento
Mt Hope
Juniper Spr.
Aztec Pass
Yampais
Inds.
Santa Maria Cr.
Inscription Spr.
New Mines
Mine Valley
Ft Whipple
PRESCOTT
Yavapai
Big Bug
Walnut Grove
Turkey Creek
Weaver
Bradshaw
LOS PINTOS
Settlement
Camp Lewis
East Fk
Mt Kendrick
Mt San Francisco
Colorado Chiquito or Little Colorado Riv.
Painted Desert
Sierra del Carrizo
Navajo Indians
Moquis Pueblos
Tegua Town
Hualpec
Shapaulahwee
Limestone Spr.
White Rock Spr.
Cascade Spring
Blue Peaks
Cosina Indians
Leroux Spr.
Aspen Spr.
Laguna
San Francisco Spr.
ATLANTIC & PACIFIC
PROPOSED R.R.
San Francisco Forest
Tonto Indians
Agua Fria Rancho
Partridge
de Chino
Salt Spr.
Carrizo Spr.
La Mira
Rio Puerco
Navajo Spr.
Jacobs Well
Chocolate Pool
Zuni R.
Chevelons Cr.
Colorado Chiquito
Bouches Cr.
Sierra de Tune Cha.
Navajo Indians
Zuni
Indians
R. del Chelly
Willow Spr.
Gold

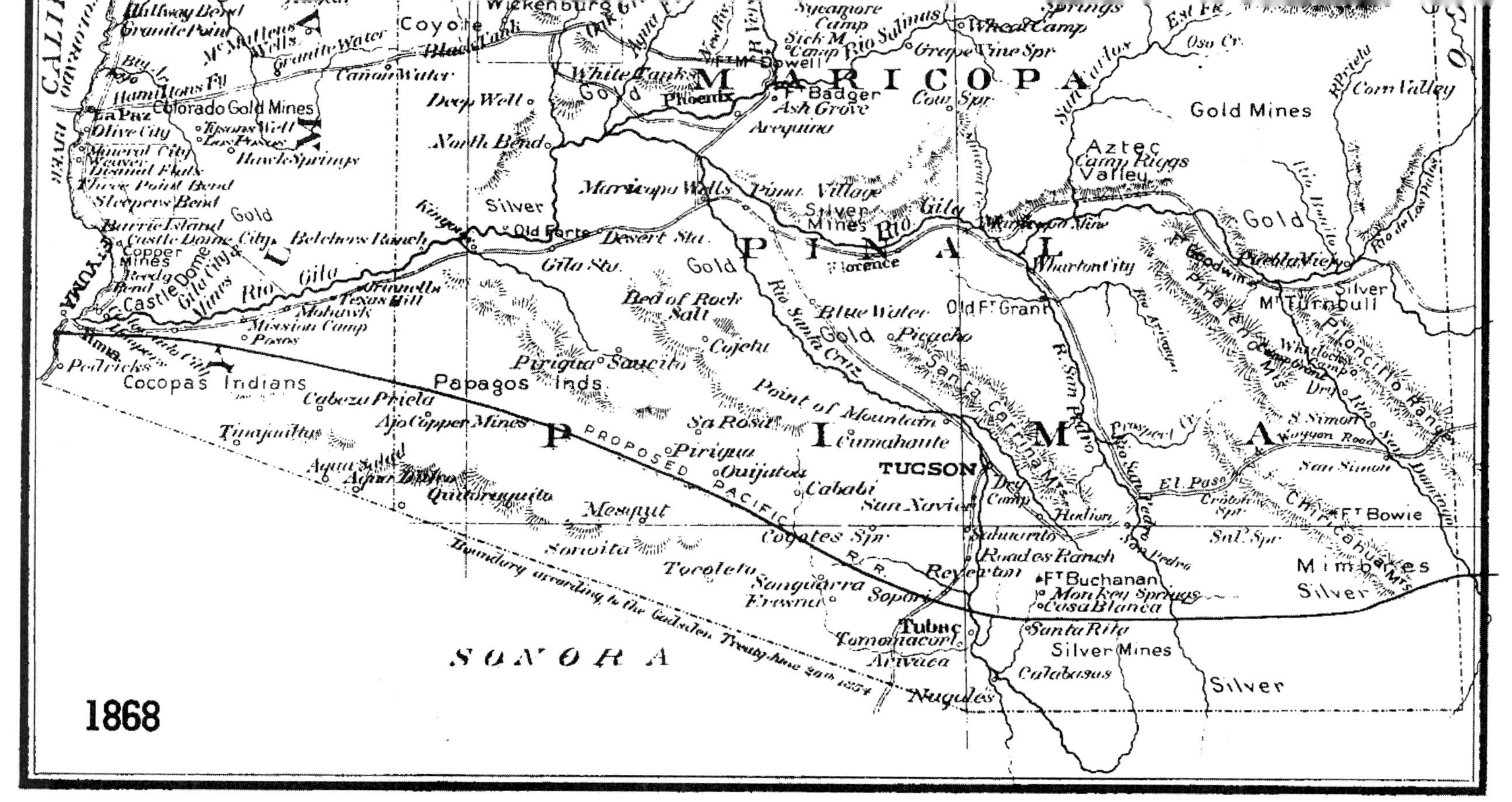

MARICOPA
PINAL
PIMA
SONORA
TUCSON
Phoenix
Florence
Tubac
Wickenburg
Coyote
Maricopa Wells
Kingston
Old Forte
Desert Sta.
Gila Sta.
Rio Gila
Rio Santa Cruz
R. San Pedro
Santa Catarina Mts.
Point of Mountain
Papagos Inds.
Cocopas Indians
Ajo Copper Mines
PROPOSED PACIFIC R. R.
Boundary according to the Gadsden Treaty June 29th 1854
Ft. Buchanan
Monkey Springs
Casa Blanca
Santa Rita
Silver Mines
Calabasas
Nogales
Tumacacori
Arivaca
Ft. Bowie
Chiricahua Mts.
Mimbres
Silver
Gold Mines
Aztec
Camp Riggs
Valley
Gold
Old Ft. Grant
Wharton City
Ft. Goodwin
Mt. Turnbull
Pinaleno Mts.
Pinal Village
Picacho
Blue Water
Bed of Rock Salt
Colorado Gold Mines
Castle Dome
Colorado City
Yuma
La Paz
Olive City
Ft. McDowell
Ft. Badger
Ash Grove
White Tanks
Deep Well
North Bend
Cañon Water
Granite Water
Sycamore Camp
Wheat Camp
Grape Vine Spr.
Cow Spr.
Corn Valley
Sa. Rosa
Cumahante
Quijotas
Cababi
San Xavier
Saguarito
Roades Ranch
Reventon
Sopori
Mesquit
Sonoita
Tinajaitas
Cabeza Prieta
Quitobaquito
San Pedro
Rio San Pedro
El Paso
San Simon
Rio San Domingo
Pioncillo Range
Silver
1868

Photos by Nell Murbarger

Counties and Towns

Pop. '80.

*Abbyes' Spring, Yuma, 10 m S W King's Well, F-16.
Adamsville, Pinal, N-19, *mail* Florence.
Aoonde, Yuma, C-21, (Ry 1) *mail* Yuma.
Agency, Apache, W-8, *mail* Ft. Wingate.
*Agency, Apache, S-8.
Agency, Yuma, B-15, *mail* Parker.
Agua Fria Valley, Yavapai, 15 m E Prescott 46
*Agua Grande, Apache.
*Ajo Copper Mines, Pima, H-22.
*Albino, Yuma, C 22.
*Alexandra, Mohave, A-11.
Alexandra, Yavapai, J-14.
*Al-too-bah Springs, Mohave, D-9.
American Flag, Pima, 44 m N E Tucson, P-23.
Antelope, Yavapai, *mail* Wickenburgh, I-15.
Antelope, Yuma, D-21, *mail* Yuma.
Antelope Spring, Yavapai, F-4.
Antelope Valley, Yavapai.
Apache Pass, Pima, V-23, *mail* Fort Bowie.
*Apache Spring, Apache, S-15.
*Apache Spring, Apache, T-15.
Aqua Caliente, Maricopa, G-19, *mail* Sentinel.
*Aqua Fria Station, Maricopa, K-17.. 40
*Aqua Viboras, Apache, N-10.
Arivaca, Pima, N-25 200
Arizona City, Yuma, 2 m S E Yuma, *mail* Yuma.
*Arizona Consolidated Mill, Yavapai, 20 m S E Prescott, J-13.
Ash Creek, Yavapai, *mail* Cienega.
*Ash Creek Station, Apache, T-18.
*Ash Spring, Pima, W-20.
Aubrey, Mohave, C-14 250
Aztec, Pima, 10 m N E Calabasas, *mail* Tubac.
*Aztec Tank, Yavapai, K-8.

*Bagley's Yavapai, N-15.
Bates, Pinal, *mail* Riverside.
Batesville, Yavapai, *mail* Brigham City.
Beale's Spring, Mohave, C-11, *mail* Cerbat.
*Bear Spring, Yavapai, K-11.
*Bear Springs, Pima, 10 m S W Camp Grant.
Beaver Creek, Yavapai, *mail* Camp Verde.
Beaver Dam, Mohave, D-4.
Beaver Head, Yavapai, *mail* Camp Verde.
Bed Rock, Yavapai, J-14...... 150
*Belcher's, Yuma, 30 m N E Mission Camp.
Benson, Pima, R-24, (Ry 1).
Berks, Yuma, *mail* Yuma.
Big Bug, Yavapai, K-14.

Big Cottonwood, Pinal, *mail* Riverside.
*Big Horse Tank, Yuma, 20 m N E Eureka.
Big Pine Crossing, Apache, *mail* Saint Joseph

Bisbee, Pima, 38 m S E Charleston, S-25.
*Bitter Spring, Yavapai, M-5
*Bitter Spring, Mohave, 10 m N Cerbat, C-10.
Black Canyon, Yavapai, *mail* Gillett.
Black Fall, Yavapai, O-9, *mail* Brigham City.
Black River Station, Apache, T-17, *mail* Ft. Apache.
*Black Rock Spring, Mohave, D-4.
*Black Tank, Maricopa, 20 m S W Wickenburgh.
*Black Water Station, Pima, 65 m N W Tucson.
*Blind Tank, Yuma, 20 m N E Yuma.
Blue Spring, Apache, V-15, *mail* Springerville.
*Blue Water, Pinal, M-20.
Bowie, Pima, V-22, (Ry 1), *mail* Dos Cabezos.
Bradshaw, Yavapai, J-15 75
Bradshaw's Ferry, Yuma, 2 m N Olive City, B-17, *mail* Ehrenberg.
Brigham City, Apache, Q-11 191
Bronco, Pima, *mail* Tombstone.
Brush Valley, Apache, *mail* Saint Joseph.
*Buena Vista, Pima, 27 m E Fort Buchanan.
Bumble Bee, Yavapai, K-15.
*Burch's Ranch, Yavapai, N-14.
Burke's Station, Maricopa, G-20, *mail* Sentinel.
Barnell's Spring, Pima, S-24, *mail* Tombstone.

*Cababi, Pima, L-23.
*Cababi Mine, Pima, L-23.
*Cabeza Prieta, Yuma, 20 m S E Mission Camp, C-21.
Calabasas, Pima, P-26, *mail* Calabazas.
*Cachise Spring, Pima, T-24.
*Cajote Spring, Pima, N-24.
Calabazas, Pima, see Calabasas.
California District, Pima, *mail* Fort Bowie.
California Saw Mill, Pima, *mail* Fort Bowie.
Callabassus, Pima, *mail* Tucson.
Camp Apache, Apache, 35 m N E Triplets, *mail* Saint Joseph, S-12.
Camp Cameron, Pima, 30 m N Tubac, P-25, *mail* Tucson.
Camp Clark, Yavapai, 20 m S E Charming Da e, I-12. *mail* Prescott.

* **Not a Post Office, and no report received as to what Post Office mail should be addressed to reach this place.**

Camp Crittenden, *mail* Crittenden.
Camp Date, Yavapai, 20 m N W Walnut Grove, *mail* Walnut Grove.
Camp Dome, Yuma.
Camp Goodwin, Pima, *mail* Camp Thomas.
Camp Grant, Pinal, *mail* Fort Grant.
Camp Huachuca, Pima.
Camp Hualapai, Yavapai, changed to Charming Dale.
Camp Mohave, Mohave, *mail* Mohave City.
*Camp Reno, Maricopa, 20 m N W Grape Vine Spring.
*Camp Riggs, Pinal, 20 m W Triplets, R-18.
Camp Rucker, Pima, V-25, *mail* Ft. Bowie.
Camp Thomas, Pima, T-19 112
Camp Verde, Yavapai, L-13.......... 75
*Camp Wallen, Pima, 30 m S Dragoon Spring.
Camp Wood, Yavapai, *mail* Prescott.
Canefield Springs, Mohave, D-10, *mail* Hackberry.
Canoe, Pima, P-24, *mail* Tubac.
*Carrizo Creek, Maricopa, R-16.
*Carrizo Spring, Apache, V-10.
*Casa Blanca, Pima, Q-25.
Casa Grande, Pinal, M-20, (Ry 1) 33
Castle Dome Landing, Yuma, B-20.
Castle Dome Mining District Camp, Yuma, *mail* Castle Dome Landing.
Catalina, Pinal, 45 m N E Tucson, P-23.
*Cave Creek Station, Maricopa, L-16.
*Cave Dwelling, Apache, U-5.
*Cave Dwelling, Apache, T-4.
*Cave Spring, Yavapai, F-4.
*Cave Spring, Apache, U-14.
*Cedar Forest, Yavapai, G-9.
*Cedar Springs, Pima, S-20.
Cedar Valley, Mohave, *mail* Signal.
Centennial Station, Yuma, *mail* Wickenburgh.
Cerbat, Mohave, C-10.
Cerro Colorado, Pima, 20 m N E Fresnal, M-25, *mail* Arivaca.
Chanes Pass, Yavapai, *mail* Brigham City.
Charleston, Pima, S-25. 350
Charming Dale, Yavapai, I-12, *mail* Prescott 35
Cherry Creek, Yavapai, *mail* Camp Verde, Agua Fria Valley or Cienega.
Chimenoa, Mohave, *mail* Aubrey.
Chino, Yavapai, J-12.
Chiricahua, Pima, *mail* Fort Bowie.
Chloride, Mohave, C-10, *mail* Mineral Park.
*Cholla, Pima, M-24.
Cienega, Pima, *mail* Tucson, Q-23
*Cienega de los Pinos, Pima, 35 m N E Tubac, P-25.
Cienega, Yavapai, 30 m N E Camp Clark.
Clifton, Apache, W-19.
*Coal Spring, Apache, 3 m W Deer Spring, W-12.

Cojeta, Pinal, K-21, *mail* Casa Grande.
*Collins' Well, Yavapai, H-10.
*Colorado Bridge, Apache V-13.
*Colorado Chiquito, Yavapai, 25 m S E San Francisco Mountains, M-10.
*Colorado City, Yuma, 3 m W Yuma, A-20.
Colorado River Indian Agency Yuma, *mail* Parker
Connolly's, Graham, T-20, *mail* Solomonsville.
Contention City, Pima.............. 150
*Cooley's Ranch, Apache, T-14.
*Copori, Pinal, see Sopori, N 25.
Copper Canyon, Yavapai, *mail* Cienega.
*Corral, Pima, 15 m N E Cojeta, K-21.
*Corral, Yuma, E-22.
*Cosnino, Caves, Yavapai, 10 m S E San Francisco Mountains, M-10.
*Cottonwood, Mohave, D 6.
*Cottonwood, Maricopa, H-19.
Cottonwood, Pinal, O-19, *mail* Florence.
*Cottonwood, Pinal, P-20.
Cottonwood, Yavapai, J-13, *mail* Prescott.
*Cottonwood Spring, Mohave, F-11.
*Cottonwood Spring, Yavapai, 25 m S W Wolf Spring, I-4.
Cottonwood Station, Pinal, *mail* Riverside.
Cottonwood Station, Graham, S-20, *mail* Solomonsville.
*Cow Springs, Maricopa, 15 m N E Silver City, P-18.
Coyote Hole, Mohave, C-11, *mail* Hardyville
*Coyote Spring, Pima, 26 m S E Cababi, L-23.
Crittenden, Pima, Q-25.
Crook Mine, Yavapai, *mail* Prescott.
*Croton Spring, Cachise, T-23.
*Cullen's Well, Yuma, F-16.

Date Creek, Yavapai, H-14, *mail* Antelope Valley.
Davidson's Springs, Pima, *mail* Tucson, Q-23.
Davis' Mine, Yavapai, *mail* Prescott.
*Deep Well, Maricopa, 25 m W Phœnix, K-18.
*Deer Spring, Apache, W-12.
Defiance, Yavapai, *mail* Prescott.
*Defiance, Apache, 15 m N W Ft. Defiance, W-8.
*Dent's Landing, Mohave, 15 m S W Aubrey, C-14.
Desert, Pima.
Desert Station, Yuma, *mail* Wickenburgh, D-17.
*Desert Station, Maricopa, L-18.
*Di Noah Spring, Mohave, C-7.
Dos Cabezos, Cachise, V-22. 126
*Dragoon Spring, Cachise, T-24.
*Dragoon Summit, Cachise, S-23, (Ry 1).
*Dry Camp, Pima, 7 m N W Cienega, Q-23. (Ry 1).
*Dry Camp, Pima, 35 m N E Croton Spring, T-23, (Ry 1).
*Dunbar's Station, Pima, S-23, (Ry 1).

Eagle Creek, Apache, *mail* Clifton.
*East Phœnix, Maricopa, 3 m E Phœnix, K-18.
Ehrenberg, Yuma, B-17............. 248
*El Dorado Mill, Mohave, A-9.
El Dorado Ranch, Pima, *mail* Fort Bowie.
Ellen Gowan Mining Co., Yuma, *mail* Castle Dome Landing.
El Paso, Pima, *mail* Tubac.
*El Riverton, Pima, 15 m N W Tubac, P-25.
Empire, Pima, Q-24.
Empire Ranch, Pima, Q-24, *mail* Empire.
*Estrella, Maricopa, J-20, (Ry 1).
*Eureka, Yuma, 10 m N W Castle Dome Landing, B-20.
Eureka Springs, Pima, S-21, *mail* Ft. Grant.
Ewell, Pima, *mail* Dos Cabezos.
Ewell Springs, Pima, *mail* Dos Cabezos.

*Fisher's Spring, Yavapai, 15 m N E Prescott, J-13.
*Fish's Ranch, Pima, Q-25.
*Flint's, Yuma, E-16.
Florence, Pinal, N-19................ 902
Fordville, Pinal, *mail* Mesaville.
Forest Dale, Apache, *mail* Saint Joseph.
*Forest Lagoons, Yavapai, H-8.
Fort Apache, Apache, T-16.
Fort Bowie, Pima, V-23, *mail* Dos Cabezos........................ 184
Fort Bowie, Cachise, V-23.

*Fort Buchanan, Pima, 15 m N E Tubac, P-25.
Fort Defiance, Indian Res., *mail* Fort Wingate, N. M., W-9.
Fort Grant, Graham, T-21........... 243
Fort Lowell, Pima, P-23, *mail* Tucson 227
*Fort Mason, Yuma, 30 m W Wickenburgh, I-16
Fort McDowell, Maricopa, M-17, *mail* McDowell 250
Fort Mohave, Mohave, A-11, *mail* Mohave City 78
*Fort Pierce Spring, Mohave, 10 m W Cave Spring, F-4.
Fort Rock, Yavapai, *mail* Prescott.
Fort Rock, Mohave, *mail* Hackberry.
*Fort Rock Spring, Yavapai, 15 m S W Cottonwood Spring, F-11.
Fort Verde, Yavapai, *mail* Camp Verde, L 13.
Fort Whipple, Yavapai, J-13, *mail* Prescott 125
*Franklin Spring, Apache, T-14.
*Fremont, Pima, H-24.
Frenchman's, Maricopa, M-17, *mail* McDowell.
French Mine, Pima, *mail* Crittenden.
Fresnal Pima, M-25, *mail* Arivaca.

Galeyville, Pima, 50 m S E Willcox, T-22.
Galeyville, Cachise, W-24.
*Gibson's Ranch, Yavapai, N-15.
Gila Bend, Maricopa, I-20. (Ry 1) 45
Gila City, Yuma, B-21, (Ry 1) *mail* Yuma.
*Gila Tank, Maricopa, 20 m S Stanwix Station, G-20.
Gila Station, Maricopa, *mail* Gila Bend, I-20.
Gillett, Yavapai, K-15............... 125
Globe City, Gila, Q-18............ 704
Goodwin, Pima, S-19, *mail* Camp Thomas.
*Grand Fall, Yavapai, O-10.
*Grant, Pima, 20 m N Croton Spring, T-23.
Grape Vine Springs, Maricopa, *mail* Globe City, Q-18.
Greaterville, Pima, 12 m N E Empire Ranch, Q-24.
Greenwood, Mohave, *mail* Signal, E-14.
*Green's Camp, Graham, S-18.
*Grindstone Tank, Yavapai, G-9.
*Grinnell's Station, Maricopa, 8 m S W Burke's Station, G-20, (Ry 1).
Groom's Creek, Yavapai, *mail* Prescott.
*Grove of Robinson, Gila, O-16.

Hacienda del Santa Ritas, Pima, *mail* Tubac.
Hackberry, Mohave, E-11............ 32
*Hac-qua-halla Water, Maricopa, 15 m E King's Wells, F-16.
*Hanging Rock, Yavapai, I-4.
Happy Camp, Maricopa, J-19, *mail* Gila Bend.
*Harauwar Water, Yuma, 15 m N Cullen's Well, F-16.
Hardyville, Mohave, A-11............ 75
Harshaw, Pima.
*Hatche's Well, Yavapai, P-7.
Hawk Spring, Yuma, C 17.
Hayden, Maricopa, 18 m S E Phœnix, K-18.
Hayden's Ferry, Maricopa, *mail* Temple, L-18.
Hermasa, Pima, *mail* Crittenden.
Herrick's, Graham, T-20, *mail* Camp Thomas.
Hershaw District, Pima, *mail* Tucson.
Heslep's Saw Mill, Pima, *mail* Greaterville.
*Holmes' Station, Gila, Q-18.
*Hooker's Ranch, Graham, T-22.
*Hooker's Station, Cachise, R-23.
*Hooper's, Yuma, 10 m W Gila City.
*Hot Spring, Mohave, A-7.
*House Rock Spring, Yavapai, K-5.
Huachuca, Pima, *mail* Tucson...... 200
*Hualapai Spring, Mohave, D-11.
*Hual-pee, Apache, R-8.
Humbug, Yavapai, *mail* Gillett.
*Hunter's Ranch, Maricopa, I-19.
*Huston's Ranch, Yavapai, O-14.

*Indian Settlement, Yavapai, F-9.
*Inscription Sprin:, Mohave, F-15.
Iron Monument, Mohave, A-11, 5 m S Ft. Mohave, *mail* Mohave City.

*Jacob's Pools, Yavapai, L-5.
*Jacob's Well, Apache, W-11.
*Jones, Graham, T-19.

*Kent's, Yuma, 15 m W King's Wells, F-16.
*Kenyon's Station, Maricopa, H-19.

*King's Wells. Yuma, F-16.
*Kirkland's, Yavapai, 15 m W Prescott, J-13.
Kirk'and Valley, Yavapai, *mail* Prescott 35

La Concho. Apache. *mail* Saint Joseph.
*Laguna, Yavapai, L-11.
*Lambey, Maricopa, I-16.
*Lano Much. Apache, R-7.
*La Paz, Yuma, B-17.
*Las Posas, Yuma, C 17.
Lee's Ferry, Yavapai, M-4........... 12
*Leroux Spring, Yavapai, M-10.
Lewiston Valley, Pima, *mail* Crittenden.
*Lime Kiln. Yuma, B-16.
*Limestone Spring, Apache, R-9.
Little Cottonwood, Pinal, *mail* Florence.
Little Giant, Gila, Q-19.
*Little Steve Ranch, Graham, U-18.
*Liverpool Landing. Mohave, B-13.
*Log House. Apache, 25 m S W Jacob's Well, W-11.
*Lone Rock, Mohave, 20 m S Hot Spring, A-7.
*Longfellow, Apache, W-19.
*Long's, Cachise, S-23.
*Lookout. Pinal, Q-21.
*Los Gigantes, Apache, V-5.
Los Metates. Yuma, 5 m S E Gila City, B-21, *mail* Yuma.
*Los Nogales, Pima, P-26.
*Los Terases, Pima, O-24.
*Lov. Read Mine, Pinal, *mail* Riverside.
Lower Agua Fria, Yavapai, *mail* Cienega.
Luttrell, Pima.
Lynx Creek Mine, Yavapai, *mail* Prescott.
Lyson's Wells, Yuma, *mail* Ehrenberg, C-17.

McCrackin, Mohave, *mail* Aubrey.
McCrackin Hill, Mohave, *mail* Signal.
*McDougall's, Pinal, P-19.
McDowell, Maricopa, see Ft. McDowell, M-17.
McDowell, Cachise, S-26, *mail* Charleston.
*McGarry, Pima, R-25.
McMillenville, Gila, Q-17........... 150
*McMullen's, Yuma, E-16.
*Mammoth Tank, Yuma, 15 m N E Castle Dome Landing, B-20.
Maple Gulch, Yavapai, *mail* Prescott.
Maricopa. Pinal, K-19, (Ry 1)....... 96
*Maricopa Mine. Pinal, 15 m S E Riverside, P-19.
*Maricopa Wells, Pinal, K-19, (Ry 1).
Martina's Ranch, Yavapai, *mail* Wickenburgh.
*Maryville, Maricopa, M-17.
*Mascal Ranch, Pima, R-24, (Ry 1).
Maskeet Station, Yuma, *mail* Wickenburgh.
Mather Toontone, Maricopa, *mail* McMillen.
*Mazatzal City, Yavapai, N-14.
*Meadow Creek, Mohave, 15 m S E Ft. Mohave, A-11.
Mesa City, Maricopa, *mail* Tempe... 151
*Mesaville, Maricopa, M-18.
Mesaville, Pinal.
Mesca, Pima, R-24, (Ry 1) *mail* Benson.
*Mescal Ranch, Pima, Q-24.
*Mesquit, Pima, J-24.
Mesquite Station, Yuma, *mail* Ehrenberg.
Meyer's District, Yuma. *mail* Yuma.
Middle Crossing, Cachise, S-24, *mail* Benson.
Millville, Pima, *mail* Tombstone, or Charleston.
Millville, Yavapai, *mail* Brigham City.
Mineral City, Yuma, B-17, *mail* Ehrenberg.
Mineral Park, Mohave, C-10...... 318
Mingville, Pima, 52 m N E Fort Grant, T-21.
*Mining Camp, Gila, Q-19.
Minnehaha, Yavapai.
*Mission Camp, Yuma, C-21.
*Moccasin Spring, Yavapai, I-4.
*Moccasin Spring, Mohave, D-6.
*Moen Ava, Yavapai, N-7.
Mohave City, Mohave, A-11.
Mohave Valley, Mohave, *mail* Mohave City.
Mohawk, Yuma, *mail* Yuma, E-20.
*Mohawk Summit, Yuma, D-21, (Ry 1).
Moing Coppy, Yavapai, *mail* Brigham City.
Monkey Spring, Pima, Q-25, *mail* Crittenden.
*Montezuma Head Tank, Maricopa, K-19.
Montezuma, Pinal, *mail* Florence.... 37
*Montezuma Well, Yavapai, 30 m N E Prescott, I-13.
Monument, Cachise, S-26, *mail* Ochoaville.
Moore's, Graham, T-19, *mail* Camp Thomas.
*Moo-sha-neh, Apache, R-8.
Morgan Ferry, Maricopa, *mail* Maricopa.
*Mormon River, Apache, U-15.
Moss Mine, Mohave, *mail* Mohave City.
Mouncopy, Yavapai, *mail* Sunset.
Mountain Ranch, Yavapai, *mail* Wickenburgh.

*Mountain Spring, Mohave, B-9.
*Mountain Spring, Pima, Q-23.
*Mount Hope, Yavapai, G-12.
Moviabia, Yavapai, *mail* Brigham City.
Mule Pass, Pima, *mail* Tombstone.
*Munson's, Graham, R-18.
Myers' District, Maricopa, *mail* Sentinel.
Myres' District, Pinal, *mail* Maricopa.
Myres' District, Yuma, *mail* Yuma.

*Navajo Spring, Apache, V-11.
*Navajo Spring, Yavapai, M-5.
Navigo Springs, Apache, *mail* Saint Joseph.
*Nelson Tank, Yavapai, 28 m S San Francisco Spring, M-10.
*New Creek, Mohave, 35 m N E Mineral Park, C-10.
New River, Maricopa, *mail* Gillett.
New Virginia, Mohave, F-14, *mail* Signal.
*Nine Mile Station, Pima, P-22.
*Nine Mile Station, Yuma, B-21.
*Nobman's Ranch, Mohave, C-10.
*Norton's Landing, Yuma, *mail* Yuma.
Nugget, Maricopa, 12 m S Globe City, Q-18.

Oak Creek, Yavapai, *mail* Camp Verde.
Oaks and Willows, Yavapai, *mail* Prescott.
Oakvale, Pinal, *mail* Globe City.
*Oatman's Flat, Maricopa, G-19.
Ochoaville, Cachise, S-26 42
*Ojo de Casa, Apache, V-5.
*Ojo Puerta, Apache, U-5.
*Ojos Gallinas, Cachise, T-26.
*Old Camp Buchanan, Pima, Q-25.
*Old Camp Cameron, Pima, P-24.
*Old Camp Colorado, Mohave, B-15.
*Old Camp Grant, Pinal, Q-20.
*Old Camp Hualapai, Yavapai, H-12.
*Old Camp Rawling, Yavapai, I-12.
*Old Camp Reno, Gila, O-16.
*Old Camp Wallen, Pima, R-25.
Old Casa Grande, Pinal, *mail* Florence.
*Old Fort Breckenridge, Pinal, 1 m S Camp Grant.
*Old Fort Mason, Pima, P-26.
*Old Indian Agency, Cachise, V-24.
*Old Presidio of San Pedro, Cachise, S-25.
*Old Well, Pinal, N-18.
Olive City, Yuma, B-17, *mail* Ehrenberg.
Oracle, Pima, 36 m N E Tucson, P-23.
*Oraybe, Apache, Q-8.
*Oraybe Gardens, Apache, Q-8.
Oro, Apache, 4 m N Clifton, W-19.
Oro Blanco, Pima, N-26 400
*Ouijatia, Pima, see Quigotoa, L-23.
Overton, Maricopa, 30 m N Phœnix, K-18.
Orrville, Yuma, *mail* Plomosa.

Pacific, Yuma, 20 m N Castle Dome Landing, B-20, *mail* Yuma.
*Padrich's, Yuma, A-21.
Pajarito, Pima, 14 m E Oro Blanco, N-26.
*Painted Rock, Maricopa, H-20.
Pantano, Pima, Q-24, (Ry 1).
Papago, Pima, Q-23, (Ry 1), *mail* Tucson.
*Papago, Rancho, Pima, L-25.
Parker, Yuma, B-15.
Patagonia, Pima, Q-26, *mail* Camp Huachua.
*Peach Orchard Spring, Apache, R-8.
*Peach Springs, Mohave, F-9.
Peacock Spring, Mohave, D-10, *mail* Cerbat.
*People's Ranch, Yavapai, 10 m S Prescott, J-13.
Phœnix, Maricopa, K-18 1708
*Phœnix Park, Apache, Q-14.
*Phœnix Well, Maricopa, J-17.
*Piacho, Pinal, 25 m S Florence, N-19.
Picacho, Pinal, (Ry 1) 21 m S W Florence, N-19, *mail* Florence.
Picket Post, Pinal, *mail* Pinal, P-18.
Pima Agency, Pinal, *mail* Terminus.
Pima Station, Maricopa, *mail* Maricopa.
Pima, Pima, O-24.
Pima Village, Pinal, L-19, *mail* Maricopa.
Pinal, Pinal, P-18 166
*Pine Forest, Yavapai, 20 m N Collins' Well, H-10.
Pinery Camp, Pima, *mail* Fort Bowie.
Pine Spring, Yavapai, N-12.
*Pine Valley, Yavapai, M-14.
*Pipe Spring, Yavapai, I-4.
*Pirigua, Pima, J-22.
Planet, Mohave, *mail* Aubrey.
*Planet Town, Mohave, D-14.
*Playas de los Pimas, Pima, 10 m S Ft. Bowie, V-23.
Plomosa, Yuma, *mail* Centennial .. 39
*Pocomatte Spring, Yavapai, G-8.
*Point of Mountain, Cachise, 20 m N W Tucson, P-23.
*Posos, Yuma, 10 m S E Adonde, C-21.
*Pottery Hills, Apache, 20 m S W Limestone Spring, R-9.
Prescott, Yavapai, J-13 1836
*Providence Wells, Pima, 10 m S E Fresnal, M-25.
*Pueblo Colorado, Apache, 20 m S W Fort Defiance, W-8.
*Pueblo Viejo Ruin, Pima, near Pueblo Viejo, U-20.
*Pueblo Grande, Apache, U-10.
*Pueblo Tocalote, Apache, S-7.
Pueblo Viejo, Graham, *mail* Solomonsville, U-20.

Queen, Pinal, *mail* Pinal.
*Quigotoa, Pima, L-23.

Railroad Pass, Cachise, U-22, (Ry 1).
*Rain Tank, Yavapai, I-8.
*Rain Tank, Yavapai, J-8.
Ramboy, Pinal, *mail* Globe City.
*Ranch, Yuma, D-20.
*Ranch, Pima, R-24.

*Ranch, Yavapai, 15 m S W Prescott, J-13.
Rancherie, Mohave, *mail* Signal.
Randallville, Apache, *mail* Saint Joseph.
Redington. Pima, 40 m N Tres Alamos. R-23 53
*Red Rock, Pinal, N-21, (Ry 1).
*Reiley's Ranch. Cachise, T-22.
Reno, Maricopa, 60 m W Globe City. Q-18.
*Revanton, Pima, O-24.
Richmond, Cachise, *mail* Tombstone.
Richmond Basin, Maricopa, *mail* McMillen or Globe City.
*Richmond Reduction Works, Cachise, S-25.
Rigg's Ranch, Pima, *mail* Fort Bowie.
*Rillito, Pima, O-22, (Ry 1).
*Rio de Tres Alamos, Pima, 15 m S W Croton Spring, T-23.
Rio Verde, Yavapai. *mail* Camp Verde.
*Ritchell's Tank, Yavapai, M-9.
Riverside. Pinal, P-19 22
*Roades, Pima, O-24.
*Rocky Island, Yuma, 10 m N W Castle Dome Landing, B-20.
*Rodes Ranch, Yuma, 15 m S W Mineral City, A-17.
Rodye Creek, Yavapai, *mail* Johnson, Utah Ter.
Round Valley, Apache *mail* Saint Joseph.
*Round Valley, Pinal, O-20.
Rucker's Camp, Pima, *mail* Fort Bowie.
Ruggles & Ewing, Pinal, N-20, *mail* Florence.

Sacaton, Pinal, M-19, *mail* Terminus.
Safford, Graham, U-20 173
Saguarro, Pima, M-25, *mail* Arivaca.
*Salado Spring, Apache, V-14.
Salero, Pima, *mail* Tucson.
*Salt Spring, Mohave, B-7.
Sample Mine, Pinal, *mail* Riverside.
San Carlos, Graham, R-19, *mail* Camp Thomas.
San Carlos Indian Agency, Pinal, 34 m S Globe City, Q-18.
*Sancito, Pima, 15 m N W Pirigua.
Sanderson, Graham, T-20, *mail* Camp Thomas.
*Sand Spring, Cachise, V-26.
Sanford, Pinal, N-19, *mail* Florence. 39
*San Francisco, Yavapai, see San Francisco Spring, M-10.
San Francisco Spring, Yavapai, M-10.
San Jose. Graham, *mail* Solomonsville, U-20 186
San Joseph, Apache, S-12, *mail* Saint Joseph.
San Louis, Pima, N-26. *mail* Arivaca.
San Pedro, Pinal, *mail* Mesaville.
*San Pedro, Pima, 15 m E Cienega.
San Rafael, Pima, Q-26, *mail* Patagonia.
San Simon Station, Cachise, W-23, (Ry 1) *mail* Dos Cabezos.
Santa Rita, Pima, *mail* Tucson.
*Santa Rosa, Pima, K-22.
San Xavier. Pima, *mail* Tucson, P-23.
*Saquarra, Pima, see Saguarro, M-25.
*Sasabi Flat, Pima, 15 m W Fresnal, M-25.
*Saucita, Maricopa, I-21.
*Saurita, Pima, P-24.
*Saw Mill, Gila, Q-18.
*See-cho-mah-wee, Apache, R-8.
Selero, Pima, *mail* Tubac.
Senator Mine, Yavapai, *mail* Prescott.
Sentinal, Yuma, *mail* Yuma.
Sentinel, Maricopa, G-20.
*Settlement, Apache, V-14.
*Settlements, Yavapai, O-7.
Seymour, Maricopa, I-16 258
*Sha-pau-lah-wee, Apache. R-8.
*Sheep Ranch, Maricopa, M-16.
Show Low, Apache.
*Shung-o-pah-wee, Apache. Q-8.
*Sickman's Camp, Maricopa, 8 m N E Fort McDowell.
Signal City, Mohave, E-13 75
Silent, Yuma, 35 m W Camp Thomas, T-19.
Silver Belt, Yavapai, *mail* Agua Fria Valley.
*Silver City, Pinal, P-18.
Silver Dist. Camp, Yuma, *mail* Castle Dome Landing.
Silver King, Pinal, O-18............. 180
Skull Valley, Yavapai, *mail* Prescott.
*Sleeper's Bend, Yuma, 14 m N W Castle Dome Landing, B-20.
*Smith's Mill, Maricopa, 5 m S Lambey, I-16.
Smithville, Yavapai, L-13, *mail* Cienega.
Smithville, Pima, *mail* Safford...... 148
*Snively's Spring, Yavapai, K-11.
Snow Flake, Apache, S-14 275
*Snow Spring. Yavapai, 5 m S Pocomatte Spring, G-8.
Soap Creek, Yavapai, *mail* Johnson, Utah Ter.
*Soap Spring, Yavapai, M-5.
*Soldier's Hole, Yavapai, H-14.
Solero, Pima, *mail* Calabazas.
Solomonsville, Graham, U-20.
Sonoitra, Pima, *mail* Tucson.
*Sopori, Pima, O-25.
*Spanish Ranch, Yuma, E-20.
*Spears' Ranch, Mohave, B-12.
*Spencer's Ranch, Mohave, E-9.
*Spring, Apache, T-7.
*Spring, Pima, 10 m S E Croton Spring, T-23.
*Spring, Apache, R-9.
*Spring, Mohave, F-10.
*Spring, Gila, R-17.
Springerville, Apache, V-15. 364
St. Johns, Apache, V-14........... 546
St. Joseph, Apache, see San Joseph, S-12.
Stanton, Maricopa.
Stanwix, Yuma, F-20, *mail* Sentinel.

Stanwix Station, Maricopa, G-20, (Ry 1). *mail* Sentinel.
*Station. Pinal, P-21.
*Steele's Station, Cachise, T-22, (Ry 1).
Stephensville, Apache, *mail* Solomonsville.
Stockton. Mohave, C-10, *mail* Cerbat.
Stone Cabin, Pima, 53 m N E Tucson, P-23.
Stoneman's Lake, Yavapai, *mail* Camp Verde.
*Strawberry Valley, Yavapai, M-14.
*Sulphur Spring. Mohave, B-7.
*Sulphur Spring, Cachise, U-24.
*Summit Spring, Apache, U-15.

Sunset, Apache, 3 m S St. Johns, V-14, *mail* St. Johns.
Sunset City, Apache, Q-11 161
*Suppai Indian Settlement, Yavapai, I-7.
Sweetwater, Pinal, (Ry 1), *mail* Terminus.
Swisshelm Mine, Pima, *mail* Fort Bowie.
Sycamore Creek, Yavapai, *mail* Cienega.

*Tank, Pima, S-25.
*Tank, Apache, Q-15.
*Tanks, Yuma, D-19.
*Tanks, Yuma, C-22.
*Tanks, Mohave, 15 m N E Stockton, C-10.

*Teamsters' Camp, Yuma, F-20.
*Tecolate, Pima, L-25.
*Tegua (town and reservoir), Apache, R-8.
Tempe, Maricopa, L-18 135
Temple, Maricopa, *mail* Tempe.
Terminus, Pima.
Tevista, Cachise, 24 m E Willcox, T-22.
Texas Hill, Yuma, E-20, (Ry 1), *mail* Sentinel.
Thomas, Apache, T-19.
Tiger Mine, Yavapai, *mail* Bradshaw.
Tiger Mining District, Yavapai, *mail* Bradshaw.
*Tinajas Atlas, Yuma, C-22.
Tip Top, Yavapai.
Tip Top Mine, Yavapai, *mail* Gillett.
*Tiri-nah-hah Spring, Mohave, C-8.
Toll Gate, Yavapai, I-12, *mail* Prescott.
Tombstone, Cachise, S-25 973
*Tomocacari, Pima, 5 m S W Tubac, O-25.
Tonta Basin, Yavapai, *mail* Camp Verde
Total Wreck, Pima, 8 m S Pantano, Q-24.
Tres Alamos, Cachise, R-23 14
*Triplets, Apache, R-18.
*Trout Spring, Apache, T-6.
Truxton Spring, Mohave, E-10, *mail* Hackberry.
Tubac, Pima, P-25.
Tucson, Pima, P-23, (Ry 1) 6994
Tule, Yuma, E-23, *mail* Yuma.
Tully, Pima, *mail* Pantano.
Turner, Maricopa, 35 m W Globe City, Q-18, *mail* Globe City.

*Tyson's, Yuma, see Tyson's Well, C-17.
Tyson's Well, Yuma, see Lyson's Wells, C-17, *mail* Ehrenberg, B-17.

Upper Crossing, Pima, S-24, *mail* Benson.
Upper Verde, Yavapai, *mail* Camp Verde.

*Val Bonito, Yavapai, 5 m N San Francisco Spring, M-10.
Verde, Yavapai, *mail* Camp Verde, L-13.
*Volunteer Springs, Yavapai, L-11.
Vulture, Maricopa, 11 m W Seymour, I-16.
Vulture Mine, Maricopa, *mail* Seymour 89

Walker, Yavapai, I-13.
Walker, Apache, *mail* Saint Joseph. 165
*Walker's Church, Apache, U-7.
Wallapai Mountain, Mohave, *mail* Mineral Park.
*Wallapi Spring, Mohave, see Hualapai Spring, D-11.
Walnut Creek, Yavapai, *mail* Prescott
Walnut Grove, Yavapai, I-14.

Wardsville, Apache, *mail* Clifton.
Washington, Pima.
Washington District, Pima, *mail* Tucson or Crittenden.
Water, Yuma, B-19, *mail* Castle Dome Landing.
*Waterpocket, Yavapai, M-5.
*Waterpocket, Yavapai, N-7.
Watervale, Pima, *mail* Tombstone.
*Weaver, Yavapai, see Weaver's Ranch.
Weaver's Ranch, Yavapai, *mail* Wickenburgh, I-15.
*Weir's Camp, Yuma, 10 m N E Parker, B-15.
Wellow Rand, Mohave, *mail* Mineral Park.
*Wheat Camp, Maricopa, 15 m N E Old Camp Reno, N-16.
Wheatfield, Maricopa, 15 m W Globe City, Q-18 74
*White Locks, Pima, see Whitlock's Cienega, U-21.
*Whitemore's Pools, Yavapai, P-7.
*White Rock Spring, Apache, T-9.
*White Tanks, Maricopa, 20 m N W Phœnix, K-18.
*Whitlock's Cienega, Pima, U-21.
*Whittmore, Yavapai, G-6.
Wickenburgh, Maricopa, I-16 104
Willcox, Cachise, T-22, (Ry 1).
Williams' Fork, Mohave, *mail* Aubrey.
Williamson's Valley, Yavapai, 10 m S E Charming Dale, I-12, *mail* Simmons 150

Willow Grove, Mohave, F-11, *mail* Hackberry.
Willows, Mohave, *mail* Signal.
*Willow Spring, Yavapai, N 6.
*Willow Spring, Apache, W-10.
Winn's, Graham, T-20, *mail* Camp Thomas.
*Winter Luck, Pinal, Q-21.
*Witches' Pool, Yavapai, G-6.
*Wolf Spring, Yavapai, I-4.
Woodruff, Apache, S-12 66

*Young Spring, Mohave, F-10.
*Yucca Spring, Mohave, C-9.
Yuma, Yuma, A-20, (Ry 1) 1200
Yuma Desert Station, Yavapai, *mail* Wickenburgh.
Yuma Meskeh Station, Yavapai, *mail* Wickenburgh.
Yuma Sentand Station, Yavapai, *mail* Wickenburgh.
Yuma Mesquit Station, Yavapai, *mail* Wickenburgh.

SOUVENIRS OF TREASURE HUNT

Bottles recovered from dumps
M-Scope located cans buried with bottles

DO'S AND DON'TS

Arizona offers an active and fertile ground for treasure hunting as much of the state is still government land or open range. The laws of decency still govern the search on private property—get permission from the owner.

Do not enter through locked gates or buildings that are locked. Everything locked is owned, no matter how long since it has been visited by the owner. Most everything adjacent to a locked building is also owned.

The treasure hunter should not be a vandal. Walls of old buildings should not be torn down or the buildings wrecked. Places of general historic interest should be respected. Historic artifacts should be preserved in every detail. This sometimes even places a limit or curtails rock hunting.

Don't be a looter. Don't be a vandal. Others will follow you so leave your camp and trail cleaner than you found it. Don't be a litterbug.

SAFETY

And a word about safety. Desert travel is different than any other you will find. Be prepared for hot and cold weather in extremes. You should carry a gallon of water for each person for each day you expect to be out, plus extra. Adequate food, of course.

For traveling be certain you get road conditions from the nearest local source. A flash flood or storm can change all existing maps over-night. Carry plenty of extra gasoline, tow ropes, shovels, and jacks—the bigger the better. Rocket flares are also recommended, for no matter how far out you are, sometimes during the next 24 hours a plane will fly over-head. Light three brush fires in the day or shoot a rocket flare at night—but only in the case of a real emergency.

As the last resort burn the tires of your car—if you do not have the strength to remove the tires, BURN THE CAR.

A Fisher T-10 M-Scope is used by Theron Fox to check to ground adjacent to old mill ruins. His daughter, Dolores, looks on intently, and serves as the shovel carrier on these expeditions.

ALVIN DANIEL MATTSON
1895 - 1970

PROPHETIC VOICE FOR THE KINGDOM

The Impact of Alvin Daniel Mattson Upon the Social Consciousness of the Augustana Synod

By
GREGORY LEE JACKSON

1986
Augustana Historical Society

Augustana Historical Society
Publication no. 35

Ross E. Paulson, Editor

ISBN: 0-910184-35-6
LC Card Number: 86-71907

Printed in the United States of America
Intercollegiate Press
Shawnee Mission, Kansas

To:

MARTIN,
BETHANY,
and
ERIN.

"Let the children come to me,
and do not hinder them,
for to such belongs the Kingdom of God."
MARK 10:14

TABLE OF CONTENTS

FOREWORD

"A.D." was the simple designation by which he was affectionately known to hundreds of former students and innumerable friends. And as oft as not his greeting would be "Let's have a cup of coffee together." For that would provide an opportunity to converse, or in contemporary idiom, to "communicate," an art he enjoyed. Down to earth, friendly, even blunt, he conveyed a sense of honesty and forthrightness too rarely evident in circles where smoothness and obliqueness are often considered the fashion. There was a certain ruggedness about "A.D." that impressed his friends, and perplexed those who didn't share his views.

His intellectual career was interesting. Drawn to philosophy and philosophy of religion he did his graduate work in these fields. But he didn't feel at home in the rarefied atmosphere of abstract thought. Sociology seemed a more congenial science as he went on in Ethics. This, however, was not the real source of his inspiration. He began to teach the Old Testament prophets. Amos gave him the theme he was to sound again and again in his preaching and teaching. He thought of the present-day congregations as he expounded the Lord's rebuke:

> I hate, I despise your feasts, and I take no delight
> in your solemn assemblies.
> Even though you offer me your burnt offerings
> and cereal offerings, I will not accept these,
> and the peace offerings of your fatted beasts
> I will not look upon.

Take way from me the noise of your songs,
to the melody of your hearts I will not listen.
But let justice roll down like waters, and
righteousness like an ever-flowing stream.

AMOS, Ch. 5

Social justice and national righteousness were indeed his main concern in his more than three decades of seminary teaching. In the light of what has happened in our country and in our churches these past few years it is startling to realize how long ago Dr. Mattson started to rouse our church to action. Not only in classroom and pulpit did he echo the words of the prophets of Israel, but on the floor of synod conventions and in church commissions. He championed the cause of the laboring man and of the poor, and everywhere he challenged Christians to rethink their attitude toward the pestilence of war and of racism. I do not exaggerate when I declare that no one more than "A.D." influenced his students who became pastors in the Augustana Church in the field of social interest and social action.

Not surprisingly he won opponents as well as converts. Yet his emphasis did not aim at the disruption of congregations. For it was not an uncharitable voice that the people heard, but the voice of one who could point to the Bible as his authority—the Bible they claimed they believed in. And whoever it was that differed with him, he could say, "Let's have a cup of coffee together." His knowledge of human nature and his sense of humor—which after all is a sense of proportion—made him remarkably tolerant of individuals and their quirks. He perceived both the comic and the tragic in humanity.

In some ways "A.D." was a representative of a pioneer period in our church, not the period of peopling new lands and cities, but of a period of transition in which the church faced a new world. It is a world of social turmoil, troubled consciences, of lip service to traditional religion but life service to modern idolatry. On this frontier he was a fearless explorer and faithful pastor. For years to come his friends and colleagues will bless his memory, and the Church will recognize the fruits of his ministry.

Conrad Bergendoff
Tribute at Memorial Service
St. John's Lutheran Church, Rock Island, Illinois
October 23, 1970

PREFACE

Two terms which have always seemed mutually exclusive are "Lutheran" and "Social Gospel." In 1930, a professor at the Lutheran seminary in Philadelphia wrote:

> If one wants to stigmatize a preacher one need only say of him that he preaches a social gospel. The implication is that he has ceased to be a true Lutheran preacher, and at least within Lutheran circles deserves little consideration.[1]

The term "Social Gospel" refers in this book to the theology of Walter Rauschenbusch. Even today, two Lutheran reference books, *The Lutheran Encyclopedia* and the *Lutheran Cyclopedia*, contain extremely critical articles on the topic of the Social Gospel, even though the authors represent the left wing and the right wing of American Lutheranism.[2] The casual observer would conclude, then, that the Social Gospel movement escaped the embrace of Lutherans in America. The fallacy of that conclusion, widespread as it may be, forms the basis for this book.

One year after Professor Fischer published his article on Lutherans and the Social Gospel, Alvin Daniel Mattson was called to be professor of Christian ethics and sociology at Augustana Theological Seminary. When he was granted tenure and installed as permanent professor in 1934, Mattson declared that Rauschenbusch's concept of the Kingdom of God would guide his thinking on social issues.[3] In his Knubel-Miller lectures at the end of his career, Mattson reiterated his fondness for the Social Gospel.[4] By the time he had retired from teaching at the seminary in 1965, Mattson had taught almost all the Augustana pastors serving in the newly formed Lutheran Church of America, or 1,100 of the pastors on the LCA ministerial roll.[5]

Mattson's career was distinguished by the fact that he alone among Lutheran seminary professors taught ethics to all the pastors of one major synod. But the most remarkable aspect of Mattson's career is that he was the opposite of almost everything that the Augustana Synod represented in 1931. Mattson was a liberal, a Democrat involved in politics, an advocate of labor unions, a foe of code morality, and a defender of the Social Gospel. The Augustana Synod was Swedish, conservative, Republican, anti-labor, legalistic, and exceedingly proud of its institutional charities (Inner Missions). Social Gospel advocates considered the theology of Inner Missions narrow and old-fashioned, while the defenders of the Inner Mission movement viewed the Social Gospel as a tragic mistake.

Mattson was not the first Lutheran to embrace the theology of Rauschenbusch. Harold Lentz has documented the brief era in which the publications of the General Synod expressed an appreciation of the work of such writers as Washington Gladden and Walter Rauschenbusch. But the movement toward confessional conservatism and merger ended the era before it became institutionalized.[6] In books and articles published before the 1962 merger of the Lutheran Church in America, "Lutheran Church in America" was used generally to describe all American Lutherans. The "old" American Lutheran Church (which was formed out of a merger in 1930) is distinguished from The American Lutheran Church which was created in a 1960 merger. Many Lutheran groups changed their names without merging, so the most common name for a given Lutheran Church body will be used to avoid confusion (See Appendix C). The purpose of this book is to show how Mattson was able to change the social consciousness of the

Augustana Synod, displacing the conservatism of Inner Mission theology with the theology of Rauschenbusch.

By the time Mattson began teaching at Augustana Theological Seminary, all traces of Lutheran approval of the Social Gospel had been replaced by a complete rejection of Rauschenbusch and the Federal Council of Churches. The Inner Mission had a carefully defined program of social improvement which included a polemic against Social Gospel theology and programs. The theology of Inner Missions was completely harmonious with the piety of the Augustana Synod, with its emphasis on the sanctified life of the believer. Moreover, Augustana was especially proud of its commitment to the method and theology of Inner Missions. That one person would enshrine the theology of Rauschenbusch at Augustana Theological Seminary and proceed to change the entire social consciousness of the synod in the course of his career, after the heyday of the Social Gospel was past, seems completely unthinkable. Yet A.D. Mattson accomplished this fact so completely that his last students found him rather conservative.

The most significant mark of Mattson's influence upon the Augustana Synod is the theological foundation of the social statements. While the theological emphasis varies from statement to statement, Augustana's were clearly different from the other Lutheran bodies. Augustana's statements were related to Mattson's concept of the Kingdom of God as the central idea in Christian social action. The life of Jesus is an example of the Christian response to social concerns. Just as Jesus recognized the worth and dignity of the individual, so must we acknowledge the rights and needs of the working man. Just as Christ foreswore violence, so must the Christian reject war as a means of settling international disputes. Just as Jesus welcomed outsiders to his circle, so must the Church welcome other races as equals within the fellowship of the congregation and in the scope of human activities. Kingdom language occurred frequently in Augustana's pronouncements. The answer to Marxism was a socially active religion, rather than simple fulminations about godless communism. Augustana's actions on war clearly indicated a different theological understanding of the issue. Augustana assumed that ethics began with Christ rather than Luther, so her statements did not show the influence of the Two Kingdoms doctrine. The other bodies, especially the ULCA, were inclined to deal with war, the draft, and armaments in relation to the just war concept traditional in Lutheran ethics.

In the Lutheran Church in America today, one can detect some difficulties inherited from the ULCA. While Augustana worked out a theology of social action based on the Kingdom of God, the ULCA pursued the quest for the historical Luther and a new understanding of the Two Kingdoms. The social agenda of the LCA is much more clearly related to the Social Gospel concerns of Mattson, while the theological justification remains that of the Luther renaissance. What appears, then, is an attempt to be sectarian or countercultural in social action while remaining culture bound in theology.[7]

ACKNOWLEDGEMENTS

I would like to express my appreciation for the considerable help given by my advisor at Notre Dame, John Howard Yoder, and the readers of the Ph.D. dissertation upon which this book is based: Stanley Hauerwas, Philip Gleason, Robert Wilkin and Conrad Bergendoff. Roland Bainton and Robert Calhoun gave me invaluable insights about Mattson's years at Yale Divinity School. Ruth Mattson Taylor generously loaned me her father's correspondence files and many other valuable items.* The Lutheran Church in America archivist, Joel Lundeen, and the staff at the Lutheran School of Theology at Chicago offered great assistance in tracking down information and literature. Additional help was provided by my mother, my wife and her family, and clergy of the Lutheran Church in America. Two congregations named Saint Timothy (in Sturgis and Midland, Michigan) were exceedingly patient during my seven years at Notre Dame. In addition, all my papers at Notre Dame have been meticulously typed by Angela Brant, a valued friend of our family. The ultimate beginning of my dissertation work was probably at Salem Lutheran Church in Moline, Illinois (formerly Augustana Synod), where I was confirmed by Pastor J. Erik Holmer, or perhaps it began when my mother took religion from A.D. Mattson at Augustana College in 1930. Later, she organized a teachers' union at her school.

GLJ

Part I

MATTSON'S CAREER AND THEOLOGY

1
MATTSON'S EDUCATION BEFORE YALE

Alvin Daniel Mattson was born in Bloomington, Illinois, on November 24, 1895. His father, J. A. Mattson, had immigrated from Värmland, Sweden, in 1869 and settled in Wright County, Minnesota. J. A. Mattson attended Gustavus Adolphus College and Augustana Seminary and was ordained in 1894. He married Anna C. Carlson. J. A. Mattson served parishes in Bloomington, Illinois; St. Hilaire, Minnesota; Winnipeg, Manitoba; Warren, Minnesota; Fort Dodge, Iowa; Manson, Iowa; Ray, North Dakota; Gwinner, North Dakota; Bock, Minnesota; and Groveland, Florida.[1] A.D. had two brothers, Karl and Earl, who became ministers and one brother, Paul, who became a teacher. He also had two sisters, Lydia and Ruby, who were nurses. A.D. was confirmed by his father in 1911 and graduated in 1912 from Manson High School. From the age of 11 he held jobs every summer, on farms and twice on a section gang of the Illinois Central Railroad.[2] Karl called the railroad job "A.D.'s first theological course." Fifty years later, A.D. still counted some of the laborers among his lifelong friends. A.D.'s father placed great value in honesty, integrity, and individuality. Hypocrisy was considered a work of the devil. J. A. Mattson thought that all men should be respected and treated as equals, regardless of their status.[3]

A. D. Mattson's education at Augustana College, where

he received his degree in 1916, can be determined from the experiences of Conrad Bergendoff, who graduated in 1915. Both were the sons of Swedish immigrants who had studied at Augustana Theological Seminary. Moreover, Rock Island was the home of the publishing house (The Augustana Book Concern) and the synod president. Bergendoff stated: "In my formative years Rock Island came to mean a viewpoint from which I saw the Christian church . . . If Swedish-America could be considered a province in the U.S.A., Rock Island was its capital."[4] Although the college president, Gustav Andreen, had been educated at Yale, he maintained contacts with Sweden and recruited teachers from the homeland. College life was insulated from the outside world. Dancing, drinking, card playing and football were banned, although football was allowed in the fall of 1918. While the college offered most of its courses in English, as of 1912, Swedish studies occupied a prominent place in the curriculum. All the faculty members were Lutheran; all but one were Swedish. Faculty members served on the synodical council, the mission board, and were delegates to synod conventions.[5] However, the school was not intended to be a barrier against learning beyond the scope of Swedish Lutheran piety. The educational reform in Sweden in 1809 and 1831 provided a university education for every pastor and greatly improved standards. Fathers of Augustana, L. P. Esbjörn, T. N. Hasselquist, and Erland Carlsson, with their university educations, envisioned a school which would combine classical education standards with nurture in Lutheran piety.[6]

When Mattson studied at Augustana Theological Seminary (1916-1919), the Repristination movement was still being felt in the synod. Lutheran leaders, such as C. F. W. Walther (1811-1887) in America and J. K. W. Löhe (1808-1872) in Europe, rejected ecumenical trends and sought to define dogma through the works of seventeenth century orthodox Lutherans: Hollazius, Quenstedt, Baier, Calovius, Schmid, and Luthardt.

Repristination influenced Augustana to remain orthodox, a style of theology which was extremely suspicious of heterodoxy and combative about doctrinal matters. Dr. Conrad Lindberg taught dogmatics at Augustana Seminary from 1890 to 1930, using the same textbook, his own *Christian Dogmatics*, which referred to Luther only marginally. According to Karl Mattson, Lindberg and T. N. Hasselquist were the real architects of the life of Augustana and "both men viewed the Lutheran proclamation through the spectacles of seventeenth century Lutheranism."[7] In 1917, the 400th anniversary of the Reformation prompted a reexamination of Lutheran doctrine, based on the works of such European scholars as Karl Holl and Ragnar Bring. This Luther renaissance centered on the life and teaching of Luther himself rather than his orthodox followers of the subsequent century. The Luther renaissance influenced the younger generation of Augustana leaders, such as Mattson and Conrad Bergendoff, even though their seminary training was orthodox.

Mattson's attitude toward the orthodox style of theology was paradoxical. He valued the training and the discipline, but felt that Lutheran orthodoxy did not address the social aspect of religion. Yet Mattson never became enamored of the new Luther theologians. Late in his career, when he taught as a substitute in the dogmatics class attended by Glenn Stone, Mattson gave some students the impression that he thought in the terms of the old school.[8] Reflecting on the influence of Lindberg, Mattson said that many of his fellow students

> . . . did not use the springboard only as a starting place. They continued to rest there permanently. It is easy to understand how this happened because as far as Dr. Lindberg's attitude to his students was concerned, there were no open questions.[9]

There is evidence that Mattson did war against the Lindberg theology, not because the theology was wrong, but because it was inadequate.[10]

Another influential professor at the seminary was Adolf Hult, who pioneered American attacks on Sweden's Archbishop Nathan Söderblom, starting in 1910. Hult was opposed to ecumenism, liberal interpretation of the Bible, history of religions, and the Common Service Book of the ULCA. Hult maintained what he called a churchly, scholastic confessionalism. He had friends in the Missouri Synod who printed his attacks against Söderblom when the Augustana publications no longer would. Hult survived the faculty revolution and became a close friend of Mattson. That the two could be such close friends, while differing on theology and politics, illustrates the sense of unity experienced in the Augustana Synod.

Sven Gustav Youngert was a professor who had studied under G. T. Ladd at Yale and was a close friend of Söderblom.[12] Youngert introduced Mattson to *The Evolution of Early Christianity* by Shirley Jackson Case. Mattson wrote:

> For Dr. Youngert, the Bible was not merely a source of proof texts but he was well aware of the dynamic origins of that Book. Christianity was more than the religion of a Book. It was a dynamic, living response to the nature of reality which the Bible reflected and thus spoke and speaks to our own day and experience.[13]

The influence of Fundamentalism upon Augustana was considerable. Fundamentalism was named after a series of booklets published between 1910 and 1912 called *The Fundamentals*. The most important points were the inerrancy of Scripture, the Virgin Birth, the bodily resurrection of Christ, the atonement of Christ, and His physical return. Fundamentalism warred against Modernism, which sought to accommodate Christianity to scientific and Biblical research. Augustana did not have the intensity of the Fundamentalist/Modernist battle which divided other schools and denominations. Although the newer methods of Biblical study were being used at the seminary, the independent Lutheran Bible Institute in Minneapolis and its periodical, *The Bible Banner*, served as opponents, for the most part, of newer trends in Augustana theology.

The most important professor for Mattson was C. J. Södergren, who taught at the seminary from 1912 to 1920. Mattson stated:

> He manifested a very sympathetic attitude for the student with intellectual problems and did a great deal to help such students find their way to understanding and clarity. For Dr. Södergren, faith was something quite different from intellectual assent to some doctrine or dogma—important as he considered right thinking to be.[14]

Södergren was an iconoclast who broached the sensitive topic of evolution and discussed the need for economic reform through socialism. According to Mattson:

> The greatest and the most dynamic influence which Dr. Södergren brought to me was the fact that he introduced me to the works of Walter Rauschenbusch. Here was a new dimension of Christianity which I had never seen before. Christianity became socially relevant.[15]

Södergren was considered one of the two gadflies of the Augustana Synod. The second gadfly was Mattson's friend, C. A. Wendell. Wendell and Södergren wrote against Lutheran Fundamentalists, taking sides with religious proponents of evolution.[16] Södergren shocked conservatives in the synod when he suggested in 1914 that the theory of evolution was not atheistic.[17] He attacked verbal inspiration in *Is the Bible Alive? Is Jesus God?*[18] G. Everett Arden states: "He pointed out that those who make the theory of verbal inspiration a tenet of faith cannot call upon the Lutheran confessions for support, for the confessions posit no such doctrine."[19] Södergren also protested the association of the synod with the exclusive confessionalism of the American Lutheran Conference. Södergren anticipated Augustana's eventual position on inspiration as well as ecumenism, since inerrancy was no longer taught when the old guard left the seminary in 1931. Decades passed before Augustana broke off merger negotiations with the American Lutheran Conference.[20] He also warned in 1925 that the Church was allied with the forces of destruction, her sins of omission heaped high for judgment.[21] While the Church was still enjoying the fruits of prosperity in the Roaring Twenties, Södergren argued that the Lordship of Christ meant applying the principles and spirit of Christ to every department of life:

> And politics is religion. So is business, and education, and art, and all our industrial and social relations. In fact, all human life and activity. If these are not to be religious, they are to be irreligious. If they are not Christian, they are the opposite. So, let us take our choice, and—the consequences.[22]

Augustana's relationship with Fundamentalism was mixed, as was Södergren's. While higher criticism of the Bible was gradually introduced to the seminary during Mattson's student days, some books were still under lock and key in the library in 1930. Augustana piety was Bible-centered, despite the investment in orthodox dogmatics. The more conservative Augustana pastors and members were literalists or Fundamentalists, but the liberals were not very liberal by today's standards. The Lutheran Bible Institutes, which were independent of Augustana, represented the Fundamentalist wing, trying to save Augustana from Modernism. Although Södergren was under attack for his modern views while at Augustana Seminary, his next job was at the LBI in Minneapolis! Mattson reflected Södergren's influence in being liberal enough to shock the Fundamentalists, but still rather conservative in his attitudes toward the Bible, as judged by one of his colleagues at Augustana. The tolerance exemplified in the relationship between Södergren, the LBI, Hult, and Mattson helps explain the reason why Mattson survived at the seminary in the 1930's. Mavericks were attacked, and they often replied in kind, but unity in the Augustana Synod was not threatened. While other bodies might split over Jonah and the whale, Augustana changed with the times, the bond of Swedish identity preserved.

Upon ordination in 1919, Mattson served three calls in Minnesota before going to Yale University. He had married Freda Anderson in 1918. His calls were to Avoca, 1919-1921, St. James, 1921-1924, and East and West Sveadahl, 1924-1926. He and Freda had two children, Ruth Elaine and Alvin Daniel, Jr.[23] In 1921, he completed his S.T.M. degree from Augustana, writing about comparative religions: "The Tools of Christianity." It dealt with the relation of Judaism and Christianity to other religions. Karl Mattson alluded to tension between the faculty and A.D. about the thesis, but the thesis and correspondence were not available to this writer.[24]

Dr. Lars Herman Beck became a neighbor to Mattson in St. James. Beck had earned his doctorate at Yale and served as the first president of Upsala College in New Jersey. Beck was one of the Augustana Synod theologians whom A.D.

labeled as outside the prevalent climate.[25] Beck encouraged A.D. to leave a comfortable parish and go to Yale.[26] Mattson accepted a call to two parishes in West Haven and Ansonia, Connecticut, in 1926, with the provision that he be allowed to pursue graduate study.

If A.D. was inspired by the social thinking of Södergren or Rauschenbusch, his publications before Yale did not indicate it. In 1921, he wrote "Objects and Opportunities of the Luther League" for the *Lutheran Companion*, apparently in anticipation of the 1921 Synod Luther League Convention in Pittsburgh.[27] Mattson discussed the work of the group in study activities, in promotion of the church periodical, and in encouraging young men to enter the ministry. No mention was made of the Kingdom of God or specific social concerns. While this kind of article would not necessarily call for such views, Mattson's later work indicated that the Kingdom of God and the theology of Rauschenbusch were relevant to all topics, including rural churches. Mattson's "unconverted state," to use his brother's term, was further indicated by his 1924 *Lutheran Companion* article, "What Kind of Theology Should We Promulgate?"[28] Mattson suggested that the theology should be based first of all on the Bible, second on the Lutheran confessions, and thirdly on the scientific world view. "As the Bible is the rule of faith, so the confessions are the rule for public teaching."[29] Those who could not abide with the confessions should withdraw from the synod. His theology did not call for social action or for special consideration of public issues. That would come later.

When Mattson completed his seminary training, Inner Mission theology defined the social ministry of the Augustana Synod. Inner Missions began in Europe through the leadership of Johannes Wichern (1808-1881) and Theodor Fliedner (1800-1864), spreading in America through the work of Augustana's friend and benefactor, William Passavant (1821-1894). Inner Mission institutions—orphanages, nursing homes, hospitals—worked with government to provide relief for the poor. Inner Mission leaders were opposed to the theology of Walter Rauschenbusch. They argued that the Social Gospel would undermine the concept of personal sin and salvation. Inner Mission theology provided Augustana with a method of dealing with the ills of society within the quietistic framework of Pietism.

2

MATTSON'S CONVERSION TO THE SOCIAL GOSPEL AT YALE

Mattson's study at Yale proved to be decisive for his career and the direction of the Augustana Synod. First of all, Mattson's theology changed during his study at Yale, from a stance of Lutheran orthodoxy to one which viewed the Kingdom of God as the sole criterion for sound doctrine. Secondly, Mattson became involved with social issues, following the agenda as well as the theology of Rauschenbusch's Social Gospel. Finally, the parishes which Mattson served in Connecticut and New Jersey were the last ones he would occupy as a parish pastor. After Yale, Mattson taught briefly in two colleges and then moved to the Augustana Seminary faculty. He spent most of his years after Yale in the Augustana Synod's only seminary, actively participating in synodical and ecumenical activities as well. Yale provided Mattson with a theology for his changing perspective on social issues, examples of ministers active in social issues, and an agenda for the Augustana Synod. The theology and social consciousness assimilated at Yale remained with Mattson for the rest of his life.

Karl Mattson named Luther Allan Weigle, Douglas C. Macintosh, and Robert Calhoun as the men who influenced A.D. at Yale.[30] Weigle became a Congregationalist minister while teaching in Northfield, Minnesota, since no English Lutheran churches were in the vicinity. At that time, the General Synod worship service had more in common with that of the Congregationalists than with the ethnic Lutheran worship of the Midwest.[31] Weigle joined the Congregational ministerium in 1916 when he came to Yale but remained a Lutheran in his theology.[32] In his 34 years at Yale, Weigle was an important leader in religious education. As dean of the divinity school, Weigle increased the reputation of the school and multiplied the number of Lutheran students there.[33] Mattson corresponded with Weigle in the years after Yale.[34] (A.D.'s youngest brother, Earl, later earned his divinity degree at Yale, and his brother Karl served as pastor of nearby Bethesda Lutheran Church, New Haven, Connecticut.)[35]

Weigle was one of the outsiders who encouraged Mattson. Weigle's background with the General Synod left him sympathetic toward ecumenism, rather than critical of it. For Vergilius Ferm, another friend of Mattson, Weigle wrote a preface to *A Crisis in American Theology*, the story of the General Synod split. (Ferm was a doctoral student at Yale and the minister at West Haven before Mattson.) Weigle stated in the preface that Schmucker was more of a pioneer than a heretic, especially in regard to ecumenism. Samuel S. Schmucker (1799-1873) taught systematic theology at Gettysburg Seminary from 1826 to 1866, training over 500 graduates. When Schmucker helped sponsor the Definite Synodical Platform anonymously in 1855, orthodox Lutherans were angered by the proposed alterations of the Augsburg Confession of 1530. Schmucker's efforts led to the formation of the more conservative General Council, which was a split from the General Synod, and the creation of the Augustana Synod in 1860, the Latin name for Augsburg (Augustana) reflecting the importance of the confession. Weigle was sanguine about the General Synod's liberal era at a time when Lutherans were trying to forget that Schmucker had ever existed. Weigle's influence can be seen in Mattson's ecumenical social ministry activities and in Mattson's regard for liberal theology.

Douglas C. Macintosh, a Canadian Baptist, was one of the most thought-provoking professors at Yale Divinity School in the 1920's, according to Roland Bainton. Macintosh taught that the truths of Christianity could be verified, as he claimed in *Theology as an Empirical Science*, which perhaps led Mattson to write his Augustana S.T.D. dissertation on "Knowledge, Emotion, and the Will in Religious Experience," which was completed in 1928.[37]

Macintosh was a moral optimist who believed that evil could be overcome. States Bainton: "This view induces a heroic attitude toward life."[38] In fact, Macintosh drew the attention of several Lutheran bodies when he was refused American citizenship for his rejection of military service during World War I.[39] However, Macintosh was not an absolute pacifist. He wanted the option to choose the war he would fight in. Macintosh's *Social Religion* affirmed the New Testament basis for social concern, for the Kingdom of Evil will come, if the Kingdom of God does not.[40] Mattson's optimism about overcoming evil definitely paralleled Macintosh's. Mattson, in his *Christian Ethics*, referred to Macintosh: "Professor Macintosh has pointed out that the universe does meet every challenge which the problem of evil presents and does make it possible for us to believe in the goodness of God." Lutheran piety, according to Mattson, had accepted evil as the result of man's total depravity, a condition not likely to be altered.[41]

The selective pacifism of Macintosh would not have been new to Mattson. The Swedish Lutherans had a tradition of opposing war, and some of them had come to America to avoid the draft in Sweden.[42] But the optimism about meeting the challenge of evil was alien to the Augustana tradition of Inner Mission. Inner Mission theology taught that evil was the result of personal sin: the cause of poverty was the sin of the poor person. Macintosh's optimism paralleled the attitudes of C. J. Södergren, Mattson's mentor in the

Augustana Synod and his most influential professor at the seminary. Mattson was not naively optimistic about bringing about the Kingdom of God in his lifetime, but he never tired of encouraging Lutherans to enter the fray before assigning the victory to evil. While Mattson was not a strong advocate of socialism, as was Södergren, he was considered a harsh critic of the abuses of capitalism.[43] Macintosh probably added to the impact of Södergren's earlier direction. Södergren once remarked to A. D. Mattson in a letter that A.D. had taken a long time to come around.

Another influential professor was Robert Calhoun, professor of church history. Direct influence upon Mattson cannot be traced. Mattson and Calhoun were both members of the Religion and Labor Foundation, but Calhoun could not recall Mattson when asked about him in a letter.

The professors at Yale who probably influenced Mattson the most were not mentioned by his brother Karl: Charles R. Brown, Jerome Davis, and Willard Uphaus. All three were proponents of the Social Gospel of Rauschenbusch. According to Calhoun, Rauschenbusch was "regarded with respect and friendliness, but not with anything like discipleship—except perhaps on the part of some individual students and a very few members of the faculty," when he delivered the 1917 Taylor lectures, which became *A Theology for the Social Gospel*.[44] The professor who was instrumental in bringing Rauschenbusch to Yale for the lectures was Charles R. Brown, professor of homiletics and pastoral care, the dean of the school (1910-1928). Mattson often mentioned him as a favorite professor. Brown had given the Beecher Lectures in 1906, published as *The Social Message of the Modern Pulpit*.[45] Brown's position was that the minister had a crucial role in smiting the conscience of those who exploited others. Brown served as a mediator in labor disputes, a role later played by Mattson. Like Brown, Mattson did not champion socialism but sought to moderate the violence of labor and the greed of unrestrained capitalism. Like Brown, Mattson gave sermons which were known and remembered for their vividness in portraying scenes in the Gospels. Like Brown, Mattson taught that ministers would ultimately be judged by the spiritual results of their work. As dean, Brown hired Jerome Davis, saying that his work would be, "...placing the social thinking of two hundred men on a sounder basis and creating fresh impulses in their hearts to preach a social gospel."[46]

Jerome Davis, described by Calhoun as a wholehearted admirer of Rauschenbusch, taught social ethics and earned a reputation as a "hard-driving activist."[47] Davis founded the Religion and Labor Foundation, which sought to educate the churches about the rights of labor. RLF was headquartered in New Haven and included many Yale faculty members on its letterhead. Liston Pope told Bainton that Davis was the most unsystematic and the most stimulating of teachers. "He would spend a part of the week in the hustings and then walk into class to tell what was rotten in the state of Denmark."[48] Davis' critique of America was published as *Captitalism and its Culture.* Davis' failure to earn tenure at Yale drew considerable coverage in one of Mattson's favorite journals, *The Christian Century.*[49]

Davis maintained contact with Mattson after the Yale years, chiefly through RLF. Davis encouraged Mattson to accompany one of the earliest groups to tour Marxist Russia in 1938. He cajoled Mattson into a second trip in 1957. Mattson's teaching style was exactly the same as Davis'. Mattson became known for his dramatic tales about social ills in the world beyond the seminary. Mattson's unsystematic style, remembered by many of his students, is evidenced in *Christian Ethics*. Mattson's interest in Russia, his critique of capitalism and his lectures show Davis' direct and indirect influence.

Willard Uphaus, who worked with Davis in the RLF, also maintained contact with Mattson in the years follow-

3

FROM YALE TO AUGUSTANA SEMINARY

Mattson's study at Yale, which included no more than two or three semesters, ended with an offer to teach at Upsala College in East Orange, New Jersey, the school which L. H. Beck had founded.[52] At Upsala, Mattson had to teach a course in the prophets, giving him an additional foundation for his theological concern for the social responsibility of the Church. Following his year at Upsala, which was still a struggling institution, Mattson accepted a call to Augustana College, where he taught Christianity from 1929 to 1931.

The death of the dean of the seminary, Conrad Lindberg, in the summer of 1930, marked a new beginning for the theological climate of the Augustana Synod. The board extended a call on August 7, 1930, to Conrad Bergendoff to serve as the new dean.[53] He was the first professor at the seminary in 30 years to have an earned doctorate. The method of hiring professors had been to elect them from the synod floor, which gave popular ministers with honorary doctorates an overwhelming advantage over candidates with more formal education.[54] The death of Lindberg caused the students and some pastors to put pressure on the seminary's board of directors to hire new teachers in addition to Bergendoff. During Bergendoff's first year as dean, four professors were relieved of their responsibilities at the ing Yale. Most of the correspondence is rather formal Uphaus did plan a trip to Augustana Seminary at the i tation of Mattson in 1937, a trip which Uphaus delayec cause of unrest on the Augustana campus.[50] Mattson t eled with Uphaus on several occasions to investigate sharecropper situation and other labor problems. Mat also recruited members for the RLF. Uphaus had beer cruited for his RLF post by Jerome Davis. Uphaus c Washington Gladden and Walter Rauschenbusch as church leaders who supported the rights of labor.[51]

end of the 1930-1931 school year.[55] Arden, who was a seminary student at that time, gave most of the credit for the revolution to student pressure.

The turnover in faculty created an unusual opportunity for a small but dedicated group of Augustana leaders. While the records are incomplete, we can conclude, from the letters exchanged at the time, that Mattson was called to serve on the seminary faculty in 1931, perhaps as a result of the efforts of this group. The group included C. J. Södergren, the former seminary professor who introduced Mattson to Rauschenbusch's theology; George M. Stephenson, who severely criticized the parochialism of Augustana; Vergilius Ferm, a Wooster College professor; and C. A Wendell, pastor of Grace Lutheran Church Minneapolis.[56] Stephenson was a member of the Augustana College and Theological Seminary board when Mattson was chosen for the position. Stephenson's contribution to Mattson's cause consisted of "remaining severely silent," knowing that silence was the best recommendation he could give. Stephenson felt that any praise for Mattson would have created "a cloud of suspicion."[57] Stephenson reported that Mattson was endorsed by members of the joint faculty committee, including Adolph Hult, the reactionary conservative in a conservative synod. Mattson's reputation, previously earned, as a conservative, probably aided in his selection. Other contributing factors would have been his parish work, his Yale education, and his reputation as a preacher.

Wendell was astonished at the good news of Mattson's selection. He was convinced that Mattson had either embraced Fundamentalism or had employed the wisdom of the Christian serpent. Wendell felt that Mattson's new position possibly meant "the dawn of a new day." But Wendell also warned that the new era of Augustana would not come without help, a struggle, and much unpleasantness.[58] Södergren shared in Wendell's astonishment and rejoicing. Writing from the Lutheran Bible Institute, Södergren viewed Mattson's call as "*another gleam of light which promises the dawn of a new day.*" (Södergren's emphasis).[59] The other gleam of light was the selection of Bergendoff as dean of the seminary. Bergendoff represented a fresh new hope for the school and the denomination.

Södergren's letter spelled out the contrast between the old Augustana and the one he wished to see in the future. Södergren had taught at the seminary for eight years, followed by ten years at LBI. He viewed the seminary in those days as dominated by "medieval scholasticism and dogmatism and mummified ecclesiasticism . . ."[60] Södergren felt that the synod was almost dead, almost without hope. He hoped that Bergendoff and Mattson would "tip the scales," since both had made the transition "from the dead past to the living present . . ."[61] Södergren urged Mattson to accomplish what he had previously failed to do as professor at the seminary, so that Augustana would not die at the root as it had already at the top.

The group had a battle plan for Mattson to follow. Stephenson urged Mattson to be wise and judicious.[62] Accordingly, Mattson did not publish a word until he was granted tenure in 1934. Ferm, indicating a common fondness for Rauschenbusch's distinction between prophet and priest, hoped that Mattson would feel anointed as "prophet rather than priest."[63] When Mattson was considering a call to Willmar, Minnesota, in 1935, Södergren expressed the feeling that Mattson was the only one who could open the window and let some fresh air in. Södergren indicated that the group would be glad to have Mattson back in Minnesota, but warned that the parish under consideration had some people who considered a sociologist to be a socialist or worse. Mattson stayed at the seminary. Södergren was teaching at the Lutheran Bible Institute in Minneapolis. Wendell was a parish pastor in a congregation serving the University of Minnesota. Stephenson was teaching at the

University of Minnesota. Ferm was teaching at Wooster College, Wooster, Ohio.

Södergren had specific advice for Mattson to follow in the effort to reform the seminary and the synod. He warned his former student not to let animosity, asperity, ambition, or envy spoil the master plan. Södergren confessed that he suffered from a tendency to add acid to his ink, spoiling his own aim when attacking synodical aberrations. He hoped that Mattson would be patient: "You may feel like Gideon in Judges 6:13, 15. But that wasn't the *end* of the story. Spread your fleece, and in a year or two God may put the hilt of His sword in your hand."[65] Nevertheless, Mattson felt almost alone at the seminary. Writing to Ferm, he said:

> You suggest that I permit myself to feel anointed as prophet. The Lord knows that I try . . . the lot of the prophet is hard but the company is good. If one could only occasionally get into physical touch with a prophet it would not be so bad. Sometimes I am seriously asking myself the question if it is worthwhile to continue.[66]

The group encouraged Mattson to stay whenever he wanted to return to parish life. He seriously considered calls to parishes in 1935, 1936, 1939, and 1948.[67] L. H. Beck and Weigle also gave support to Mattson. Weigle wrote:

> It seems to me that it would be most unfortunate for you and men of your understanding of Lutheranism to surrender it to the type of obscurantism that you describe as in the saddle officially at present. In the end I believe you can win out. At least it is worth trying.[68]

The new president of the synod, P. O. Bersell, also encouraged Mattson to remain at the seminary during one of the episodes (not specified), and Bersell never regretted that act.[69]

A few outsiders (Södergren, Ferm, Wendell, Stephenson, Weigle) gave Mattson the support he needed to endure many lonely years at the seminary. While Södergren had hoped that Bergendoff and Mattson would work together for a change, the opposite sometimes occurred. Although they were personal friends, Bergendoff and Mattson ended up on opposite sides of many issues. Bergendoff was considered high church because he favored the liturgical reforms of the Common Service Book while Mattson was low church. Mattson led faculty resistance against some of Bergendoff's liturgical improvements. Mattson would take stands he felt were right, even if friction resulted. He would defend a cause, even if it resulted in threats of withdrawal of monetary support for the institution by members of the church at large. Bergendoff had to deal with the complaints about these controversial stands. In 1948, Mattson and Bergendoff took opposite sides over whether the college should be split from the seminary. Mattson favored the division, while Bergendoff did not.[70]

In general, Mattson followed the advice of his supporters. He remained patient and reasonable, answering the sharpest rebukes with even-tempered explanations of this theological position. He was unusually conciliatory with people, eager to talk over the issues dividing them, often over a cup of coffee. Mattson was deeply and passionately hated by some pastors and laity during his early years as professor, but he won over the opposition by consistently teaching his Social Gospel, until almost all of the Augustana pastors, synod presidents, and professors were taught by him. The outsiders won the victory for which they had prayed.

4

MATTSON'S THEOLOGY

The impact of Mattson upon the social consciousness of the Augustana Synod owes much to his distinctive theological articles and books. The letters from his students reveal Mattson's ability through repetition to imprint his basic maxims on the minds of his audience. Since he used his books (especially *Christian Ethics*) in class, they are direct evidence of his teaching style and the content of his thought. Moreover, his books and articles were variations on the same themes, so that one can ascertain his favorite theologians and straw men. Decades after graduating from Augustana, Mattson's students were able to quote verbatim individual statements from his lectures, such as "Morality is the cement which binds and holds society together."[72] Since many of those students remembered Mattson as the most influential professor at Augustana, one can hardly overestimate the impact of his theology on the Augustana Synod and, indirectly, on the Lutheran Church in America. However, Mattson's different theological approach was not adopted by his students automatically. (Many found virtue in the theologians he attacked or ignored.) The students were required to take ethics, an unusual departure for a Lutheran seminary. By the time other seminaries caught up with Augustana in teaching ethics, Mattson's students were imbued with a theology foreign to traditional Lutheranism and no longer acknowledged among the liberal Protestant bodies. (The term "Social

Gospel'' receded from the annual index of *Christian Century* in the 1930's and disappeared by 1934, when Mattson was tenured.)

Mattson's theology reflected two main sources of authority, the Bible and Walter Rauschenbusch. Both sources are essential in understanding Mattson and his influence on Swedish Lutherans. Mattson's use of the Bible displayed the Augustana Synod's Rosenian piety, which emphasized daily study of the Bible. Rosenian piety was derived from the impact of Carl Olof Rosenius, (1816-1868), a Swedish lay leader influenced by Wesleyan piety. Rosenius, the most important figure to influence Augustana pioneers, taught salvation through grace alone. However, he emphasized that the Christian should manifest evidence of the Holy Spirit in a life of holiness. Pietists therefore refrained from the sins of society and opened themselves to charges of works-righteousness. Rosenian piety included Bible study, prayer, a sanctified life, and a warmth of emotion which traced its roots to the revivals held at the beginning of Augustana's history in Sweden. The Augustana Synod placed more emphasis on adherence to the Scriptures than to the Reformers. Augustana parishes enjoyed large Bible study classes, and Augustana pastors preached exegetical rather than thematic sermons. Biblical authority did not displace Luther in the Augustana Synod, but it did subordinate Luther to the Bible. As one of Mattson's students said, ''My feeling is that Mattson did not feel that Martin Luther was the last word on questions of ethical and social problems, but that Christ was.''[73] In contrast to Lutheran bodies more involved in doctrinal repristination, Augustana debates were best settled with appeals to Scripture, rather than to the Augsburg Confession or to the Book of Concord. The emphasis on Luther was not lacking in the Augustana Synod, which certainly felt an intense loyalty to the confessions, but it was not as great as outsiders have assumed. The position of code ethics alone speaks more for the influence of Wesleyan piety (via Rosenius) than the confessions. In fact, code ethics obtained authority from Augustana's understanding of New Testament sanctification, which meant (at first) abstention from alcohol, cards, dancing, and sexual immorality.

Mattson was not the main teacher of the Bible at the seminary, but he did offer electives in the Old Testament prophets, and the Epistle of James. He also wrote a few articles on Biblical topics for Lutheran periodicals. Mattson's articles on the Bible were among the few he wrote which did not emphasize social action or rural church ministry. His publications and his teaching in the area of Scripture testify to the importance of Biblical authority in Mattson's own thought. He used his knowledge of the Bible to support his claims about the relationship between faith and social ministry. Citing Scriptures well known to the Augustana constituency, Mattson attacked Lutheran "quietism," as he called it, and advocated a social understanding of the Kingdom of God.

Mattson's second authority, Walter Rauschenbusch, was not cited as often as the Bible in his publications, but echoes of Rauschenbusch are found in most of Mattson's writings. From the beginning of his teaching career to the end, Mattson considered Rauschenbusch the most important figure in ethics. He quoted others (E. Stanley Jones, Richard Ely, Washington Gladden, J. H. W. Stuckenberg, Archbishop Nathan Söderblom, and Toyohito Kagawa), but Rauschenbusch remained the pivotal theologian for Mattson. This is crucial for realizing Augustana's unique position among Lutheran bodies. Mattson taught what others critiqued, whether it was the works-righteousness of Rauschenbusch (according to conservatives) or his optimism (according to liberals). While some of Mattson's students claimed that their professor was not a Social Gospel advocate but rather a critic, the evidence reveals a different story. Mattson found fault with the term "Social

Gospel,'' but only insofar as it implied that the Gospel could be either individual or social. Mattson urged that the Gospel included both individual conversion and the application of the Gospel to social issues. In saying this, he emphasized that all Christians have social responsibilities and that all reform must be based upon faith in Christ. In this he paralleled the reforming zeal and the pastoral concern of Rauschenbusch. For Rauschenbusch and for Mattson, the main theme and the support for Christian social action was the Kingdom of God.

Still it seems perplexing that Mattson found a hearing while speaking for a theology rejected by so many other Lutherans. Why was Mattson not driven out of the seminary and replaced by someone more traditional? While Mattson suffered for many years, he was able to call upon certain aspects of Augustana piety receptive to the Social Gospel. The seminary had rejected the timeworn dogmatics of the late dean, so the theological climate was in flux during the 1930's. Aiding Mattson's cause was the bitter attack by Missouri Synod leaders upon the synod for entertaining the Swedish theologian, Nathan Söderblom, during his 1923 visit to America. Söderblom was a world figure, idolized by most Swedish Lutherans, including Bergendoff. Söderblom (1866-1931) taught theology before being named archbishop of Sweden in 1914. He wrote that Christianity was unique among world religions in offering a communion with God mediated through Christ. Mattson found in Söderblom an authority who supported activism in Christianity rather than quietism, an optimistic attitude of trying to better the world, rather than a pessimistic attitude of withdrawal from the world. Söderblom also emphasized the Kingdom of God in his theological writings, a fact not ignored by Mattson in his citations. When Augustana leaders were invited to the world church conference in Stockholm, Sweden, in 1925, they found that the topic of the meeting was the Kingdom of God. The event marked a turning point in ending the parochialism of the Augustana Synod.[74] In addition, Mattson was able to call upon the Augustana tradition of serving others through the Inner Mission movement fostered by another Augustana patriarch, W. A. Passavant. Finally, the piety of Rauschenbusch was not alien to Augustana members. Rauschenbusch called upon the teaching and the example of Christ in his exhortations to create a new social order. Thus, the emphasis on the social responsibilities of Christians and the Biblical basis for reform all contributed to an atmosphere of acceptance in the Augustana Synod.

Mattson's publications were mostly argumentative, not systematic, and aimed at a specific group of people: pastors and members of the Augustana Synod. Some publications reached a wider Lutheran audience, but most were written for Swedish-American Lutherans. He published *Christian Ethics* in 1938, revised in 1947. *Christian Ethics* was translated into Chinese and published by the Lutheran Literature Society at the Taoshing Publishing House, going through three editions, and was used widely in Bible schools and theological seminaries in Southeast Asia.[75] Nels Ferre required *Christian Ethics* in his course at Andover-Newton Theological School. He wrote in 1940:

> I can't tell you what a delightful experience I have had the last two days reading your book. It definitely is a contribution to Christian Ethics. It is penetrating both in principle and application. It is exactly the kind of book my students need because it is soundly Christian throughout.[76]

Christian Ethics enjoyed wide circulation in the Augustana Synod, unlike Mattson's *Christian Social Consciousness*, 1953. The second book is a clearer, more succinct explication of Mattson's theology; it includes many of his favorite maxims and stories. A third source of Mattson's views on social issues is his *Polity of the Augustana Lutheran Church*, 1941, revised 1952. Mattson taught the required polity course, so all pastors bought the book, which was based on Lindberg's earlier book on polity.[77] Mattson's final book on social action originated in his Knubel-Miller lectures, *The Social Responsibility of Christians*, 1960.[78] The ULCA lectures, given at several seminaries, were an honor for Mattson. Most pastors of the ULCA had an opportunity to read Mattson's lectures, since they were sent to all ULCA churches through grant money.

Mattson's research in the area of rural churches led to *Mid-West Rural Churches of the Lutheran Augustana Synod*, 1944, a booklet revised and retitled *Town and Country Churches*, 1946.[79] The revised edition was published by the National Lutheran Council. Mattson included a prayer by Rauschenbusch at the end of both editions, but the booklet was devoted mainly to practical strategies in the parish. Mattson's study reiterated his basic claim that the Church must take responsibility for conditions in the community. J. F. Oberlin (1740-1826) was Mattson's example of a pastor who built up his parish by building up the community. Oberlin was a German Lutheran pastor who served a remote and troubled area of Alsace for 59 years. He helped the rural community build schools, roads, bridges, warehouses, and banks, working to improve all aspects of life in the area.

God as Creator

All of Mattson's work reveals an affirmation of natural law as the foundation for ethics. Since God created the universe, man must obey the laws governing the world. More than once, Mattson quoted Luther's comment on the Decalogue:

> . . . so we read Moses, not because he concerns us or that we must obey him, but because he rightly

> corresponds with natural law. Again he says, 'I keep the law of Moses, not because Moses has commanded it, but because it is planted in my nature and Moses rightly corresponds with nature.'[80]

Thus all concepts of law, morality or ethics ultimately are derived from God's creation and man's perception of that creation. While man may misinterpret the meaning of justice, the existence of moral codes indicates a common understanding that good and evil can be defined. Even atheistic states, such as Marxist ones, define good and evil based upon the Judeo-Christian heritage of Karl Marx. Man may deny the existence of God, or (like Kant) be unable to prove God's existence, or subvert the meaning of religion, but the moral order testifies to God's design. However, the revelation of God through nature is insufficient. God also reveals himself through history and through Jesus Christ. No understanding of God or ethics can be complete or satisfactory without the knowledge of Christ.[81] God's activity in history is especially evident in the crucifixion of Christ. Only through Christ can God's complete revelation be perceived, that God's love for man might be returned and also shown to man's neighbor.

Mattson did not expend great effort in defining God, since God could not be found at the end of a logical syllogism (a well-known Mattson maxim).[82] The purpose of dogmatics is to describe the content of faith, but speculative theology cannot inspire one to faith in God, any more than one can experience gravity by reading Newton's physics. Mattson felt strongly that Barth repeated the mistakes of the Lutheran orthodox by making the Christian faith too propositional, too transcendent. Mattson often referred to Barth as a Fundamentalist, one of his worst charges. The neo-orthodox, according to Mattson, were unable to connect their speculations with the problems of mankind.

"The fact is that theological systems are not and have never been the dynamic for social reconstruction."[83] Mattson thought that modern theology abandoned the immanence of God in favor of the transcendence of the Creator.

Mattson did not think that any person or church became socially concerned as a consequence of theological formulations. "The social concern of the Christian is not the end product of any theological system, liberal or orthodox, but it is given in his sense of a divine presence with its compelling imperative."[84] People must experience the hurts of society first hand in order to grasp the relation between faith and ethics. God seeks man, actively revealing Himself through the spiritual influences surrounding man.[85] God reveals Himself, but not all are sensitive to the revelation. Those who subjectively receive God's objective revelation repeat the burning bush of Moses' experience and apply the truth not only to themselves but to all mankind.

Man

Mattson rejected predestination, because it did not mesh with the facts. Man may refuse the grace of God, and therefore has responsibility through his free will. "The cure lies in the medicine, but the patient is responsible for his illness if he refuses to take it."[86] The purpose of ethics is to define the duties of the Christian on the basis of his experience of God's revelation through Christ. Mattson stated:

> In considering the Christian life we are interested not only in deeds but in motives, not only in acts but in character, not only in doing but in being . . . Luther said that good deeds do not produce a good man, but a good man does good works.[87]

Mattson differentiated between a man being prevented from doing evil (in jail) and a man refusing to do evil, between a good deed being done for the wrong reasons (personal gain, fear), and one done for the right reasons.

Man's sinfulness can be defined as opposition to God or as refusal to carry out duties to man. In contrast, love is the fulfilling of the law, the love of God and the love of neighbor. "A lack of love, or lovelessness, is the heart of sin."[88] Child labor and impure foods are both examples of man's ability to tolerate evil.

Moral Judgments

When Mattson discussed man's role in the world, he invariably used a combination of authorities for determining values; Kant, the Old Testament prophets, Jesus' teaching about the Kingdom of God, and the interpretation of Walter Rauschenbusch. The use of Kant was perhaps derived from Mattson's association with Luther Weigle at Yale.[89] Mattson was introduced to the social implications of the prophets when he taught the subject for one year at Upsala College.

Mattson did not deal extensively with Kant, but referred to the philosopher in his books and articles consistently. Kant answered two basic problems for Mattson: (1) how does one deal with the distinction between good and evil, considering differing value systems throughout history and around the world? (2) how can one justify the intervention of the Christian in the issues of public life? Mattson found harmony in Kant's treatment of the ultimate worth of the individual, as an end rather than a means to an end, and the Biblical view of man as God's creation. Morality as a force points to God's authority and leads man to establish morality in all forms of life.

Mattson often reviewed the prophetic books, one by one, to prove how often their religious statements dealt at the same time with social problems: food, wages, oppression, and business concerns. Throughout his career, Mattson made a sharp distinction between the prophetic and the priestly role of the minister, a distinction Rauschenbusch made in *A Theology for the Social Gospel*.[90] Mattson used the prophets not only to plead for social concerns in a church where Inner Mission theology prevailed, but he also used prophetic authority to call upon the resources of all Christians in combating social evil. While the Augustana Synod was not "high church" by contemporary standards, Mattson found all efforts at liturgical reform both priestly (in the worst sense) and indicative of a moribund social consciousness. Mattson felt that the preaching of the Word was essential, while all forms of priestcraft were not. Mattson, as seminary class advisor, asked pointedly whether the pastors would be prophets or priests.[91] When the Service Book and Hymnal came out in anticipation of the LCA and TALC mergers, he wondered often and loudly about the relevance of Elizabethan English and praying for deliverance from the horns of the unicorn (Introit, Palm Sunday). E. E. Ryden, Jr. created a unicorn for Mattson out of a live goat and a "plumber's friend." (Ryden was almost expelled by Karl Mattson, but A.D. loved the joke.)[92]

Mattson quoted with approval Rauschenbusch's passage on the difference between the priest and the prophet.[93] The priest is a religious professional, jealous, tampering with history, opposed to free inquiry, selfishly exploiting religion for the interests of his class. The prophet has a personal experience of God, is an enemy of priestly religion, cares for religious rights, and has a keen feeling about God's opposition to oppression and injustice. Mattson compared the vested interests of the priest to the prophetic role of Luther, who broke with "the sacerdotalism of the Middle Ages."[94] In *Answer to Emser of Leipzig*, Luther claimed that the priesthood was a man-made custom, not Scriptural. A group of people, captive in the wilderness could, according to Luther, set apart someone to serve as minister without the approval of bishops. Mattson felt that

Lutherans had allowed their church to become priestly, escapist, and unconcerned with social problems.[95] When he retired, many of his students quoted his favorite passage in Amos, when they wrote of their gratitude for his work:

> I hate, I despise your feasts,
> and I take no delight in your solemn assemblies . . .
> But let justice roll down like waters,
> and righteousness like an ever-flowing stream.
>
> AMOS 5:21-24

Bergendoff used the same quotation in his funeral tribute to Mattson.[96] To be a prophet was Mattson's aspiration and his goal for every seminarian and church member. When he asked that businesses (and church institutions) place people ahead of dollars in ethical decisions, Mattson was reflecting his concern for the ultimate worth of the individual and the prophetic role of the Church. Both Kant and the prophetic tradition pointed toward the question of "what is the highest good?" which Mattson discussed through his main theological theme: the Kingdom of God.

Kingdom of God

Mattson left little doubt about the importance of the Kingdom of God in his writings, nor was he reticent about giving credit to Rauschenbusch for this insight. When Mattson gave his address at his installation as tenured professor in 1934, he said:

> I could think of no subject more intimately related to all the fields in which I am interested as a professor than the subject, 'The Kingdom of God.' Here is a subject which touches philosophy, ethics, sociology, church polity and runs like a red thread through all Scriptures.[97]

In 1960, he reiterated his perception of the Kingdom of God as crucial for any type of Christian social responsibility:

> When the meaning of the kingdom of God is grasped, religion immediately becomes social in its outlook because the kingdom of God is, in itself, a social concept. Many years ago I determined to find out what those who manifested a sense of social responsibility had, theologically, that was absent in those who failed to emphasize the social responsibility of the Christian. The answer was not difficult to find. Almost invariably a sense of social responsibility was connected with an insight into the meaning of the kingdom of God.[98]

Mattson then quoted Rauschenbusch for support of this thesis: ''If theology is to offer an adequate doctrinal basis for the social gospel, it must not only make room for the doctrine of the Kingdom of God, but give it a central place.''[99] One can therefore understand how the Kingdom of God became a litmus test for Mattson in his theological formation. Mattson found warrant for its importance in its use in both Old and New Testaments, and in the use of the term by Jesus Himself.[100]

Mattson made an unusual observation in his discussion of the Kingdom of God in *Christian Social Consciousness.* Lutherans writing about theology or ethics either choose Luther or the seventeenth century orthodox theologians as their authorities, but Mattson used his Kingdom of God litmus test to show the error of Lutheranism. Mattson felt that any theological system not giving the Kingdom of God central place would be malformed.[101] Protestants and Catholics both have erred in giving forgiveness of sins the central place in their theology, or in misunderstanding the meaning of the Kingdom of God. Therefore, Mattson only accepted those theologians who expressed a theological conception of the Kingdom of God consonant with his. Mattson was not setting up his own standards, from his perspective, but choosing Scripture as a test of theological soundness. In this he was more like Luther, but certainly atypical for a Lutheran of his time.

Mattson did not want to deny the importance of the doctrine of forgiveness:

> The doctrine of the forgiveness of sins is a very important doctrine. It is a specific article in the Apostle's Creed itself. Without forgiveness there is no reconciliation with God for man. We must not detract from the significance of this doctrine but it does not exhaust the meaning of the Christian faith.[102]

Mattson did not think that the Kingdom of God was the state into which the forgiven Christian went, nor was it a synonym for heaven, nor was it equivalent to the visible Church, nor was it a temporal millenium. Mattson pointed out that the Church is mentioned in the Gospels only twice, while the Kingdom is mentioned over one hundred times. As he stated:

> We must not minimize the significance of the church but it does not have the central place that the Kingdom of God does in the teaching of Jesus. Jesus calls us to first seek the Kingdom of God, and then we must view the church in its relationship to the Kingdom.[103]

Mattson implied that the emphasis on forgiveness had led to the individualism and quietism of churches. He argued that the Christian should not only emphasize the second article of the Apostles' Creed, but also the first and third. God created the world and through His Holy Spirit sanctifies the world, as people grow in character and service to the Kingdom.[104]

Mattson's concern with New Testament authority also manifested itself in his love for the Epistle of James, which was not Luther's favorite book. Mattson taught that not all sins were equal, and used James 2:10 to support his argument. Mattson was not explicit about which sins he considered more significant, perhaps because he was wary of casuistry. One might surmise that Mattson failed to specify personal sins because he felt the emphasis on personal morality had displaced any concept of economic or social justice in the Augustana Synod or in Lutheranism. Mattson was inclined to view sin as that which did harm to the self or to others. Thus he could not state that dancing itself was evil, but he could question the effects of movies on youth.[105]

Mattson also departed from typical Lutheran ethics in his treatment of forgiveness in relation to sanctification and character. Sanctification is almost entirely absent in Lutheran theology, but Augustana placed considerable emphasis on the concept in its early days.[106] Sanctification did not receive much attention in Lutheran theology because of the perceived dangers of works-righteousness and the emphasis on sanctification in non-Lutheran groups, such as the Baptists and Methodists. The Lutheran state churches of Europe were not concerned with sanctification and therefore did not produce university theologians who dwelt on the subject. Since the Augustana Synod was founded by those who rebelled against the worldly character of the Church of Sweden, sanctification was a major emphasis of the pioneer days. Sanctification was the goal of the Augustana code and the purpose for church discipline. The believer, by shunning the allure of the world, grew in Christian character. Those who could not keep the standards of the faith were warned, then excluded from the parish. This was, of course, the result of Wesleyan influence through

Rosenius and other Pietist leaders of the Awakening in Sweden. A question and answer column from Mattson's teaching days reveals that little preaching on sanctification was being done in the synod by the 1930's.[107] Augustana's concept of sanctification was an either/or proposition; the Christian either rejected all worldly pleasures or the significance of the faith. The hodgepodge list of sin diminished as some sins became socially acceptable: Masonic lodges, smoking, dancing, drinking, card playing, theatre, and divorce. Augustana liberals reduced the list, while conservatives fought for continuance of complete sanctification. Luther did not reject growth in the Christian faith, but Lutherans have seldom used sanctification as a term in ethics, concentrating on the meaning of justification instead.[108]

Mattson's atypical approach was to retain sanctification, but use the term in a different sense than that which Swedish-American Lutherans understood. He was not inclined to attack the Augustana code head on. He wrote:

> Salvation from the ethical point of view is not fully complete. Christians grow toward it (1 Pt. 2:2) work it out (Phil. 2:12) and may be nearer to it than when they first became believers (Rom. 13:11). The Christian should grow 'toward the fullness of the stature of Christ.' Through salvation the image of God in man should be more and more fully restored (2 Cor. 3:18).[109]

As official recognition of sanctification was diminishing in the Augustana Synod, Mattson gave it new meaning. He wrote that character and salvation were intimately related. "Character is achieved in and through salvation."[110] The difficulty with the ordinary concept of salvation in the revival meeting was that the process stopped with the initial act of repentance. A sense of sin led to God's gift of faith, but a true conversion experience meant a "complete change of personality so that the convert is headed another way than before." (Mattson's father came from Värmland, Sweden, where revivals flourished.) The Christian life was one of repentance, and repentance was "more a character than an act. Repentance is to be looked upon as a type of life rather than an episode."[111] Thus, conversion was not a matter of "accepting Christ" in the revivalistic sense, but a new life in Christ, in which the believer pointed toward one goal.

Conversion, for Mattson, was not simply turning from paganism to Christianity. He felt that one could be a Christian and have a conversion experience. This was likely to happen between the ages of 12 and 24, but it could happen later.[112] Confirmation was a time at which a deeper faith could be discovered by the adolescent. Mattson's own change of heart about the social implications of the Gospel was termed a conversion by his brother Karl, and A.D. left little doubt that he desired a similar conversion in all his students, colleagues, and audiences. The conversion he experienced, the conversion he desired for others to have, was not a conversion to the theology of A. D. Mattson, but to a complete recognition of the meaning of the Kingdom of God. He pointed out that Rauschenbusch had experienced a burning bush encounter with God at the edge of Hell's Kitchen in New York City. The encounter had turned a typical minister into an extraordinary reformer:

> He saw the effects of poverty and unemployment. Malnutrition, disease and crime in the tenement districts touched the heart of the young pastor and he became convinced that such an environment was neither conducive to the saving of souls nor a safe place for saved souls. And thus, social needs became for Rauschenbusch also a channel through which his religious life flowed. Here

> human need and a sense of God had again met. The call of Moses was similar to the call of Rauschenbusch. Where human need and God meet in the consciousness of an individual something is apt to happen in society. This is the road that will lead to a social awakening in the church.[113]

We do not have an account of Mattson's conversion to the same ideal, though Rauschenbusch recorded his own in *Christianizing the Social Order*, but we do have the effects of Mattson's change in his life and his theology of the Kingdom of God.[114]

Mattson defined the Kingdom of God in his *Christian Ethics* as "the Christian's highest good."[115] This was established when Jesus said, "Seek first his kingdom and his righteousness; and all these things shall be added to you," (Mt. 6:33). The phrase also expressed "the very essence of Christ's life purpose."[116] Jesus preached in Galilee saying, "Repent and believe in the Gospel: the time is fulfilled and the kingdom of God is at hand." The term faded from church usage for a number of reasons. The epistles avoided the term because of revolutionary or nationalistic connotations, or because Gentile readers would not have been familiar with the term. Early church fathers thought of the Kingdom as a temporal kingship to be established by Christ in Jerusalem. "When Augustine identified the millenium with the earthly reign of the church, the doctrine lost its ecclesiastical standing (*The City of God*, Book XX, sections 7-11)."[117] The 1925 Stockholm conference on Life and Work (attended by Augustana Synod president, G. A. Brandelle and Pastor G. Rast) agreed that the Church is the means by which God brings in the Kingdom. For Augustana, the conference was the denomination's first experience of being part of the worldwide Church. For Söderblom, it was an opportunity to influence the Church with a dynamic interpretation of the Kingdom of God. For Mattson, the beloved archbishop and the epochal conference supported a new direction for Augustana's social consciousness.[118]

God is active in human history, so theology cannot be a "matter of conserving and perpetuating doctrines but will concern itself with the resistance which is to be overcome and the great ends which are to be gained."[119] Mattson defined the Kingdom of God as "the rule of God in the hearts and lives of men." In the Lord's Prayer, he found great significance in the connection of the petition "Thy kingdom come" and "Thy will be done on earth as it is in heaven."[120] God's Kingdom comes only to the extent that His will is obeyed in all human activities. "*It is the very energy of God pressing in upon human affairs.*" (Mattson's emphasis).[121] Mattson stressed not only the activity of man in establishing the Kingdom of God, but also (and especially) the activity of God. The Kingdom of God is a gift, just as salvation is a gift. "Faith itself is a gift of God but only that faith is vital which energizes in love."[122] As God establishes His Kingdom, He takes us into His service. Whatever man does for the Kingdom of God is in fact God's activity in man. Attacking the old-time religion of Lutherans, Mattson argued that:

> To wait for the coming of the Kingdom in the spirit of quietism is not true to the genius and the dynamic power of the Christian faith. A gift is bestowed upon us but that gift is a call to a task, in which God uses men as His instruments.[123]

This concept of the Kingdom then gives the Christian a distinct philosophy of history.

Mattson compared several philosophies of history with the Christian view. The Hegelian philosophy absolutized the State, creating a synthesis between the warring elements of society. Marxist philosophy argued for the revolution of the laboring classes to produce the opposition to capital, so that a new society could be formed. Both philosophies made man the determiner of his own destiny. But God remains the sovereign of history. "Man is responsible for his damnation and his social maladjustments, but God is sovereign."[124]

Mattson realized that the Social Gospel had been criticized for excessive optimism, which two world wars and "more sober thinking" destroyed.[125] Mattson was not willing to reject the idea of progress, which had been attacked by the neo-orthodox. However, the naive optimism that society constantly improves deserved all the scorn it received. The only kind of progress is that which God accomplishes through history, and it may include the destruction of nations and cultures. Excessive pessimism can be as great a danger as naive optimism. Spengler's view of history as cyclical offered no hope for the Christian, no dynamic for social betterment.[126] Mattson did not expect to see the Kingdom of God realized in his own time, since God's ways are mysterious and since each battle must be won slowly. He acknowledged:

> . . . the ideals of the Kingdom of God will undoubtedly never be fully realized in history, but again, this does not imply that there can be no progress toward those ideals. The Christian is devoted to a realization of such progress.[127]

As Christians, we follow the path of duty and leave the future to God.[128]

Mattson knew that the Social Gospel was held in low esteem by some theologians. Even his brother Karl, who studied under Reinhold Neibuhr at Union Theological Seminary, had a different theological approach. (Mattson, who did not agree with Reinhold Niebuhr's theology, enjoyed quoting him to the effect that Rauschenbusch was the real founder of the social Christianity and its most brilliant and most satisfying exponent.)[129] Mattson acknowledged that the exegesis of Rauschenbusch could be challenged by New Testament research, and that Rauschenbusch's hopes for stopping the transmission of sin through redeemed social institutions were naive. But Mattson attached the greatest importance not to the current status of Rauschenbusch but to the authority of Scriptures. Mattson felt that not only the teachings of Christ were authoritative for the Christian, but also the life of Christ as an example for the believer. This not only reflected Luther's teaching that Christians should be little Christs; it also was harmonious with the piety of the Augustana Synod. Augustana members could not argue with Mattson's basis for his theology, but they disagreed with his interpretation of Scriptures. Mattson was particularly effective with those students of the Lutheran Bible Institute wing who separated personal piety from public responsibility. Mattson enjoyed revealing to his most conservative students that they were not being true to the prophets, Christ, or Luther.

Mattson's primary assault was on the quietism or individualistic piety of Lutherans, who felt that the highly developed institutions of the Inner Mission were in fact a Christian response to social needs. Mattson did not think that hospitals, orphanages, sailors' missions, and old-age homes were bad, but that they were inadequate responses to social ills. He gave as an illustration a city without water. The Christian response would be to give the thirsty a drink of water. One approach would be to bring in as many pails of water as humanly possible. A better approach would be to build a pipeline and solve the problem.[130] Mattson's often repeated example of the Good Samaritan (quoting E. Stanley Jones) asked whether one should bind the wounds of the beaten man or make the road to Jericho safe. Mattson faulted the Inner Mission for binding up the wounded without dealing with the source of the injury. "Charity is a Christian virtue but so, also, is justice."[131] Just as the disciples of Rauschenbusch forgot that morality needs religion, so also have the disciples of Luther forgotten that he assumed Christians would participate in the social order.[132] Luther's emphasis on the individual was an antidote to the political nature of Christianity of his time. He condemned the oppression of the poor, demanded reform of university education, and advocated laws to address the needs of society.[133] Mattson argued:

> . . . Luther's followers have continued to make use of his individualistic emphasis and have forgotten what he considered an axiom, namely this, that religion is concerned with the social order.[134]

Furthermore, Luther refused to bow to the temporal powers when he felt it would compromise his Christian convictions at the Diet of Worms. Yet Lutherans have turned his distinction between the power of the State and the power of the Church into an abject submission to the temporal powers. Quoting H. Richard Niebuhr, Mattson noted that Lutherans have substituted two parallel, separated moralities for Luther's closely related ethics. Mattson added dryly: "At any rate, the followers of Luther will derive little comfort for their quietism in the writings of the Reformer himself."[135]

5

THEOLOGY FOR SOCIAL ISSUES

Mattson's main causes were: labor, the rural church, peace, and politics. In *Christian Ethics* and *Christian Social Consciousness*, he dealt more fully with issues that became part of Augustana's social statements. His theological approach explains the direction of Augustana's social involvement. Since he chaired the Commission on Morals and Social Problems of the Augustana Synod for its entire existence, served as a member of the parallel commission in the American Lutheran Conference, and served on the National Lutheran Council's committee, his perspective on social issues clearly influenced their formulation and expression. While the National Lutheran Council's committee never achieved much, the American Lutheran Conference and the Augustana Synod did work through their committees to address social issues. Mattson's theological perspective set apart Augustana as a Lutheran body, ahead of the others in expressing concern for the problems of society, distinct in its theological expression.

Labor and Economics

Mattson was not an ardent socialist, but neither was he an ardent capitalist. One of the major problems in the world was the unequal distribution of wealth and the oppression of the poor. Whether he called upon the prophets, or the "Amos of the New Testament" (James), or the example of Christ, Mattson attacked Christianity for blessing the *status quo*. According to Mattson, the Gospel did not endorse any one set of economic prejudices.[136] The Church could speak about economic matters because the Bible did not separate the religious realm from the economic situation. The problem with capitalism was the profit motive, which made the worker a means to an end. In order to maximize profits, too many businessmen engaged in cut-throat competition, strove for lower wages, and cut corners on safety measures. The end result was suffering by the many for the sake of a few. Mattson observed that:

> People with kind and benevolent dispositions do make use of the capitalistic system, but the characteristic institution of the capitalistic system is the corporation, which is impersonal, soulless, and conscienceless.[137]

Although he did not approve of the totalitarian stance of Russian communism, Mattson felt that the Russian system had proved that human abilities could be harnessed apart from the profit motive. He also felt that true Christian communism, as practiced in the Book of Acts, could be compatible with American ideals. He often referred in his lectures to the Koinonia community in Americus, Georgia, which he had visited. Mattson believed strongly in cooperatives, helping to start them, keeping in contact with other believers, and promoting them in his books. The Rochdale Cooperative in England was his example for a means of overcoming economic adversity through a sharing of capital and labor.[138]

Mattson was more famous for his activities in the labor movement itself than in his efforts with cooperatives. The situation of the worker distressed him, especially when he saw poor wages and pathetic working conditions excused as a means to uphold the prosperity of a business. For Mattson, Christianity meant that persons were more important than dollars. His support of the union at the Augustana Book Concern and at John Deere (which was seen as harmful to the synod's interests) exemplified his compassion for the individual.

Mattson could use Amos and James to support his position, and he was fond of quoting the statements by churches favorable to organized labor. But his own theological position grew out of contact with social needs. Theology does not produce compassion; first-hand experience does. A person who realizes that Christians are responsible for economic injustice will seek to redress the wrongs done by society. Once the assumption of non-involvement is destroyed, the conclusions about solutions follow naturally. Mattson endeavored to turn compassion for the individual into preventative measures. Justice demands that the Christian help legislate the given morality of natural law. A correct theology is necessary but not sufficient for reform.

The problem with the Church is that the institution remains a middle-class ghetto. Involvement in economic issues may open the Church to the lower class, but the work must be done simply because the need exists, not because it may strengthen the Church.

Mattson's concern for the rights of the working man was proclaimed throughout his teaching career at Augustana. The first evidence of his involvement is found in his membership in the Religion and Labor Foundation (RLF), which began in 1932 under the leadership of Jerome Davis and Willard Uphaus, two of Mattson's professors at Yale. By 1937, Mattson was serving on the executive committee with Douglas Macintosh and H. Reinhold Niebuhr. Other members of the RLF were Roland Bainton, Robert Calhoun, Harold Fey, Halford Luccock, and Henry P. Van Dusen. Mattson's friendship with Davis and Uphaus led to other involvements, such as the trips to Russia (1938 and 1957), mentioned previously, and trips to the South to study the sharecropper situation, the first in 1936. The trips to the South introduced Mattson to the plight of the Black sharecroppers and acquainted him with such men as John L. Lewis of the United Mine Workers, Martin Luther King, Jr., and the interracial community of Koinonia near Plains, Georgia. Mattson's interest in labor issues also led to his friendship with Paul H. Douglas, former U.S. Senator from Illinois.[139] Although Mattson joined other organizations, such as Fellowship of Reconciliation and Promoting an Enduring Peace (another of Davis' concerns), most of his work was done through RLF. The motto of RLF was "to translate the social creed of church and synagogue into the economic life of the local community and the nation." RLF published a magazine called *Economic Justice*. When Mattson wrote an article for *Economic Justice* in 1937, copies of the magazine were sent by RLF to all Augustana pastors.[140]

Mattson's friendship with Davis and Uphaus led him to take sides on the Spanish Civil War, opposing the Fascists. A delegation of Spaniards came to the Rock Island area to voice their opposition to Fascism, but they were not allowed to speak. The incident, in November of 1936, made the local papers. The delegation found that one meeting place after another would not accommodate them, so they finally refused to appear, "giving as their reason that they would not force themselves on any community."[141] Mattson had supported the group's right to speak. Mattson's opposition to Fascism later led to one of the most dramatic moments of his life. When he traveled to Chicago in 1938 to preach at Concordia Lutheran Church, the Silver Shirts' representative warned the pastor that Fascists would attend the service. The word went out that the Fascist sympathizers would shoot Mattson out of the pulpit. Police were placed in the audience.[142] The incident added color to the Mattson legend and distinguished him from the prophet whose courage manifests itself only in the classroom.

Mattson was not simply an observer of the labor situation. He and some of his students helped to organize locals. Myron Lindblom wrote to tell A.D. that he had organized a union in the factory where he worked while he was finishing seminary.[143] Malvin Lundeen, later Augustana Synod president, wrote as a parish pastor to A.D. for advice on labor disputes in his community.[144] Oscar Benson, as president of the Illinois Conference of the Augustana Synod, sought Mattson's advice on a labor speaker for the Conference.[145] Mattson's advocacy for labor caused a stir more than once, especially when he served as a member and president of Augustana Book Concern board. The ABC was the publication house for the entire synod. Mattson was president of the board for three years, using his position to help unionize the ABC. Tensions developed and the typographical union issued an ultimatum. Bersell, Augustana Synod president, wrote to Ivar Johnson, a member of the board, to express his views on the union. Bersell did not blame Mattson for his role in unionizing the ABC, but he did blame "the big union bosses" for making "outrageous demands."[146] Bersell was not willing to accept the ultimatum and cast his vote against it. This did not stop Mattson. Months later, as president of the board, he wrote to R. Leekley, a union official, about how they should proceed with the matter.[147] Mattson was concerned that the men who worked at the ABC should have a living wage, even if it meant increased cost of books for the church. The episode caused tension between Mattson and the ABC management.

In a dipsute at the J. I. Case company in Bettendorf, Iowa, in 1960, Mattson and Father William T. O'Connor, who served together as co-chaplains of the UAW, offered to help mediate the problem. Henry Timbrook of the UAW agreed, but the manager of J. I. Case felt the two chaplains were not neutral.[148]

When a union membership drive came up at the John Deere Company of Moline, Illinois, Mattson circulated a letter at the company in 1960 using his Augustana Seminary letterhead. Augustana Synod president Malvin H. Lundeen wrote to him, while the Kennedy election issue was erupting, that Mattson did not have the right to use Augustana's name with regard to personal issues. Lundeen asked for a letter from Mattson to Deere which would explain that Mattson was not representing the Church in his action.[149] Mattson replied that he had supplied a labor organizer with a statement on the rights of workers to organize. Since Augustana and most other churches had recognized the rights of workers to unionize, Mattson refused to repent of anything he had done. He did not feel that the use of his stationery implied Augustana support of his statement. He offered to spend an evening talking the whole labor matter over with Lundeen.[150]

In 1962, the Quad-City Federation of Labor, AFL-CIO, honored both Father O'Connor and A. D. Mattson for their service through the years. Hundreds of union men came to the dinner to show their appreciation. In April of 1966, Senator Paul H. Douglas paid special tribute to Mattson for his work on behalf of labor at a Lutheran School of Theology seminar.[151]

While Mattson was not a firebrand, the opponents of labor saw him as one. He fulfilled the vision of Charles Brown in trying to speak for the rights of the worker while endeavoring to quell labor violence. He tried to mediate labor disputes, although his contribution was not always appreciated by factory owners. For the fund raisers and money managers in the Augustana Synod, Mattson was an albatross. Critics of his positions tried to use their contributions as weapons to silence him, but to no avail. Mattson's unrelenting courage eventually won him the respect of church leaders, especially since more and more of them were Mattson alumni as the years passed. But Mattson was proud of the fact that he had friends in low places, where most churchmen could not get a hearing. For him, the Gospel must be preached and lived for all classes of mankind, not just for those who endow ecclesiastical institutions. However, Mattson did not want to hurt Augustana by his actions. He thought that Augustana would be strengthened and prospered by making the Gospel relevant to working people.

Church and State

While Augustana pastors were ordained without having heard of Luther's Two Kingdoms doctrine, Mattson did discuss the concept (though obliquely) when treating Church and State in *Christian Social Consciousness.*[152] Mattson indentified the two realms as relating to one another, having separate functions. The church is not a political unit, so neither a theocracy nor caesaropapism is to be desired. The relationship of the Church to the State is to serve as a leaven in society. "The church must, in the name of God, speak to the state, for the state is also God's institution. Furthermore, it is the duty of the church to enlighten the conscience of its membership to the end that the will of God may be accomplished in the social realm."[153] This is exactly what Luther expressed in various writings, that the Church should abstain from temporal authority while still applying the Gospel to the secular realm. Mattson did not invoke the name of Luther, but the concept is familiar enough:

> There are two realms and church and state have separate functions but these realms are not parallel lines which never meet. They constantly cross each other and while it is the province of the state to wield temporal power, it is the province of the church to speak to the state, in the name of God, with respect to His will. All this is to be done to the end that the kingdom of the world may become the Kingdom of our Lord and of His Christ.[154]

A. D. Mattson exerted his influence through his work in politics, the labor movement, and in rural church work. The first two arenas brought him a measure of fame in the Quad-Cities. In rural work he established himself nationally as one of the experts, to such an extent that some students feared he was giving up his earlier social issues. In addition to these activities, he was constantly in demand as a speaker and a preacher, whether at educational conferences, church youth groups, Sunday services, or church anniversaries. This kept him in constant touch with the membership of the synod, and since he stimulated the people in his sermons as he did in some of his public activities, he was well thought of as a minister.

Mattson was an early supporter of Franklin Roosevelt. When Mattson spoke on the local radio for the F.D.R. campaign, several Augustana professors did not speak to him for years.[155] (Mattson's parents, who were Republicans, heard the broadcast and were shocked.) Dr. A. Henry Arp, mayor of Moline, Illinois, wrote to him to thank him for "the stand which you took in behalf of our wonderful president, Franklin D. Roosevelt, and the support which you gave our cause during the recent successful campaign."[156] Others were not as pleased. One person sent a poster which said: "Carrie Nation of Kansas Started to Ruin America 35 Years Ago. Don't Let Landon of Bone-Dry Kansas Finish the Job Carrie Started. One with Roosevelt." The poster had a note written in pencil: "Hope you are satisfied." The poster and many angry letters were a response to a mailing which Mattson and C. L. Esbjörn sent to all Augustana pastors:

> A vote for Landon is a vote against the World Court.
> Republican Platform: 'We pledge that America shall not become a member of the World Court' —a peace agency approved by three Republican

> presidents.
> Landon himself says: 'I doubt if civilization can survive another war. There is no greater responsibility resting on the government than the preservation of peace.'
> Clearly, then, the economic problem is entirely secondary. Besides, many of us believe that is already being satisfactorily solved. Let us vote therefore to save civilization, and thereby save America, from destruction by war. Law or mass murder—which?[157]

One pastor felt that Mattson was working for a communist-supported candidate. Another felt that Mattson was working against the temperance movement and against morals.

In 1948 Mattson caused another tempest when he nominally headed the Henry Wallace movement in the Quad-Cities. President Bersell wrote to one area couple a conciliatory letter:

> I have full confidence in Dr. Mattson's honesty of purpose and I am in sympathy with his fundamental proposition that an opportunity be given for a dispassionate hearing of all sides in a political debate. . . Furthermore, I call your attention to the fact that Dr. Mattson is a professor in the theological seminary and is not connected with Augustana College to which you promised your gift in the recent appeal.[158]

During the same year he was considering running for Congress, after being asked by some labor representatives to enter the primary as a Democrat.[159] Mattson asked Bersell how it would work out and whether it was ethical. Bersell did not oppose the move, but cautioned that a loss would be especially embarrassing for Mattson. Olof Olsson and

Julius Lincoln were Augustana pastors who had served in state offices, so the precedent had been set in the synod. Olsson, ordained in 1863, was elected to the Kansas state legislature. Lincoln, ordained in 1893, served in the New York State legislature. Bersell remarked:

> You are a member of the wrong party and if I were in your district I would not be able to vote for you. You are in the wrong company that has gotten us into the mess that we are in, but perhaps that only gives added reason why some good men should enter the lists and champion the cause of righteousness. Seriously speaking, the whole situation intrigues me very much and my advice to you is to follow your own desire and be ruled by your own conscience and you will come out all right as far as both your ministerial and professional status are concerned.[160]

Mattson decided, however, that he could not run unless as an independent. "As a Christian pastor I cannot identify myself with anything except my Christian faith." The newspapers learned of his candidacy, increasing the temptation for Mattson to run.[161]

Mattson filled one large letter file with the materials and letters involving the 1960 election, which he marked: "Kennedy, 1960." Mattson and 19 other Lutherans signed a statement which said:

> It is apparent that the religious issue is still vital to the voters of the coming election in spite of all efforts of the candidates to avoid it. In view of the repeated clear statements of Sen. John F. Kennedy, we feel that a vote against him because of his religion would be a breach of our tradition of separation of church and state. Furthermore,

> because of Sen. Kennedy's forceful and imaginative stand on foreign policy, civil rights, and social welfare, the undersigned support his candidacy for the presidency of the United States, and thus demonstrate their confidence in his ability to be, not a 'Catholic' or 'Protestant' President, but a great American President.[162]

The signers, mainly Lutheran seminary professors, included George W. Forell, Joseph Sittler, Axel C. Kildegard, James A. Scherer, Jaroslav Pelikan, Sydney E. Ahlstrom, George A. Lindbeck, Warren Quanbeck, A. C. M. Ahlen, Don H. Zinger, and Franklin Sherman. The story appeared on Sunday, November 6, 1960, just before the election, having been released through the New York office of the National Lutheran Council.

Dr. Malvin H. Lundeen, then president of the Augustana Synod, immediately sent a telegram to Mattson and five other professors, stating:

> I respect your right as a private citizen to support for the presidency whomsoever you wish, but I must protest your use of the name Lutheran in connection with a statement issued by a group of theologians including yourself, because of its implication that it is an official Lutheran position.[163]

News releases pointed out that Mattson taught at Augustana Seminary, and the wire story listed him as one of 20 top-ranking Lutheran theologians. Neither item was overlooked as the critics replied.

Lundeen and Dr. Fredrik A. Schiotz, president of the Evangelical Lutheran Church, issued a joint statement on Monday, November 7, 1960, which said:

> The Associated Press story appearing in many Sunday newspapers entitled 'Top Lutheran Theologians Back Kennedy' conveys the impression that it has a measure of official standing. This is completely erroneous. Neither our Churches not our theological seminaries endorse political candidates, whatever the party. While we defend the right of an individual to speak his mind, we strongly deplore individuals allowing the name 'Lutheran' to be identified with a political endorsement.[164]

Lundeen also issued a statement to the *Lutheran Companion*, which outlined the matter (without making reference to the 1960 convention statement) and drew three conclusions.

> 1. Every member has the right and duty to vote.
> 2. Augustana and its institutions do not endorse candidates.
> 3. Pastors, professors, and church executives who publicly endorse a candidate perform a disservice to the Church.[165]

The 1958 synod convention had voted that:

> It is the responsibility of the pastor to assess political and social trends in the light of the Word of God and share his insights in his preaching and teaching with the people of his congregation. The congregation should assume responsibility for encouraging political thinking on the part of its members through such means as forums, study groups and committees. That Christians, as citizens of the state, should be concerned with the affairs of government, become acquainted with political issues, bringing their Christian

> witness to bear on party politics at all levels, and exercise their right to vote. Christians who are qualified should be encouraged to seek public office.[166]

Lundeen did not bring this statement into the discussion, but concluded from "this unfortunate incident:"

> Without a doubt, the finest contribution we as pastors can make to our national way of life at any time is to be faithful in the primary task to which God has called us, viz., to preach and teach the Gospel's redeeming truth in Christ. Let us be prayerfully concerned that we do our work in this area with an ever greater effectiveness! One of the fruits of such a faithful ministry will be a growing sensitivity to the real content of Christian citizenship, to be exercised as a private right and responsibility of every member of the Church.[167]

Lundeen affirmed the individualistic approach to Christian ethics, bypassing the 1958 and 1960 statements of the convention, both of which endorsed study and action on political matters by the Church.

Mattson objected, however, to the suggestion that the signers were implying institutional endorsement:

> The statement which was issued does not even imply anything of the kind. The statement says, 'The undersigned supports his candidacy.' That means in plain English that each and every signer was speaking for himself, and himself alone. He was not even speaking for the group which signed the statement. In the interest of the record, I want to set this matter straight.[168]

Mattson's wife died the week the issue erupted. While the family gathered for the funeral, the phone continued to ring, as people called to denounce Mattson for his action.

Letters and telegrams poured in, most of them condemning Mattson. Many letters came from individuals who warned that Mattson's stand had placed their financial support of the synod in jeopardy. Others included tracts about the dangers of Catholicism in general. Several letters came from church councils. Almost all the letters were signed and carbons sent to various church officials.

Dr. A. C. M. Ahlen of Northwestern Lutheran Theological Seminary wrote to the *Lutheran Companion*:

> Speaking for myself and for no one else, I signed the statement in question because of the political preaching that had been going on for weeks in several Lutheran pulpits. Had it not been for this fact, I certainly would have kept silence; and I am reasonably sure so would my cosigners. According to some persons' way of thinking it was perfectly proper for some clergy to turn their pulpits into political rostrums, but it was entirely wrong for Dr. Mattson to issue a public statement under the circumstances. This kind of reasoning I do not follow.[169]

Writing to Mattson, Norman A. Hjelm, who later served at Fortress Press and then as Director of the Department of Communication of the Lutheran World Federation, commented:

> It was with a sigh of relief that I saw your name included in the list of Lutheran theologians who, according to the *Chicago Sun-Times*, endorsed the candidacy of Senator Kennedy for the Presidency. I have for some time been at work attempting to

> create a more enlightened attitude towards the problem among my parishioners and this statement has served to offset some of the viciousness in recent issues of *The Lutheran Companion*. . . Today my household, at least, is awaiting the outcome which you will know when you receive this letter. Let us hope that we live with Democrats for a while. . .[170]

Mattson became one of the first Lutherans to receive national attention on a national issue. His example doubtless led many of his students to follow the spirit of the 1958 statement on citizenship and involve themselves in politics.

Rural Churches

While the exponents of the Social Gospel concentrated on the city, Mattson also directed his attention to rural needs. Raised in rural parishes, he understood the needs of the farmer and the difficulties of the rural church. His sensitivity to the relationship between poverty and spiritual growth was distinct from that of many church leaders. Many ecclesiastical authorities had hailed the Depression as God's means of humbling people and bringing them back to church.[171] Mattson, in contrast, wrote that the Gospel could not be nurtured in distressed economic situations. Criticizing the spiritual isolation of the typical rural church, he pointed out that the best minister cares deeply about the community life and the needs of the farmer. Mattson's favorite example was Pastor John Frederick Oberlin, who worked for roads, schools, medical care, and economic improvement as he served a poor rural community in Alsace, France. Unfortunately, most rural pastors surveyed did not consider their task to include any revision of the social or economic system in which they found themselves.

Mattson's concern for the rural church was based on a

fear for its survival. He noted that churches involved in helping farmers retain their property prospered with the farmers. Even ecology (then an unknown word) affected the rural parish. When the Dust bowl destroyed farms, the rural churches serving them disappeared as well. He did his best to show that the Lutheran tendency to withdraw from the world was neither noble nor protective. He wrote:

> Wherever and whenever religion has functioned virtually in all human history, it has been an integrating center for life in its totality, and that kind of religion is also the kind which preserves the rural church.[172]

Mattson not only saw the relationship between the social implications of the Gospel and the rural church, he also predicted the plight of the urban church at a time when the downtown churches were dedicating their latest building improvements. He stated:

> In the cities the church has been able to function as an organization rather successfully with its middle-class constituency. However, the crisis will come to the urban church as it has come to the rural church, with equal force, unless the urban church will learn from the rural church.[173]

The urban church did not learn, so many city parishes fled their changing neighborhoods and re-established themselves in the affluent, white suburbs.

Rural churches were a part of Mattson's interest from the 1940's to his retirement. Mattson discussed the problem of rural churches with S. E. Engstrom, executive director of the board of Home Missions of the Augustana Synod. Engstrom wrote to Mattson in 1943 to tell him that the board was giving him a call to study rural churches for three months. He wrote: "The seriousness of this rural Home Mission problem is not felt by everyone yet. We sincerely hope that the facts of your study might bring forth and help to call attention to this situation."[174] Out of this study came *Mid-West Rural Churches of the Lutheran Augustana Synod.*[175] Mattson organized study conferences and spoke at them. He traveled to rural churches and spoke at farmers' meetings. He felt that the rural church must focus on the material and the spiritual needs of the community, from forming farm cooperatives to protecting the environment. In 1951, Mattson wrote to Engstrom that the efforts which had been made from 1941 to 1946 had produced good results in membership increases. Mattson pleaded for additional emphasis on the rural churches.[176] Engstrom agreed and a committee to study the matter was formed in 1952.[177]

Separating Mattson's interests into categories of commission work, labor relations, political activities, and rural church work was done only to create some sense of order in describing his career. Mattson did not lose interest in any social issue. He tended instead to add concerns to his work, all of which fit into his concept of relating the Gospel to society as a whole. While he felt that the reform of society was an end in itself and needed to be a constant goal, he also thought that by being concerned about the world, the Church would gain in strength and membership.

Peace

Mattson did not write extensively about war, although Augustana's social statements (and his students' recollections) reflected an intense interest in pacifism. Mattson was not an isolationalist, nor did he oppose only the wars which failed to meet his approval. Mattson was a consistent pacifist throughout his teaching career. In *Christian Ethics* he discussed three types of Christian attitudes toward war. The first type holds that the Christian has a duty to obey the government in time of war, leaving the moral responsibility to the governing powers. Although Luther himself held this view, a fact not acknowledged by Mattson, he held that such an attitude is not based upon New Testament Christianity, since the Apostles themselves defied the secular authorities with the words, "We must obey God rather than men." (Acts 5:29).[178] The second type holds that a Christian may take part in a just war. But Mattson stated:

> However, as soon as we yield this point in favor of participation in war, we need to remind ourselves that all wars are justified by those who wage them, at least until they are ended.[179]

The third type, the pacifists, refuse to fight evil with its own weapons, realizing that such action only increases evil. Barbarism cannot be fought by adding to barbarism. The Christian pacifist believes that war is antithetical to the spirit of Jesus, who said, "Put your sword back into its place; for all who take the sword will perish by the sword." (Mt. 26:52)[180]

Mattson believed that love, not hate, would win the victory. Christian love is not just an emotion expressed, but activism to achieve a goal. The causes of war are selfishness, a competitive spirit, excessive nationalism, and an unequal distribution of wealth. The causes of war must be dealt with, and war must cease to be an instrument of national policy.

6

RETIREMENT AND DEATH

After the battle over Kennedy's election and the fracas over the union at John Deere, Mattson engaged in no more battles. The loss of his wife may have decreased his flair for controversy, but Mattson did not withdraw from social issues. The creation of the LCA in 1962 changed the context of his service. He continued to teach at the seminary until 1964 and then returned to teach an extra year at the request of the seminary board. He was honored several times for his contributions to labor and to seminary education. The seminary asked him to come back to present special discussions on polity and social issues. Churches continued to invite him to speak. Jerome Davis, writing on Promoting an Enduring Peace stationery, invited him to take another trip to Europe in 1966.[181] He was appointed to the social trends committee of the National Lutheran Council in 1965. Mattson spoke at a pastoral institute for the Kansas Synod, LCA, in 1968, on "Prophetic Word and Pastoral Responsibility." In 1966, he was sending a query to Hyde Park, New York, about the religious attitudes of Franklin Roosevelt.[182]

Mattson died in Bemidji, Minnesota, on October 19, 1970. His only son, A.D., Jr., died less than a year later. His brother Karl had died in 1964. The memorial service for A.D. was held in St. John's Lutheran Church in Rock Island, Illinois, on October 23. Conrad Bergendoff said in his tribute:

> In the light of what has happened to our country and in our churches these past few weeks, it is startling to realize how long ago Dr. Mattson started to rouse our church to action. Not only in classroom and pulpit did he echo the words of the prophets of Israel, but on the floor of synod conventions and in church commissions.[183]

A.D.'s pastor from St. James Lutheran Church in Rock Island said in his funeral sermon:

> He believed in the church. But both as a parish pastor and as a teacher he sought to move the church out from idolatrous self-worship into the mainstream of life. Not only by his persuasiveness as a teacher and his ability to motivate others, but personally, individually, he brought the healing, redeeming word 'where cross the crowded ways of life. . .'[184]

In articles appearing before and after Mattson's death, he was remembered as a man who was the champion of the underdog, a patient counselor of troubled students, a warm-hearted person, a pastor influenced both by the Old Testament prophets and the Social Gospel.

7

MATTSON AND PARAPSYCHOLOGY

One aspect of Mattson's life which has drawn considerable attention, across the United States, has been his belief in para-normal experiences. The discussion among his former students and other Lutherans has arisen because of the publication of *Witness From Beyond*, edited by his daughter, Ruth Taylor.[185] After Mattson's death in 1970, a clairvoyant from England, Margaret Flavell Tweddell, began holding sessions with Ruth Taylor's family. The transcripts from those sessions were edited for the book, which has also appeared in paperback. Some of Mattson's students have expressed disbelief that Mattson ever took psychic experiences seriously. However, Mattson became interested in psychic experiences at Yale, due to the research being done at the psychology department and the interest of Macintosh. Mattson did not express interest in psychic phenomena in his writings or official letters. According to one colleague, his interest grew after the death of his wife in 1960. His deeply felt loss and his interest in para-normal experiences were acknowledged in two letters from his former colleagues. (He may have discussed the subject in personal letters to his family, but family letters were not in the files used by the writer.) One of Mattson's best friends on the faculty, Hjalmer Johnson, wrote:

> Nor did AD regard his assurance of survival as justification for a negative attitude toward all the phenomena of parapsychology. On the contrary, he believed that psychic phenomena, under whatever name they are subsumed, should receive increasing scientific study leading to just evaluations of conscientious work in these significant fields. AD's interest in parapsychology developed strongly during the time of his graduate studies at Yale University Divinity School, and it continued to grow throughout his life.[186]

In 1965, Mattson had offered to translate Nathan Söderblom's book on the mystic Sundar Singh, but the offer was declined by J. B. Lippincott.[187] Late in life, Mattson was increasingly drawn to theologians who took world religions into account. Mattson taught comparative religion at the seminary, and expressed a fondness for Tillich and Chardin in his retirement years. (His son wrote a dissertation on Tillich and Chardin.) Clearly, though, the years in which Mattson taught and wrote were dominated by the thought of Rauschenbusch.

Part II

MATTSON'S INFLUENCE AND FUTURE IMPLICATIONS FOR LUTHERANS

Introduction

Mattson's influence, which continues to be felt, came about chiefly through his role as professor of ethics and sociology at Augustana Theological Seminary for three decades. The second area of influence was in the social statements of the Augustana Synod, where Mattson served as the chairman of the Commission on Morals and Social Problems from its inception in 1937 to the LCA merger in 1962. Mattson also had some impact upon other Lutheran bodies through his work on social statements in the American Lutheran Conference and through his publications. In addition to being a pioneer in the area of Lutheran social action, Mattson established himself as one of the three Lutherans known for expertise and leadership in rural parish work. In the Quad-Cities, where Augustana Theological Seminary was located, Mattson was known for his involvement with labor unions and his activities in the Democratic Party. While Mattson cannot be given sole credit for the changing social consciousness of the Augustana Synod, no other person contributed so much to the transition from quietism to activism among Swedish Lutherans in America.

8

MATTSON AS TEACHER

Mattson exerted his profoundest and most direct influence through the 1,100 students he taught, most of the Augustana ministerium. Some took the electives he offered in Amos, James, and comparative religion. His teaching style was quite unusual. He began his classes in ethics and polity by reading from his lecture notes, which later became books. The students learned that Mattson was at his best when answering questions, and he was ready to respond to any query. Mattson had humorous stories to illustrate certain points, so seminarians often slanted their questions to elicit those stories. Many of his students still remember the stories verbatim and enjoy performing the impersonations of A.D. they polished at the seminary. In the years intervening, many have come to feel that the countless repetition of anecdotes and aphorisms from Mattson had a greater impact than the polished lectures of other professors. H. Conrad Hoyer recalled:

> However, after taking up the responsibilities of a parish pastor, I found myself drawing more and more on the insights which Dr. Mattson had presented and less and less on the contributions of the professors who at the time seemed more stimulating. Other classmates have made the same comment to me from their experience.[1]

Wilton E. Bergstrand, who served as executive secretary of the Augustana Synod's Luther League (youth ministry), felt that the use of repetition was Mattson's deliberate teaching device.[2] Mattson sought the interruptions and became quite frustrated when a class conspired to let him lecture without pause for an entire period.

Unlike many professors, Mattson least enjoyed the responses of students who agreed with him. He loved to bait the conservative seminarians, especially those from rural parishes, by making attacks on fundamentalism, the Republican Party, and quietism. One method was to let the outraged student make a claim about the Biblical proof of a certain idea. One seminarian exclaimed, "The Bible says: 'Prayer changes things.'" Then A.D. would hand the roused student a Bible and say, "Look it up for us." He waited with unfeigned glee while the student thumbed fruitlessly through the Scriptures. His attacks on the Republican Party and capitalism, in a constituency which abhorred liberalism and socialism, caused considerable dismay among students and pre-Mattson pastors who learned of his teaching. He would comment about the *Chicago Tribune's* former right-wing political sentiments: "I read the *Chicago Tribune*, but I also read the Bible to get the other side of the story."[3] His critique of Lutheran quietism was that people wrongly believed the teachings of the Bible to be solely concentrated on individual salvation. He continually emphasized, often using James or the plumbline of Amos, that Christianity has profound social implications.

If a student had come from a progressive parish, such as Salem in Chicago, or had been influenced by Edgar Carlson and other Augustana liberals, Mattson was not shocking. But some seminarians were so distraught by his classes that they considered leaving their chosen profession. Others angrily sought to prove Mattson wrong. Mattson never gave up on his conservative opponents. He waited in the seminary cafeteria for a chance to continue his arguments, offered to have coffee with anyone who disagreed, and went to students' rooms for additional discussions. His personal interest in students, which exceeded that of other professors, won them over. Arthur O. Arnold, former acting president of Lutheran School of Theology at Chicago, stated:

> Anyone who was shocked by him, at first, learned to appreciate him and inevitably was influenced by his interpretation of the gospel. Even when in later years graduates and some colleagues with whom he differed went beyond him in their social views, they have been quick to credit A.D. with a tremendous influence on them and the church.[4]

Lawrence H. Holt, who was involved in Lutheran Social Services, expressed the opinion of many:

> No one left the seminary without at least being aware that Christ was concerned about people and the conditions under which they lived, and if we are to be true to our calling as His followers and minister in His Name, we had better be concerned too and try to show this concern in our ministry.[5]

While Mattson's social concerns may not seem new or remarkable now, he was virtually alone at first in his advocacy of those ideas which are taken for granted by many in the Lutheran Church in America today.

Mattson made the Gospel relevant to society by bringing his experiences and special speakers into the classroom, also by taking students out of the classroom and into social institutions. His trips to the South and to Russia, his experiences with labor and party politics, and his rural travels all contributed to his anecdotes about how religion could affect the world. Not content simply to exegete the book of Amos, he told of the condition of Black sharecroppers on Southern farms owned by large corporations. Pastor J. Erik Holmer, retired minister of Salem in Moline, Illinois, remembered:

> In his Social Ethics classes the memory that lingers most was of his feelings and reaction after he had visited in the South and spent his days among the 'sharecroppers' particularly those that were owned by Singer Sewing Machine. It was a surprise to me that such tactics as 'bosses' who rode around to make certain that none of the sharecroppers would leave, were actually happening here in our country. He was very vivid in his portrayal of the men riding about on horses and the use of long whips to keep control.[6]

Mattson often spoke of his experiences with organized labor, telling the students of the hostile attitudes expressed in the local community. One time he met with union leaders at an open meeting to which a reporter was invited. The door was accidentally closed and locked before the journalist arrived. The headline in the next day's paper was: "Seminary Professor Meets with Union Officials Behind Locked Doors."[7] Mattson's anecdotes helped the seminarians see the other side of labor/management disputes. Since Augustana College depended upon gifts from local corporations and felt obliged to apologize for Mattson's pro-labor views, the students experienced first-hand the institutional pressures exerted by the business world. Labor leaders often spoke to Mattson's classes, as did Mattson's acquaintances in government, rural parish work, and cooperatives. The special speakers and Mattson's reflections from his many trips gave the students a wider perspective in social ministry.[8]

Mattson was not content to bring the outside world into the ivy-covered buildings of Augustana Seminary. He also took the students on field trips, to such places as the East Moline State Hospital (for the mentally ill). E. Theodore Bachmann, a ULCA professor, was so impressed with the way Mattson used these trips that he copied them in his course on social missions at Maywood Seminary in Illinois.[9] Most of Mattson's students, including those who felt no direct influence from his teaching, attended a union meeting with A.D. Others became involved with cooperative associations, where a group set up a store in which the members of the association could buy food and other items wholesale. For Mattson, the Gospel could not be preached by men who had no feeling for the daily experience of people. He wanted to show the future pastors how they could take part in union activities, politics, social institutions, and special interest groups in order to improve man's condition and extend God's rule.

Mattson's influence on his students can only be understood in relation to his attitude about social ministry and the Church. Mattson was not simply a humanist with a sentimental attachment to the Bible. He felt that the Church could only grow if all elements of society became the object of ministry. He did not distinguish between the urban parish and the rural parish in his quest for reform. The urban pastor and the rural pastor both had unique opportunities to become part of the community, whether through work for racial justice in the city or through participation in farmers' organizations in the country. He frequently pointed out that the church which cared about the community grew in membership. In this regard he was quite different from many LCA professors who felt that social ministry in a parish would lead inevitably to a decline in membership, since the more conservative members would be scandalized and quit.[10] Mattson did not consider the alienation of members a prophetic role of the modern church. For him, membership decline was a visible sign of congregations' disinterest in the needs of their own communities.

Mattson never preached directly on social issues, but he used graphic sermon illustrations about sharecroppers and miners. He was considered an outstanding preacher with a powerful voice and a gift for creating vivid word pictures. When he described the crucifixion, listeners felt the pounding of the nails. Mattson felt that emotion in a religious service was good, although he was opposed to the emotionalism of a revival service. He shared with the typical Augustana Lutheran a profound sense of God's personal relationship with the individual, a faith which seeks service in the name of Christ. The social implications of the Gospel were shared by Mattson when he was invited to speak about such issues to Lutheran and non-Lutheran church groups. Then he advised them on advance publicity, provided information for a news release, and often received large follow-up stories in the local paper. Thus he gave congregations the opportunity to see that a Rosenian pietist could become involved in the sufferings of sharecroppers, conditions in Russia, labor disputes, and pacifism. He traveled throughout the Augustana Synod in many capacities: preaching on seminary choir tours, distributing communion at nearby churches, addressing church groups, and consulting with rural parishes. One of his first trips was to show the California Lutherans that he was not the dangerous heretic they feared, but the years of teaching gradually gave him more receptive audiences.[11] He became known for shocking audiences, so journalists were fond of quoting him, and he made enemies throughout his career. However, the correspondence files reveal him as a person who did not enjoy turmoil. He was quite hurt when people accused him of base motives or destructive tendencies, but his conscience compelled him to speak out when a minority report was needed.

Mattson's influence on his students cannot be measured as directly as the social positions of the Augustana Synod.

As chairman of the social ministry committee throughout its existence, Mattson had a direct hand in every statement accepted by the synod. The impact upon his students can be represented by what they have said in reflecting upon their changing social perspectives. Some statements have been drawn from the retirement letters presented to Mattson, others from questionnaires sent to about 100 of his former students and colleagues. Additional information has come from letters sent by those who learned about this research and by those pastors who volunteered insights informally at conventions and church conferences attended by the author. Mattson's students have served and continue to serve as LCA pastors, professors, college presidents, synod presidents, missionaries, church executives, churchwide agency personnel, and in special ministries. Mattson's chief concerns were: community issues, labor, rural churches, racial justice, pacifism, and politics. Since Augustana was not progressive in those areas before Mattson's time, the extent of clergy involvement in those issues can be traced to his influence. Even in taking an interest in the rural parish, Mattson was ahead of his time.

9

COMMUNITY ISSUES

One of Mattson's main concerns was that pastors relate directly to community issues. Most Lutherans accepted the theological perspective of Inner Missions, that Christians can reform society only through individual participation in secular institutions, with the hope that an evangelized populace will carry out the will of God in society. Mattson compared this to the limited role of "pure" theology advocated by Hitler's government, a theology concerned only the speculative thought and liturgical practices.[12] Mattson's students were taught to address the problem rather than simply minister to victims of injustice. Charles V. Bergstrom was strongly influenced by Mattson's example as an involved Christian.[13] As a parish pastor, Bergstrom was instrumental in exposing police corruption in Springfield, Massachusetts. The Augustana's Synod *Lutheran Companion*, March 12, 1958, commended him for his work.[14] Bergstrom wrote about Mattson:

> He influenced my work to the extent that it helped me in seeing the pastoral ministry as a total ministry within the congregation and the corporate church, but also to the world and eventually to my present position in the Lutheran Council Office for Governmental Affairs.[15]

As executive director of the Office of Governmental Affairs, Lutheran Council in the USA, Bergstrom has been responsible for advocating social issues related to the federal government in Washington, D.C. Violating Inner Mission ideals, he has spoken to congressional committees about Lutheran concerns and reported significant issues to Lutherans through his office's publication, *Focus on Governmental Affairs*. Bergstrom's work is supported by the LCA and ALC through LC/USA. Another prominent LCA pastor in Washington, D.C. was the chaplain to the House of Representatives, appointed in 1979, James D. Ford, a 1957 Augustana Theological Seminary graduate. Ford received his best grades in Mattson's classes and appreciated Mattson's antidote to the individualistic piety of Augustana.[16]

While Augustana piety focused upon ministry through such institutions as orphanages and hospitals, Mattson encouraged his students to extend their ministry to secular organizations and structures, so that God would rule over all parts of society, not simply ecclesiastical institutions. When Bernard Spong was a pastor in Gary, Indiana (1945-1951), he became known as the "Crime Buster" for his efforts in cleaning up police corruption.[17] Spong wrote about Mattson:

> It was his influence and willingness to take sometimes radical and drastic actions in the world of politics and the real affairs of everyday life of human beings that helped me to take actions in the communities where I have served.[18]

Many of Mattson's students have reported similar involvements in their communities as a natural part of their parish ministry. They point with obvious pride to their roles in advocating changes in the communities or in taking unpopular stands about racial injustice, labor relations, and pacifism. In the 1960's, two of Mattson's students (F. Jan Bengston and Gerald Christensen) went with a rabbi to the school board of Gary, Indiana, about the firing of five assistants to the superintendent of schools. The school board was notified that the ministerial association supported the assistants and that a teachers' strike would follow any firings. No one was fired at that time.[19]

Another indication of the community concerns of Mattson's students is the extent of parish involvement in various local service groups. Even today, the more conservative Lutheran parishes (Wisconsin Synod and Missouri Synod) shun ecumenical ministeries as a symptom of unionism, based on the unhappy experiences of the Prussian Church Union. Augustana's ecumenical outlook, fostered by Conrad Bergendoff, and Mattson's teachings, led to a different style of parish ministry. One example is Bethlehem Lutheran Church in St. Charles, Illinois. The senior pastor, Arthur M. Holmer, graduated from the seminary in 1949. In 1979, benevolent work comprised 40% of the parish budget. (The Illinois Synod average that year was 16%.) At Bethlehem the most active committee has been the social ministry committee. The church subsidized a full-time day-care center, sponsored Laotian families, supported schools for Blacks, and gave financial support to a mission church nearby. The congregation also contributed to Tri-City Family Services, FISH (a volunteer service group), and other activities. Pastor Holmer wrote about Mattson: "His lectures and his life had a profound influence on my thinking and activities."[20] While Augustana inherited a special passion for social ministry from William A. Passavant, Mattson's students have extended the meaning of social ministry through the Lutheran parish.

10

LABOR

One of Mattson's most remarkable accomplishments was in making his students sympathetic to the needs of labor. Mattson was one of the few Lutheran clergy who actively espoused the cause of organized labor. His interest began at Yale with the Religion and Labor Foundation and never waned in the decades after. The Augustana constituency was profoundly anti-labor, an attitude shaped by hostility towards socialism, Democrats, and Roman Catholics. In contrast, Mattson attacked capitalist excesses, demonstrated labor's complaints, and shared chaplaincy of the local union with a Catholic priest. Mattson did not succeed in making all of his students support labor with unalloyed zeal, but many confessed that Mattson was the first to show them labor's side of the issue. Others took active part in union activities while at the seminary, and later. Some now wonder what Mattson would say about union tactics today. Ruth Mattson Taylor, his daughter, has said that "A.D. felt that labor's rights should be protected, but he would certainly oppose any excessive power manipulations by labor which would be unfair or a detriment to society as a whole."

One of Mattson's students most active in labor issues is John A. Nasstrom, a 1951 graduate of the seminary. Nasstrom works in California for the Division of Mission and Ministry of LC/USA. According to LC/USA news release:

> The division serves as an agent for identifying issues and concerns for the Church in mission, for sensitizing church bodies to these issues, for counseling the Church in decisions related to planning, and for involving church bodies in a corporate witness to the community.[21]

Nasstrom has worked with Caesar Chavez' United Farm Workers, with support provided by LC/USA and California Lutherans. Born in Pontiac, Michigan, Nasstrom was prepared for Mattson's ideas by the discussions held by his father and uncles on the hypocrisy of churches and the issues of labor justice. Profoundly affected by Mattson, Nasstrom has identified with social issues and community concerns ever since ordination. As a parish pastor in Butte, Montana, Nasstrom served as chaplain to a labor council, member of the city recreation board, and helped start a community planning council. His concern with social ministry led him to accept a position with Lutheran World Relief and Church World Service in Brazil. Nasstrom represents Mattson's concept of the Kingdom of God as "the energy of God pressing upon human affairs."[22] One person who has marched in support of the UFW lettuce strikes is Dr. Carl W. Segerhammar, president of the Pacific Southwest Synod from 1962 to 1975, who was a Mattson student in the 1930's. Both men reported that Mattson influenced their social consciousness.[23]

Mattson not only taught about organized labor and brought labor leaders into the classroom, but also involved students in labor unions. Glenn C. Stone, editor of the influential *Lutheran Forum*, an independent journal, was a 1952 graduate of the seminary. Stone served as Mattson's student assistant during his senior year. While an undergraduate at the University of Chicago, Stone felt that many liberal or radical views were incompatible with Christianity. He stated: "I would say that A.D. helped to make clear for me the social dimensions of Christian ethics in a way which enabled me subsequently to evaluate issues from a less rigid point of view.''[24] Stone did not appreciate the labor movement before entering seminary, but Mattson convinced him of the importance of organized labor and the need for the Church to relate to it in a positive way. Mattson used his labor contacts to get a job for Stone, working for a union local at its grocery cooperative. Stone carried potato sacks from boxcar to warehouse and got involved in union activities. A union organizer for the farm implement factories suggested that Stone abandon preaching and become a union organizer. Stone has served as an editor since 1962, when he began at the *National Lutheran*.

Mattson's views on labor were so unusual for a Lutheran that conservatives and liberals alike were affected by them in a positive way. Edgar M. Carlson, a 1933 seminary graduate, is considered the second most influential person in changing the social consciousness of Augustana. Through Mattson, Carlson's attitude toward labor unions was altered. Carlson is one of many who attended labor meetings with Mattson.[25] Others found themselves more understanding when labor disputes arose in the communities where they served. Mattson's influence kept them from automatically taking an anti-union stance. N. Everett Hedeen is one of many pastors who took part in labor/management panels to promote better industrial relations. Hedeen organized a panel in 1945 in Kansas City, holding monthly meetings. When the group sponsored a two-day conference for the community, Mattson was one of the guest speakers. Hedeen was impressed by Mattson's ability to identify with the working man. He wrote: ''To hold the respect of these hard-fisted men without compromise and still maintain a visible understanding is no easy acceptance path.''[26]

One labor leader who knew Mattson and worked with him for a number of years was Dick Fallow. He reported that Mattson was respected and admired for his courageous stand on controversial issues. Union members liked Mattson's "warmth and down to earthness, appreciating that he didn't talk down to his listeners." The union members usually called him "Doc." Fallow saw Mattson as a person who worked to build alliances between those groups which sought to improve the lot of humanity. On a personal level, Fallow wrote that he appreciated Mattson's inspiration, guts, skills, and compassion.[27] As co-chaplain to the Quad-City Federation of Labor, AFL-CIO, Mattson became friends with Cecil Quails, United Auto Workers International Representative. Mattson was a great help during the 1946 strike at the J. I. Case Company and the 1952 strike at Farmall, two farm implement plants in the Quad-Cities. Quails recalled: "Especially at these times, the workers were in need of spiritual guidance and assurance. Reverend Mattson was always available helping to calm fears and to give encouragement, giving faith to those who needed it." Mattson also pointed out to workers their real purpose and their duties to their brother members.[28]

Mattson was carrying out one of the major strategies of the Social Gospel leaders who felt the Church was abandoning the working class and therefore heading toward decline. But Mattson did not use his influence for empire building. When offered the chance to run for Congress, after receiving official permission from the synod president, Mattson declined. His eagerness to serve in Congress was offset by his desire to change the social consciousness of future pastors. When he was strongly tempted to return to the parish, his friends begged him to remain in the seminary and carry out his special role. Since he joined organizations rather than starting them, he did not distinguish himself as a pioneer in most areas, with the exception of rural ministry. However, his goal was to change individuals in their ability to relate their faith in Christ to their responsibilities in the Church and in the world. Theodore N. Swanson, a 1954 Augustana Seminary graduate who has served as a professor and missionary, recalled Mattson saying:

> I've visited a lot of congregations. I've asked pastors, 'What have you accomplished in your ministry?' I've been given all sorts of tours of church buildings, with pastors telling me about building Sunday School additions and parking lots. I have yet to have a pastor introduce me to a person and say, 'This person's life has been changed through the Gospel.'[29]

As Swanson has noted in his letter, Mattson was able to acquaint seminarians with social implications of the Gospel without disparaging the personal dimension. For Mattson, all ethical decisions were grounded in religious faith.

11

RURAL WORK

Mattson's interest in rural churches stemmed from his background as a child and as a pastor in rural parishes. His interest led to a survey for the National Lutheran Council (precursor of LC/USA) and then to a position with Augustana's mission board, sharing his time with the seminary, 1945-1950. Since most pastors remain in the city or work towards a call to the more prosperous metropolitan areas, rural parishes have not been viewed by the clergy as desirable calls or lifelong vocations. But Mattson attached as much importance to the distinctive mission of rural and small town parishes as he did to urban and suburban congregations. Because many Augustana parishes were in the Midwest and West, Mattson was able to prepare students for ministry in agricultural areas. Just as he was one of the first ethics professors in a Lutheran seminary, he was also one of the few to train pastors specifically for rural social ministry.

When the National Lutheran Council published *Inside Rural America* in 1962, the author noted that only three Lutheran leaders had shown an appreciable amount of concern for the rural parish before 1945.[30] Mattson was one of them. The other two were Dr. T. F. Gullixson of the (Norwegian) Evangelical Lutheran Church and Dr. Martin Schroeder of the ULCA's Midwest Synod. Mattson established a rural sociology course at Augustana in 1938. The course had been requested by students as early as 1935, but

Mattson had some difficulty in having the course approved. Later he helped persuade the president of Iowa State University at Ames to offer a summer course in rural sociology for clergy and seminarians. Through the Augustana Synod, Mattson organized conferences on rural ministry at many locations. He was in contact with the acknowledged experts on rural parishes in all denominations, Protestant and Catholic. De Vries noted:

> A characteristic of Dr. Mattson was continually to keep in contact with current developments at the grass roots level of rural America. He took the initiative to meet and know farm organization leaders, other denominational people interested in the problems of the rural church, colleagues in colleges and universities, and members of rural congregations.[31]

Mattson saw the social implications of the Gospel in rural areas. His booklet on rural ministry concluded with a prayer by Rauschenbusch.

Mattson's approach was spelled out in several articles as well as his booklet. He expressed considerable anguish over the neglect of the rural parish, which he saw as a school of character for those who resided in agricultural areas and for those who emigrated to cities. His major stress was that rural churches must minister to the entire community, not to people of one ethnic or denominational heritage. This came at a time when missions were still being established based on ethnic divisions within Lutheranism, with a Swedish church placed near a Norwegian or German congregation. By taking an interest in the entire community, the rural parish could provide needs which would directly help the congregation's growth. For example, the pastor who knew how to help farmers obtain credit from government sources would be instrumental in stabilizing a community. Soil conservation was a crucial concern, for care of God's creation is just as important as worship and education. Mattson noted that careless soil management led to the loss of hundreds of congregations during the Dust Bowl and that economic depression in the 1930's forced countless churches to close. He fought against the attitude from earlier days that the spiritual ministry of a church could be divorced from the material concerns of people. Mattson advocated lifelong dedication to rural areas, based on proper seminary and post-graduate pastoral training. Mattson tried to make rural churches accept responsibility to the disadvantaged, surveying the area to ascertain community needs.

Mattson was distraught over official indifference to rural concerns but he was consulted by Lutherans of various jurisdictions in matters of rural and small town ministry. Rural pastors often wrote to him to express their appreciation for the insights from his classes they were using. Others wrote to him to help answer questions about salary, constitutional matters, ethical concerns, and advice on whether to accept a new call. When Mattson retired, Pastor G. Adolph Johns wrote from Mankato, Minnesota:

> When I became a pastor in North Dakota, you were kind enough to visit us in Bismarck. You were willing to accompany me as we visited small rural congregations in the vicinity of Bismarck. Then, I recall that you devoted considerable time in presenting the implications of the Christian gospel to Farmers Union groups in North Dakota.[32]

Mattson enabled rural pastors to see their work in the light of a special and much-needed ministry to all people, not as a form of punishment in preparation for a better call.

12

RACIAL JUSTICE

Mattson's influence in regard to racial justice has been affirmed by his students. His contact with the most obvious problems of oppression apparently came during his trip to the South in 1936 to view the sharecropper situation, since most of the sharecroppers were Black.[33] He made another trip later and became acquainted with Martin Luther King, Jr., and the Koinonia community near Plains, Georgia. In 1937, Eric J. Gustavson, one of Mattson's students, took a trip through the same area and agreed that, after seeing the suffering, one could never be the same again, as Mattson had said in his lectures.[34] The sharecropper information received wide circulation through Mattson's lectures and talks at parish meetings. According to Conrad Hoyer, Mattson was not looked to as a philosophical leader when Lutherans dealt officially with racial justice matters, but some students traced their awakening to the problem to his classes. Mattson did not belong to racial justice organizations, but many of his students became quite active in the movement for racial equality in the 1960's. As Richard A. Olson, adult education leader for the Division for Parish Services, LCA, pointed out:

> When I was on internship I became involved with the Lutheran Human Relations Association in San Diego. I can't say that A.D. ever mentioned the LHRA but his interest in justice certainly

> would have encouraged me to reach out to those new opportunities to understand our Black brothers and sisters.[35]

As a whole, the graduates of the 1950's and 1960's were not as easily shocked or disturbed by Mattson, since most of them had been exposed to his earlier students, but the newer students felt their social concerns supported by Mattson.

Some students were emphatic in giving credit to Mattson for their awareness about racial injustice. Pastor Gerald Nelson wrote:

> When a community was hamstrung by one man and the community didn't seem to care, I wondered why I felt differently than they. When pressure was applied not to baptize five Negro children and receive their mother into membership, I wondered why I spoke out so strongly about it. On a journey which would bring me to Selma, Alabama, I wondered why I was going. The answer had to be, God's Word. But it was A. D. Mattson who brought me to the realization that God's Word speaks to social concerns.[36]

The most publicized case in a congregation with conflicting racial attitudes involved two of Mattson's students, one the pastor (L. William Youngdahl) and the other a synod president and former pastor of the parish (Reuben Swanson). Lutheran Film Associates filmed Augustana Lutheran Church, Omaha, Nebraska, as it became embroiled over a decision to have an exchange visit between members of Augustana and a Black church. The movie, "A Time for Burning," captured the struggle from the social ministry committee meeting to the resignation of the pastor.[37] President Reuben Swanson later served as LCA secretary (the second highest elective post in the LCA). Both Youngdahl and Swanson were active in racial issues and gave credit to Mattson for his influence. Youngdahl wrote while still serving Augustana Lutheran Church:

> Over the years you have aroused a dormant social consciousness in many prospective pastors. You have led us to see that the minister must be both priest and prophet. You have always spoken and acted fearlessly when the welfare of man is at stake.[38]

Swanson wrote that he was one of many students who disagreed, even somewhat violently, with many of Mattson's thoughts at seminary.[39] However, Mattson made Swanson aware for the first time of injustices to which he had not been exposed while growing up in a rural area. Mattson made him understand ministry as more inclusive and wide ranging.[40]

The film, according to many pastors, exacerbated the tension of Augustana Lutheran Church and led to Youngdahl leaving the LCA for the United Church of Christ. However, other parishes with less visibility achieved considerable progress in terms of promoting racial understanding and integrating parishes in changing neighborhoods. Pastor Paul V. Bergren, a 1942 graduate, who owes to Mattson his social consciousness, was involved in integrating housing in Deerfield, Illinois, from 1959 to 1962.[41] At his last parish, Christ the King in the Loop, Chicago, Illinois, he introduced "Where Cross the Crowded Ways of Life," a favorite hymn of the Social Gospel leaders, as the theme of the congregation.[42]

One of the most successful efforts in adapting a ministry to a changing neighborhood was achieved by a succession of Mattson's students at Salem in Chicago, Illinois, near the University of Chicago campus.[43] The Salem story is not one of Mattson's sole influence but of many factors working together to accomplish a difficult transition. The pastors who have served Salem make up a remarkable list:

Dr. Conrad Bergendoff (1921-1931), later seminary dean and college president;
Dr. Oscar A. Benson (1931-1942), later Illinois Conference and Augustana Synod president;
Dr. Constantine Trued (1943-1949), later pastor at Immanuel, Detroit;
Pastor Philip A. Johnson (1949-1958), later with the National Lutheran Council and the Council on Religion and International Affairs;
Pastor James A. Claypool (1958-1961), later with the Division for Parish Services, LCA;
Pastor Norman A. Nelson (1961-1970), later a pastor in Downer's Grove, Illinois;
Pastor Karl J. Mattson (1971-1977), later the Gettysburg College chaplain.[44]

After the pastorate of James Claypool at Salem, Norman Nelson came from Saron in Chicago to serve the integrated parish. (Johnson has described his work in *Call Me Neighbor, Call Me Friend.*)[45] Nelson participated in the community organization, Park Manor Neighbors, started by Pastor Philip Johnson. He also belonged to the steering committee of the Chicago Urban League's Council of Religious Leaders. Nelson worked to introduce Black history and civil rights interpretations into the traditional Lutheran confirmation instruction. Membership and financial support grew, despite controversial parish stands on busing and the Viet Nam War. Nelson wrote that Mattson's teaching, and the emphasis learned in his home church from one of Mattson's students, combined with his parents' views to encourage his ministry among the working class.[46] Karl J. Mattson wrote that his uncle "introduced factors into my personal equation that made me decide to take churches in the urban scene."[47]

Mattson helped create a climate which encouraged urban ministry as a special calling. When F. Jan Bengston, a 1953 graduate, published a booklet titled *Toward an Inclusive Lutheran Congregation in an Interracial Community* (Chicago, 1961), he sent a copy to Mattson with a note: "You started me on this way. Thought you'd like it."[48] Mattson's attitude toward solving injustice was illustrated by a case where a Black seminarian was refused a haircut at a unionized barber shop. The outraged seminarians wanted to picket the shop, but Mattson objected. He first went to the barber to discuss the matter, and when that failed to produce results, went to the state union officials. The officials told the barber to stop discriminating, and the barber complied. He told Mattson, when A.D. went to get a haircut, "You won." The incident was never given any publicity, so few people are aware that it happened.[49] The episode demonstrates Mattson's preference for understanding rather than confrontation, but his willingness to use his influence to help someone. In the Quad-Cities, he prodded the unions to accept Blacks and he questioned the policy about admission of Blacks to local hospitals.

13

PACIFISM

Mattson found the most receptive audience when he spoke on behalf of pacifism. The Swedish Lutherans, many of whom traced their move to America for avoidance of universal military training, had a strong strain of antimilitarism. Mattson took an early stand in favor of pacifism in *Christian Ethics* and belonged to such organizations as Promoting an Enduring Peace (PEP), and Fellowship of Reconciliation (FOR). Mattson felt that war was antithetical to the spirit of Christianity, that the causes of war must be removed (economic injustice, trade barriers), and that a Christian could refuse military service based on a higher obedience to God's will. He recruited people for membership in PEP and FOR. He advised people on their duties in regards to the draft, Conscientious Objector status, and alternative service. When the Korean War began, he encouraged seminary students not to register for the draft.

14

POLITICS

Mattson's politics were the least acceptable to the Augustana membership, which was traditionally Republican ever since the anti-slavery stance of Esbjörn. Esbjörn and other Augustana pioneers were horrified by slavery, so the synod identified early with anti-slavery Republicans. Mattson was an active and highly visible supporter of the Democratic Party, except for his support of Henry Wallace in 1948. His activities not only violated the Republicanism of Augustana's members and leadership, but also departed from the traditional non-involvement of clergy in public affairs and politics. Locally, Mattson's political activities caused considerable anguish for the school's administration, since individuals threatened to withdraw their support. From his support of Roosevelt in 1936 to his endorsement of Kennedy in 1960, Mattson was able to outrage Swedish-American Lutherans from all over the U.S.A. Through his seminary teaching, however, he was able to convert some of the most conservative Republican seminarians into enthusiastic Democrats. Mattson was generally known for this ability, which both Arthur Holmer and Joel Lundeen have attested to in their letters.[50] Although this effect was not universal, it widened the perspectives of students who thought that Christianity and the Republican Party were synonymous.

15

CHURCH LEADERS

A special role of Mattson in his influence of the Augustana Synod was the training he gave to future leaders of Augustana and the LCA. The LCA's work was organized into four divisions, two of which have been directed by Mattson's students. Louis Almen was the executive director of the Division for Professional Leadership and later served as president of Thiel College in Pennsylvania.[51] David Vikner was executive director of the Division for World Mission and Ecumenism. A 1944 graduate of the seminary, Vikner wrote that Mattson broadened his views and gave him a theological and ethical base of his views. He noted:

> Gradually, over the years, I have come to see the mission of the church to be an integrated program of proclamation, service and social action, and believe that A.D. was one of the early influences that put me on that track. In the world mission scene today, integrated mission is an accepted fact and is being implemented in a variety of ways where the LCA is involved.[52]

The importance of an executive director's perspective can be seen in the recent LCA statement on world mission, written by Vikner and circulated throughout the denomination, "Mission is. . . Not." The statement contrasts the older ideas about mission and what world mission is today. One sentence reads: "World mission is not only the verbal proclamation of the gospel; it is bringing the full impact of the gospel by word, service, and social action."[53]

For those students who became involved in ecumenical activities, Mattson's emphasis on the Social Gospel gave them insights into the theological ethics of Protestant bodies, such as the Methodists, which were influenced strongly by the Social Gospel and were indifferent about the two kingdoms. H. Conrad Hoyer was a staff member of the National Council of Churches for 12 years (1960-1972). A 1936 graduate, he did not consider himself as a social crusader but did not hesitate to speak out on ethical aspects of social issues in his career as parish pastor and ecumenist.[54] Many of Mattson's students have been or still serve as presidents of LCA regional synods, such as Illinois, New England, Minnesota, Pacific Southwest, Pacific Northwest, and Iowa. By the time of the LCA merger, most of the Augustana leadership had been trained by Mattson. The synodical presidency may have less direct effect than some would claim or fear, but it does have impact on the use of funds and the direction of special ministries. The personal example of the synod president may also affect the social consciousness of the constituents. The former president of the Pacific Northwest Synod said of Mattson:

> Because he was such a strong personality, as well as a very likable individual, he made a strong impact on me relative to my being involved, interested, and aware of the social issues of the day. That impact has continued to affect me as I have sought to interpret the Gospel in the light of what we need to do to relate to those social concerns in today's world.[55]

Fjellman recalled earlier, as Reuben Swanson had, that he did not immediately agree with Mattson: "We acknowledge that you were a prophet and that we were reluctant learners."[56] Raymond L. Lingwall, the former president of the Iowa Synod, wrote:

> Unquestionably, your influence on me as a teacher was the deepest of any that I have experienced, either in college or seminary. Many of your former students have indicated to me their experience was the same. I get a great deal of satisfaction out of hearing my son and other present seminary students quote you or make reference to your expressions and attitudes.[57]

16

MATTSON'S DECREASED INFLUENCE AFTER THE LCA MERGER

Mattson was opposed to the merger which created the Lutheran Church in America, according to Eric Wahlstrom, a former colleague.[58]

Mattson participated in the Joint Commission on Lutheran Unity which led to the merger, working on social concerns. His fears were that Augustana would be swallowed up in the merger, that Lutheran Social Services (Inner Missions) would supplant the church's role in speaking out on social issues, and that Augustana's stand against the Masonic orders would be compromised.

Harold Haas reported that Mattson did not become a member of the LCA Board of Social Ministry and was rarely, if ever, a part of its social concerns development. (According to Ruth Mattson Taylor, Mattson's daughter, Mattson was never invited to participate in the LCA Board of Social Ministry, undoubtedly because his theological approach stressing the centrality of the Kingdom of God in dealing with social issues differed from the Two Kingdoms approach stressed by leaders from the ULCA.) This is supported by Haas' statements below:

The thing that impresses me most about A. D. Mattson is the fact that he influenced generations of (Augustana) theological students. In these circles there was a great appreciation for him, and what he stood for, and did . . . I remember once having to substitute for him at a discussion session at some conference. The session was filled with his former students who were still attracted by him. I also had the impression, however, that many had come to argue about some of his theological grounds.

A. D. Mattson's chief contribution may have been within the Augustana Lutheran Church but it was significant there and carried forward. His concerns were right and the church had to catch up theologically so as to include those concerns.

I do not know if A.D. had a different agenda from others pressing for more social concern by Lutherans. I doubt that the agenda was different. The way of getting there, theologically, was. It is important to remember, however, that A.D. was a pioneer in many respects. Until the 1950's there seemed little grounding for social concerns in Lutheran theology among any of the American Lutheran Church bodies. (There were, of course, individual exceptions.)[59]

A. D. Mattson's theology did seem to clash with that of other socially minded Lutheran leaders. He did not seem sympathetic to the theological approach that has been emerging among other Lutherans (e.g., the ULCA three volume Christian Social Responsibility series published in 1957-). On the other hand, when A.D. was invited to give the Knubel-Miller lectures on Christian Social Responsibility in 1960, many were disturbed at the invitation because of his theological approach.[60]

EPILOGUE

The full extent of Mattson's influence can only be indicated. When most Lutherans were taking shelter in the individualized theology of Inner Missions, Mattson was introducing seminary students to Rauschenbusch's critiques of Lutheran piety. According to Glenn C. Stone, who has observed the Lutheran church scene for years, Augustana had an earlier and deeper involvement than any other Lutheran body in social issues, even before social action came into vogue in the 1960's.[61] The influence of Mattson is being continued through his students, as Louis Almen observed when he saw *The Lutheran* cover story about labor activist John Nasstrom:

> In a moment of reverie I could hear the voice of A. D. Mattson, social prophet, honored professor at Augustana Seminary, and mentor of Nasstrom and many delegates speaking in behalf of the statement (on economic justice, at the 1980 LCA convention). A.D. would have been proud to hear his former students 'dig in' on current issues... As a result of his long teaching career he shaped the social thinking of well over a thousand contemporary LCA clergy. He has undoubtedly had a decisive impact upon the current attempt at social relevance by the Lutheran Church in America.[62]

Almen's statement brings to mind the letter written by Mattson, age 39, when he was ready to quit teaching at the seminary:

> You suggest that I permit myself to feel anointed as a prophet. The Lord knows that I try . . . the lot of the prophet is hard but the company is good. If one could only occasionally get into physical touch with a prophet it would not be so bad.[63]

For many people, that hope was fulfilled for them when A. D. Mattson spoke vividly about social ills and urgently about their role in the Kingdom of God.

Part III

MATTSON

SPEAKS FOR HIMSELF

The Social Responsibility of Christians

The Knubel-Miller Foundation
Lectures—1960

With special permission of Ruth Mattson Taylor,
who holds the copyright to
The Social Responsibility of Christians
(the compilation of
the Knubel-Miller Lectures
given by Dr. A. D. Mattson in 1960),
we are herewith reprinting
that material in its entirety.

TO MY GRANDCHILDREN

with the hope that the kingdom of

God may increasingly become a

reality in their consciousness

PREFACE

Theological liberalism and a social ethical emphasis are not synonymous. I am grateful for many insights which liberalism has contributed to my theological development, but I am not a liberal. I hope it will be quickly apparent that I do not belong to a fundamentalist camp, either. Likewise, I have always had—and still hold—many reservations with respect to the type of theology which developed after the close of the First World War, and is now the fashion in many circles. There is a classical Christian tradition—we might say an orthodox tradition—and in this tradition I feel most at home. Modern scholarship has made significant contributions to a more adequate understanding of that tradition, but there is a main channel; and in that stream I trust that the theological presuppositions of these lectures will be found.

Many, in both orthodox and liberal traditions, have become alarmed at the lack of an ethical emphasis in some theological circles during the last quarter of a century. Where the ethical has been emphasized at all, it often has been ethics without content. In this series of lectures I shall try to point out some of the attitudes in modern theology which tend to destroy its ethical relevance. The ethical impact of the Christian faith upon society will, of course, be the primary consideration.

I am deeply indebted and grateful to Walter Rauschenbusch for his influence upon my thinking during the time

I was a college and seminary student. The impact of his works has been an inspiration through the years. I am also mindful of the influence of Nathan Söderblom, which will be apparent in these lectures. Both of these giants, at the time they were at the height of their prestige, did much to develop a sense of social responsibility in the young student, and the years have not dimmed their significance.

A. D. Mattson

1

THE MEANING OF SOCIAL RESPONSIBILITY

The Christian Faith Involves an Ethic

Back in 1930, Alfred E. Garvie reacted negatively to the type of theological development which was taking place on the Continent, and the efforts which were being made to "make it the fashion of the hour" in England, also. He said "there is an almost Manichaean, Gnostic dualism in this theology between the relative and the absolute, world and God, God's imminence and God's transcendence. Man's sin, great and grievous as it is, has not so corrupted the world that it has ceased to be the world God made, preserves, and rules, in which He still is and works."[1] Garvie sensed what was taking place in the postwar theological climate, and many who have followed the theological developments of the last thirty years have often been alarmed at the progress of the trend which Garvie so clearly saw. Paul Holmer, in a recent issue of the *Christian Century,* expresses his apprehension when he says that "much of recent theology—neo-orthodoxy if you will—cuts the nerve of ethical endeavor."[2] The position is often emphasized that the exigencies of the historical situation make it impossible to apply the Christian

[1] Alfred E. Garvie, *The Christian Ideal for Human Society* (West Rindge, N.H.: Richard R. Smith, Inc., 1930), p. 467.

[2] Paul Holmer, "Modern Theology, Another Evasion?" *Christian Century* (Chicago), January 22, 1958, p. 103.

ideal. There is a truth involved in this attitude which must be recognized, but we must never allow a compromising position to become the ideal. After all, it is not the historical situation which is determinative for the Christian, it is the will of God. We need to guard against committing idolatry by making the historical situation determinative. If the historical situation is to be determinative, then it is no longer God who is sovereign and, like the situation in Marxian communism, historical forces become God. In the last analysis, based on such a position, ethics loses its religious basis.

Christian social responsibility is ethical responsibility. A kind of Gnostic dualism which emphasizes justification but neglects to stress the "birth of a new self who finds his place in the world of existence by devotion to the will of God,"[3] will not be the classical Christian faith, and it will not be the answer which the world seeks and needs.

The biblical tradition places the ethical concern in the nature of God himself. The "wisdom" literature of the Old Testament is a pregnant example. The word wisdom meant, primarily, "moral principle." Wisdom was virtually the equivalent of goodness. It was spiritual insight, a true discrimination of values, and an understanding of what is most worthful. Wisdom had its roots in religion, so to be wise meant to estimate the values of life from God's standpoint. For the wise man, God was at the center of life and governed thought, word, and deed.[4] In Proverbs 8:22 ff., wisdom is spoken of as the first creation of God, which is now present among men as the mouthpiece and representative of God. Wisdom is the impersonation of a moral quality. The ethical quality of wisdom is also emphasized in Ecclesiasticus, where it is identified with the "law that Moses commanded."[5]

[3] Carl F. H. Henry, *Christian Personal Ethics* (Michigan: William B. Eerdman's Publishing Company, 1957), p. 394.

[4] Prov. 1:7.

[5] Ecclus. 24:3 ff.

In Wisdom of Solomon 7:22 ff., wisdom is the "artificer of all things" and "the brightness (effulgence) of the everlasting light and an unstained mirror of the power of God," and it penetrates and permeates all things.

In the works of Philo, the Logos idea is the equivalent of wisdom. In the fourth Gospel, Jesus is identified with the Logos;[6] and in the Letter to the Hebrews Jesus is spoken of as "the effulgence of his (God's) glory."[7]

Similar to the fourth Gospel and the Letter to the Hebrews are the Epistles of Paul, when they apply terms to Jesus which had originally been applied to wisdom. In fact, Paul calls Jesus "the wisdom of God"[8] and then he adds he was made "unto us wisdom from God, and righteousness and sanctification, and redemption. . . ."[9] He says in Christ "are all the treasures of wisdom and knowledge hidden."[10] As wisdom was the first creation of God, so also is Christ "the firstborn of all creation."[11]

It is evident that the role which wisdom played in the Old Testament and in the Apocrypha is transferred to Jesus in the New Testament. Jesus was the manifestation of the wisdom or the "moral principle" of God. He was the revelation of perfect goodness. Whatever else the doctrine of the divinity of Christ means, it does mean that Jesus revealed God in the goodness and the moral quality of his character. Jesus Christ is the "image" of God.[12] The divine is manifest in the moral perfection of the life of Jesus, and thus the ethical is bound up with the very being of God himself. The essence of the moral is a unity, and it is identical, though not in degree, for both God and man.

[6] John 1.
[7] Heb. 1:3.
[8] I Cor. 1:24.
[9] I Cor. 1:30.
[10] Col. 2:3.
[11] Col. 1:15.
[12] Col. 1:15.

Social Ethics and the New Testament

It was Jesus himself who said, "Truly, I say to you, as you did it to one of the least of these my brethren, you did it to me."[13] This does not mean that Christ is troubled from a distance by the needs of our fellow men, but that love's identity and unity places our human woes upon him. Saul, when he journeyed to Damascus to persecute the Christians there, heard Christ say, ". . . why persecutest thou me?"[14] Christ, as Paul conceived it, identified himself with these persecuted men and women. "In all their affliction he was afflicted. . . ."[15] Again, the Christian faith places a social concern in the nature of God himself.

As "God is love" so also is the Christian life one that is lived in love to God and the neighbor. Love to God and love of fellow man belong together. According to the First Epistle of John, "If any one says, 'I love God,' and hates his brother, he is a liar; for he who does not love his brother whom he has seen, cannot love God whom he has not seen."[16] The ground of the Christian ethic is not to be found in any kind of hedonism, utilitarianism, eudaemonism, or in that which makes for good human relations, but in the love and will of God. This love cannot be separated from the love of fellow man for love is a unity. Any such separation is an illusion. A lack of ethical love separates man from the life which is in fellowship with God. Failure to love our neighbor cancels our love to God because God is love. If God's nature is love, then we must love in order to love God.

Anders Nygren has had considerable trouble in dealing with the concept of love in relation to God, as the concept is difficult to fit into his theory. Instead of speaking, as Jesus did, about love to God, he feels that faith is the term to use

13 Matt. 25:40. 14 Acts 22:7.
15 Isa. 63:9.
16 I John 4:20.

when we speak about man's relationship to God.[17] He holds that the concept involved in "agape" in the Johannine writings is fluctuating and that the distinction between "motivated" and "unmotivated" love is not clearly maintained.[18] Precisely so. The facts do not fit the theory. "Agape" does not always mean "unmotivated love" as Nygren maintains it should, and he makes the mistake of overlooking the flexibility in the use of words. He rejects emphatically the idea of "loving God in our neighbor."[19] He rightly emphasizes that there are differences between man's love of God and man's love of fellow man, but he fails to see that Christian love is a unity which includes both God and man as the author of I John emphasizes. Here again the Christian finds himself faced with a social responsibility which proceeds out of the very nature of the Christian life and experience. If we fail to assert the unity of love, which I John emphasizes, our theology and religion may simply become an escape from social responsibility, and it is to be noted that there is very little emphasis on social responsibility where this unity is not maintained.

Religion and morality belong together in the New Testament. Jesus would not allow what were considered to be religious observances to negate the manifestation of love to fellow man.[20] A classical example is found in Mark 7:9–13, R.S.V. Jesus said to the Pharisees: "You have a fine way of rejecting the commandment of God, in order to keep your tradition! For Moses said, 'Honor your father and your mother'; and, 'He who speaks evil of father or mother, let him surely die'; but you say, 'If a man tells his father or his mother, What you would have gained from me is Corban' (that is, given to God)—then you no longer permit him to

[17] Anders Nygren, *Agape and Eros* (Stockholm: Svenska Kyrkans Diakonistyrelses Bokforlag, 1930), p. 94.
[18] *Ibid.*, p. 118. [19] *Ibid.*, p. 70.
[20] Mark 3:1-6.

do anything for his father or mother, thus making void the word of God through your tradition which you hand on. And many such things you do." Jesus here, in a very radical way, has abolished any separation between religion and morality. Religion and morality are not identical, and we cannot confine religion to the ethical, but they are inseparably united in the Christian faith.

In the last sentence of the first part of the *Small Catechism,* Luther emphasizes this relationship when he says, "We should therefore love him, trust him, and cheerfully do what he has commanded." Luther's explanation of the First Article emphasizes the same idea when he says, "For all of this I am bound to thank, praise, serve, and obey him." In his explanation of the Second Petition he says that faith in the Word of God leads to "a godly life here on earth." Love to God becomes an empty form if it does not manifest itself in love to neighbor. This relationship is so intimate that the author of I John could say, "this is the love of God, that we keep his commandments."[21]

A seldom quoted passage from scripture, which describes a sense of social consciousness and responsibility, is a prayer from the primitive church. The social implications of this prayer are so often overlooked that we shall quote it in its entirety. Peter and John had been released from prison, and when they returned to the company of their fellow believers this prayer was offered:

> "Sovereign Lord, who didst make the heaven and the earth and the sea and everything in them, who by the mouth of our father David, thy servant, didst say by the Holy Spirit,
> 'Why did the Gentiles rage,
> and the peoples imagine vain things?

[21] I John 5:3.

> The kings of the earth set themselves in array,
> and the rulers were gathered together,
> Against the Lord and against his Anointed'—
> for truly in this city there were gathered together against thy holy servant Jesus, whom thou didst anoint, both Herod and Pontius Pilate, with the Gentiles and the peoples of Israel, to do whatever thy hand and thy plan had predestined to take place. And now, Lord, look upon their threats, and grant to thy servants to speak thy word with all boldness, while thou stretchest out thy hand to heal, and signs and wonders are performed through the name of thy Holy servant Jesus."[22]

The members of this primitive church knew it was imperative for them to take a stand with respect to the political and cultural situation in which they found themselves. A union of Roman political authority and vested religious interests had crucified Jesus. Political forces of the time were powers opposed to God and his will. Herod and Pontius Pilate were political instruments opposed to God. Government may be an instrument in the service of God or it may be a power which is opposed to God, and this fact was very clear to this primitive Christian community. Its members were conscious of the responsibility to take a position in relation to the political forces which surrounded them. This was their Christian social responsibility.

The apostle Paul has sometimes been interpreted in a manner leaving little room for any dynamic for a sense of social responsibility; but it was Paul who wrote "God was in Christ reconciling the *world* to himself," and has committed to us the ministry of reconciliation.[23] Here Paul sees the Christian gospel in terms of a reconciliation of the world to

[22] Acts 4:24-30.
[23] II Cor. 5:19.

God, and this involves a sense of social responsibility. The Christian faith, in Paul's conception, was more than a matter of individual salvation, or ecstatic feeling, or a rejoicing in the hope of a heaven after death. Paul's hope involved the reconciliation of the world to God.

The Christian sense of responsibility for the social order is also found in the last book of the Bible—a book where we might least expect to find it. The holy city, or the new Jerusalem, is a city that comes down to earth from out of heaven. It is not heaven itself.[24] The millennial hope in the Book of Revelation is a social hope which emphasizes the Christian's concern with the social order. When Revelation was written, Rome was the mistress of the world and the church was feeble and persecuted. The millennial hope involves that the roles will ultimately be reversed. God's people will see a fruition of their labor and suffering even in this world. This hope is an inspiration for social welfare and social justice. God has not abandoned his world or the realm of history. As long as the temporal lasts, evil may again manifest itself. The author of Revelation takes sin very seriously, but the Christian still maintains his hope for the social order and history.[25] We have no outline of history in advance, but we do have a hope which includes history because this is God's world.

The passage in the New Testament which emphasizes social responsibility, and which is used more often than any other, is the third petition of the Lord's Prayer. From its primitive days, and to the present time, the church and Christians have prayed:

> Thy kingdom come,
> Thy will be done,
> *On earth* as it is in heaven.

[24] Rev. 21:1-2. [25] Rev. 20.

We pray that God's will may be done *on earth* and thus assert a sense of responsibility for the social order. Someone has said that the first casualty in prayer is the one who really prays; and we cannot really pray the third petition of the Lord's Prayer unless we have a sense of social responsibility. God desires that his will be done in the things of earth, and the Christian cannot be indifferent to them if he is to be faithful to the object of his faith. And as Christians we cannot wait, for God's will does not wait.

The New Testament is replete with a sense of social responsibility. As we become aware of this fact, the meaning of our social responsibility becomes clear. The relation of the Christian to God involves more than a dual relationship. God and the individual soul are involved, but our relationship to God involves a trinity: God, the individual soul, and our neighbor. As our relationship to our neighbor enters the picture, we find ourselves in the realm of the social and social responsibility. As the consciousness of our relationship to God develops, the sense of solidarity with our fellow men increases. The Christian is a sinner who stands in need of God's forgiving grace, but justification is not something which is unrelated to the rest of life or social responsibility. Luther put it this way: ". . . for where there is forgiveness of sins, there are also life and salvation."[26] The forgiven sinner lives in an atmosphere which becomes meaningful for life. The forgiven sinner is called to a life of service, and God will only be served as we recognize our God-given responsibilities to our fellow men. There is no bypass to God, from the point of view of Christian faith, which ignores our relationship to our neighbor. There are attitudes connected with the worship life of the church which give the blasphemous impression of a kind of Divine egocentricity on the part of God. Worship of God without ethical emphasis and

[26] *Small Catechism.*

devotion is an insult to him who finds his highest honor in serving. Luther said it is the glory of God that he is a blessing to us.[27]

Social Welfare

Christian social responsibility is an integral factor in the Christian faith and life, and it manifests itself in two directions. In the first place, it is directed to minister to the physical and temporal needs of our fellow men. Social missions and inner missions are terms well known in the history of the church. The Bible is full of this type of ministry—from cover to cover. The healing ministry of Jesus and Paul's collection for the poor are well-known examples. Social service is a Christian obligation and Christians universally have recognized it as such. When certain groups in the church are confronted with the criticism that they are quietistic, by way of defense they often will point to the charitable institutions they have established and maintained. Hospitals, orphan homes, homes for the aged, homes for epileptics, and many similar institutions, are manifestations of a faith which energizes in love, and there would be something lacking in a Christianity unconcerned with the human needs to which such institutions minister. The Christian's concern for his neighbor will and should manifest itself in caring for the indigent.

The Spiritual and the Material

In rendering service as described above, the Christian does not set up an antithesis between spiritual and material realms. Such an attitude is well illustrated by Dr. Gibson,

[27] *Gloria eius est, quod beneficus in nos est* as reported in *Lectures on Romans* from *D. Martin Luthers Werke* Kritische Gesamtausgabe (Weimar, 1883-). Hereafter referred to as *WA*.

the Bishop of London, to whom the religious care of plantations and slaves in America had been entrusted. In 1727 he wrote: "The freedom which Christianity gives is a freedom from the bondage of sin and Satan and from the dominion of man's lusts and passions and inordinate desires. . . ." but, as to slavery, ". . . it makes no manner of change in it." The Lutheran Synod of South Carolina, in 1846, heard its president say, "Lutherans having slaves should exercise their right as masters to bring them to attend divine worship in the churches where they hold their membership; and if such slaves desire to enter into church relations, let them be advised to unite with the churches where their owners enkindle their devotions at the altars of God." Slaves had souls that could be made eternally happy, but often there was no concern about the temporal slavery of these people.

The Christian does not minister in the form of material blessings in order to bring a spiritual blessing to the recipient. The Good Samaritan ministered to the physical needs of the man who had fallen into the hands of robbers on the road between Jerusalem and Jericho. There is nothing in the parable that indicates he was concerned about an Evangelistic message before he left him at the inn. Here was need, and that need was met; and the Good Samaritan was commended by the Lord for his act. The material and the spiritual are not different categories. The spiritual may manifest itself through the material things of life. The word "spiritual" may be used to describe the incorporeal, but it does not mean a lack of interest in the material. Paul exhorts his readers to present their material bodies as a spiritual worship.[28] The spiritual involves having a nature in which spirit predominates, or it is the human spirit led and guided by the Spirit of God.

Material things may be used for spiritual service. Moses

[28] Rom. 12:1.

rendered a spiritual service when he delivered his people from their Egyptian bondage. Moses was concerned about developing a right relation to God on the part of his people, but when he delivered them from their slavery he acted because they needed to be freed. Jesus "did not heal in order to commend himself or to overcome opposition or prejudice, for some of his miracles resulted in stirring up opposition and he knew they would so result. He did not heal to attract a crowd, for, as in Mark 8:30, he sometimes '. . . charged them that they tell no man. . . .' He does not seem, even, to be concerned with making use of the evangelistic opportunity to preach to those he healed. His ministry of healing was just not done casually, as if secondary and unimportant. He put forth both physical and spiritual energy to heal men. He refused to perform works of healing as signs. He is not described anywhere in the Synoptic Gospels as using his cures as texts for sermons."[29] This statement is by the Christian Medical Association of India, and it indicates the proper perspective on the Christian attitude toward temporal needs. To urge people to establish hospitals so that we may get a chance to preach to their sick is hardly an honest motive. To be sure, the Christian desires to share the whole Christ with his fellow men; but when we minister to the sick we minister because they are ill, and not for some other reason. We care for the orphan because he is an orphan and for no other reason. Wherever there is need, we desire to minister because there is need. Any other motive violates the fundamental nature of Christian love.

A labor leader once asked me if my interest in the labor movement was prompted by the desire to get labor people to join the church organization. My answer was, in effect, "I certainly am interested in seeing labor people share in

[29] Seward Hiltner, *Religion and Health* (New York: The Macmillan Company, 1943), p. 42.

the blessings of the church, but I am interested in seeing justice done to labor even if I find it impossible to induce them to affiliate with the church. Christian love functions in the presence of need simply because there is need." This point of view is of more than academic interest, as is well illustrated by an article which appeared in a southern labor newspaper a few years ago. It speaks of the "tent preacher" who appears "from distant places with a full knowledge of all our wickedness and of all our spiritual needs, and comes in raving about our spiritual and moral truancy, and carries on night after night, crying himself prostrate about our spiritual and moral delinquency, and tells us of the great things we are to inherit if we follow his teachings—after we are dead. . . .

"It is amazing that ministers are so deeply concerned that we workers shall miss none of those golden blessings promised us after we are dead, but concern themselves so little with the tribulations of millions of Americans who struggle homelessly and hopelessly through this vast wilderness of unemployment, beridden of hunger and sickness of body and soul, seeking friends and relief from this stifling tragedy, but finding only people who wish to save our souls.

"Our Bible teaches that Jesus Christ not only loved the soul of mankind but their body as well. He not only healed the festered spirit of men, but usually their body first. The sick he made well, the hungry he fed—and then he preached, which inspires us to ask, can a preacher love our wicked soul so profoundly without having some affection for our body? Can a sick soul be healed as quickly and efficiently in a hungry, pain-racked body as in a body well and comfortable?

"We read, we listen, and we wonder. 'Beware of false prophets, who come to you in sheep's clothing, but inwardly are ravening wolves.'[30]" Such is labor's grievance.

[30] Matt. 7:15.

Social Action

The Christian is interested in serving his fellow man simply because there is need for such service, and this disposition encompasses both physical and spiritual needs. It means caring for the helpless and the indigent, but there is another direction in which Christian social responsibility manifests itself. The Christian is also concerned about the conditions which produce the need for charity. The Good Samaritan performed a Christian service when he came to the man who had fallen among robbers ". . . and bound up his wounds, pouring on them oil and wine; and he set him on his own beast, and brought him to an inn, and took care of him."[31] The Christian has an added interest in such a situation from the point of view of his social responsibility. The Christian is also concerned about making the road between Jerusalem and Jericho safe, so that men may travel that road without falling into the hands of robbers. Such manifestation of Christian love may not be as dramatic or sentimental as the former, but it is ofttimes more effective. The Christian is interested in rescuing the drunkard, but he should also be interested in the situations in the structure of society which produce drunkards. The average rescue mission performs a real Christian service in caring for the indigent, but the Christian should also be interested in doing something about the slum areas of our large cities, which produce many of the dregs of society with which the Rescue Mission deals. It is a Christian service to minister to the victims of flood waters, but it is likewise a Christian obligation to seek the prevention of floods. Christianity is concerned about the cure of the victims of social maladjustments, but also with preventing people from becoming victims.

[31] Luke 10:34.

Recently a church member was trying to justify the concern of her church for the laboring man by pointing out that an organization in the church had distributed baskets of food to the needy at Thanksgiving and Christmas. To be sure, it is an act of Christian love to feed the hungry, but it is a more significant attitude to be concerned about working conditions which bring about such need for food. Various groups and organizations connected with the church in Germany have made a significant effort to establish friendly relationships with the industrial workers, particularly since the end of the Second World War. A very significant aspect of this approach has been a concern for justice for the worker as against mere charity. Charity is a Chrstian virtue but so, also, is justice. The giving of alms where there is need is not to be depreciated as a social responsibility for the Christian, but there must also be a concern for situations which produce the need for alms. We must care for the aged who cannot care for themselves. This may be done through building and maintaining homes for the aged, but it can also be done by an adequate social security program; and the latter is as involved in the Christian attitude as the former. The promotion of an effective social security program may be a much more effective approach to the problems of the aged than the establishment of homes for these people. There always will be a need for charity and there always will be people who cannot take care of themselves, but Christian social responsibility implies a concern for the elimination of those things in the structure of society which produce indigent people. This is the distinction between "welfare" and "social action." Both are necessary and both are involved in Christian social responsibility. It is in the realm of social action that the church and Christian too often have failed to recognize their social responsibility. It is at this point that an awakening must take place if the church is going to meet the crisis of our age in a realistic fashion. As men seek for meaning and direction for life, they will not find it in the ministry of the church unless the church comes to grips with the problems involved in social action. The old taunt song about "pie in the sky" and the Marxian challenge about religion being the opiate of the people may involve historical reflections which may cause serious soul-searching on the part of Christians and the church. Social responsibility involves a sense of responsibility for the character of society. Holding out the hope of heavenly bliss cannot be a substitute for such things as adequate housing, decent wages, security for old age, and an opportunity to educate the young.

The Realm of Culture

We have already stated that the Christian faith involves God, the individual soul, and our fellow men. Any attempt to distinguish between "individual" and "social ethics" soon reveals that any such line of demarcation becomes rather tenuous. However, there is a realm of experience which is relatively private in nature. Our friendships, love, marriage, and our interior hopes and worries are peculiarly our own individual experiences. In addition to this rather private aspect of human experience, there is another realm. It has to do with the whole field of history, work, industry, government, and society in general. It is the realm of culture or civilization. H. Richard Niebuhr has well defined this realm when he says: "Culture is the 'artificial secondary environment' which man superimposes on the natural. It comprises language, habits, ideas, beliefs, customs, social organization, inherited articrafts, technical processes, and values. This 'social heritage,' this 'reality sui generis,' which the New Testament writers frequently had in mind when they spoke of 'the world,' which is represented in many forms but to which Christians like other men are inevitably subject, is what we mean when we speak of culture."[32] Our religion is not excluded from this realm. God will, in the long run, have to be recognized as the Lord of all of life or we shall fail to recognize him as the Lord of those areas to which we have attempted to confine his activities. A Catholic theologian in Germany has said that Hitler was concerned to confine the studies of theological students to areas which dealt with liturgies and "pure theology" (which meant theology detached from culture). Neither the Fascists nor the Communists have ever been particularly concerned with such theological disciplines. They have, however, been tremendously concerned with religion at the point where it touches the realm of culture. The martyrs and the persecuted heroes of the faith, in our age and in many other ages, have experienced the wrath of the demonic forces of life when they have come to grips with the cultural aspects of their environment. The experience of the church in modern times makes it clear that we cannot confine religion to the sacristy or to a theological "ivory tower." It will, in the long run, be increasingly difficult to keep it in these limited areas unless we come to grips with the social problem. The kind of religion which is confined to the four walls of the sanctuary and to the so-called realm of the "inner life" does not have the answer that our generation seeks and needs. The Christian life is not lived in a vacuum, but in a concrete historical situation with which it is involved. The Christian must seek to live his life as a Christian in the historical context in which he finds himself, or his faith will lack vitality. Even the pillar saint cannot sever various connections with the social order without perishing.

The realm of history, culture, and civilization is involved

32 Helmut Richard Niebuhr, *Christ and Culture* (New York: Harper and Brothers, 1951), p. 32.

in Christian experience, and when we recognize this fact we soon discover that there are social situations which transcend the individual will and which cannot be dealt with from the point of view of the individual will. There are problems which are specifically social in character. There are problems which can be solved by the will of the individual. But there are also problems which can be solved only as the patterns and forms of society are altered. Among the latter are: war, the relations between capital and labor, poverty, the concentration of wealth, child labor, racial relations, crime, amusements, population problems, and the care of dependent classes. These problems involve situations which are not subject to the immediate will of the individual. For example, an individual may will not to strike his neighbor, and thus prevent such action from taking place. However, when war comes, no amount of willing on the part of the individual will prevent the inflicting of suffering on people. In war, men participate in a situation which is not amenable to their immediate wills. The individual has little to say about the declaration of war, or his participation in it. It is difficult to imagine applying the spirit of Christ to our enemies in a war situation. The problem can never be solved on the basis of individual attitudes. It must be faced as a social problem, and the only solution is to be found in the abolition of the war system as an instrument of the policy of nations. The United Nations organization was established for the purpose of accomplishing this and other objectives. As a Christian, I feel it to be my obligation to support this effort to solve this great social problem in a social way. I hate war but, apart from efforts of this kind, I am helpless to cope with the problem.

An individual may be perfectly honest in his dealing with banks. He may will that depositors in a bank shall not lose their savings, but to insure this fact will require something more than is involved in his individual willing. The depression of the 1930 decade taught us it was necessary to establish new government regulations for banks if people were to be protected; and it is a Christian obligation to be concerned that such protection be provided.

Anyone who has even elementary knowledge of the problems involved in the relations of capital and labor must realize that a solution must be sought in a manner quite different from the manner in which individual problems are solved. Experience has taught us that laws and organization are necessary to cope with the problems involved. Without organization and a social approach the individual worker is ofttimes helpless.

Child labor is another example of a problem which cannot be left for its solution to the individual will. History tells us that the abuse of children in the early days of our modern industrial development was stopped only through social legislation.

One of the best examples of the manner in which social situations effect Christian ethical conduct is found in the economic realm. As Christians, we participate in an economic order. In the measure that such a system is unchristian, we are not, to that extent, living the Christian life; and the only remedy for such a situation is to create a system where it is possible to practice more adequately that which is ethical from the Christian point of view. In other words, the problem can only be solved as a social matter. The isolated individual is helpless to do anything about it. For example, a Christian employer may try, as an individual, to deal fairly with the employees; and the result of such an attitude may be bankruptcy for him because of competition with other employers who are not benevolent in their attitudes to their employees. This problem must be solved as a social problem if it is to be solved at all. There are many businessmen who have come to the conclusion that it is impossible to operate a single, isolated business on Christian principles.

The difference between approaching a problem and its solution from an individual and a social point of view can be illustrated by imagining a city which has no water to meet the needs of its inhabitants. Every Christian would recognize that it is a Christian duty to give a thirsty fellow man a drink of water. The situation might be met in two ways. A pail of water might be brought from some source of supply. The person desiring to minister to the needs of the people might visit as many individuals as possible with a pail and cup, and thus provide as many as possible with water. Another way to meet the situation would be to employ engineers to build a pipeline, and thus bring a supply of water into the city. The latter would certainly be the better way to solve the problem, and it need be no less Christian in spirit than the former. Until we understand that there are situations and problems which can only be approached from a social point of view, we shall never understand the full implications of Christian social responsibility.

A sense of social responsibility involves recognition of the fact that there are certain patterns or forms of society in which the Christian life cannot express itself. The realm of social relationships also presents us with the fact that there is a relativity with respect to the possibility of expressing the Christian ideal in various forms of the social structure. Some of these patterns are better and some are worse as media of expression for the Christian life.

The fact can be illustrated if we imagine a missionary approaching a cannibalistic tribe for the purpose of Christianizing the people. The missionary could not ignore their social customs or patterns, or their cannibalistic practices in their social relationships. The absurdity of ignoring the patterns of society impresses itself upon us if we can imagine such a missionary ignoring the cannibalism of the people and simply teaching them to use a table prayer before eating. This would be a separation of the religious and the ethical. The Christian life just cannot express itself in connection with such social customs, and they must be abolished before there can be any Christian life. We cannot be indifferent to the forms and patterns of culture, if we are to take our Christian life seriously.

Another example may be taken from family relationships. The Christian ideal for marriage is monogamy. Within the framework of the monogamous family, the Christian ethic can be exercised. Many sins occur in the monogamous family relationships, but their cause is not to be found in the structure of the family relationship itself. The monogamous family pattern supplies an organization for this social unit where Christianity can be practiced. The most profound insights and experiences of the Christian can be expressed with figures from family life. The words "father," "mother," "brethren," and "sisters" come from the monogamous family relationship and are capable of symbolizing some of the deepest experiences connected with the Christian faith. The only adequate form for Christian living in the family relationship is to be found in the monogamous pattern. In other words, the structure of the family is important for the expression of the Christian life.

The doctrine of "vocation" is a tremendously dynamic concept as we meditate upon the meaning of Christian social responsibility. However, historically the life-giving stream has often vanished in the sands of the desert. It did so in Roman Catholic monasticism. It may be that monasticism arose partly as a protest against the false notion that God's forgiveness is something that can be had cheaply from God; but one of the fundamental weaknesses of monasticism is that it tries to withdraw from the ethical problem, and cuts itself off from responsible action in the world. A modern monk, describing how he found satisfaction in a Trappist monastery, used these words: "What wonderful happiness there was, then, in the world! There were still men on this miserable, noisy, cruel earth who tasted the marvelous joy of silence and solitude, who dwelt in forgotten mountain cells, in secluded monasteries, where the news and desires and appetites and conflicts of the world no longer reached them."[33] Here is an excellent illustration of a conception of "vocation" which does not lead to any sense of social responsibility.

As we look at history, we cannot be too contented over the issues of the doctrine of "vocation" in Lutheranism or Calvinism. The very emphasis on the doctrine in contemporary theology is mute testimony that the issues have not been what we should expect or would desire. Only as we come to recognize the "deadly corporateness" of sin will the dynamics of the doctrine of Christian vocation be adequately realized. Without a sense of social responsibility as we have described it, the doctrine will never be vital; but set in the framework of social responsibility, it becomes a dynamic Christian social responsibility.

There is a tendency to look upon Christian social responsibility and social action as an addendum to Christian experience. Such an attitude stems from a misunderstanding of the nature of the ethical. As man is confronted by God, he not only is made aware of his dependence but also senses his responsibility; and thus the ethical is given in the religious experience itself. The call of Moses involved a concrete content.[34] Moses was given a sense of social responsibility

[33] Thomas Merton, *The Seven Story Mountain* (New York: Harcourt, Brace and Company, 1948, p. 316.

[34] Exod. 3.

in that call. This concern was not a consequence of his religious experience, it was an integral part of it. The religious experience did not come first and the concern for his people and their slavery as an appendage. When Moses sensed the call of God, he was made aware that the concrete content of that call was to deliver his people from bondage. God spoke to Moses and impressed upon him a sense of social responsibility. A social interest is an integral part of religious experience, if such experience is true to the genius of the Hebrew-Christian tradition.

2

THE NEED FOR A CHRISTIAN SOCIAL EMPHASIS

The very subject for these lectures indicates that there are those who feel that the subject needs to be emphasized. There has always been need for a social emphasis from the point of view of the Hebrew-Christian tradition. Human sin and nature being what they are, it is imperative to stress continually this aspect of our faith.

The Prophetic Recognition of Social Responsibility

The great prophets of the Old Testament, in their day, found it necessary to stress the social significance of their faith. Professor John Wick Bowman has isolated various types of religion found in the Old Testament.[1] He speaks of the religion of the altar, the religion of the book, the religion of the throne, and the religion of maturity. The latter is the great prophetic movement. The prophets were the "pioneers to Christianity," as Walter G. Williams puts it.[2]

The prophets of the Old Testament were particularly emphatic that the ethical cannot and must not be separated from vital religion. When we add to this the attitude of the prophets to superstition as a substitute for religion,[3] we dis-

[1] John Wick Bowman, *The Religion of Maturity* (Nashville: Abingdon-Cokesbury Press, 1946).

[2] Walter G. Williams, *The Prophets—Pioneers to Christianity* (Nashville: Abingdon Press, 1946).

[3] Isa. 8:19-20.

cover that the prophets exemplify the two chief roads on which, historically, religion has advanced to higher levels—the elimination of the magical and the recognition of the ethical.

The first of the great literary prophets, Amos, manifests his genius by his emphasis upon the ethical in religion. In the book of Amos we have not only monotheism, but an ethical monotheism. In a classical passage he says, as the spokesman of God, "I hate, I despise your feasts, and I will take no delight in your solemn assemblies. Yea, though ye offer me your burnt-offerings and meal-offerings, I will not accept them; neither will I regard the peace-offerings of your fat beasts. Take thou away from me the noise of thy songs; for I will not hear the melody of thy viols. But let justice roll down as waters, and righteousness as a mighty stream."[4] Here was a sense of social responsibility. A lack of justice meant death just as sure as a lack of water in the desert.

The ancient peasants called the eschatological end of all things the day of Jehovah. God would vanquish their enemies and place them in a position of supremacy. But the prophet Amos ethicized the popular eschatology, and he says, "Woe unto you that desire the day of Jehovah! Wherefor would ye have the day of Jehovah? It is darkness, and not light. As if a man did flee from a lion, and a bear met him; or went into the house and leaned his hand on the wall, and a serpent bit him. Shall not the day of Jehovah be darkness, and not light? even very dark, and no brightness in it?"[5]

What God demands of his people is social morality and justice. This is the fundamental law of the universe which God created and which is ruled by him. This was the teaching of Amos as a new way of life. We shall, perhaps, never know what the total attitude of Amos was to the cult of his day, but it is clear that he is condemning the cult as he knew

Amos 5:21-24. [5] Amos 5:18-20.

it. Dorothy Clarke Wilson has Amos looking inside the Most Holy Place in the Temple at Bethel, and when asked by the high priest if he believes that "Yahweh really lived in the little dark room" he answers, "You ought to know, you're allowed to go inside, aren't you?"[6]

The same spirit permeates the book of the prophet Isaiah. The first chapter is, perhaps, a summary of the message of the "king of the prophets," and in this chapter it is said that the herds of beasts trampling the temple courts, the burning of fat, the reek of blood, and the clouds of incense, were an abomination and a weariness to God. Festivals and solemn meetings, prayers and prostrations, were iniquity from which God turned his face. What God wanted was a right life and the righting of wrongs: ". . . your hands are full of blood. Wash you, make you clean; put away the evil of your doings from before mine eyes; cease to do evil; learn to do well; seek justice, relieve the oppressed, judge the fatherless, plead for the widow."[7]

Speaking for the Lord, Hosea said, ". . . I desire goodness, and not sacrifice . . . "[8] and Jesus was fond of quoting his words. Jesus loved Hosea and the words of the prophet are often found on his lips.

The attitude of Micah is identical. He says, "Wherewith shall I come before Jehovah, and bow myself before the high God? shall I come before him with burnt-offerings, with calves a year old? will Jehovah be pleased with thousands of rams, or with ten thousands of rivers of oil? Shall I give my first-born for my transgression, the fruit of my body for the sin of my soul? He hath showed thee, O man, what is good; and what doth Jehovah require of thee, but to do justly . . . love kindness . . . walk humbly with thy God?"[9]

[6] Dorothy Clarke Wilson, *The Herdsman* (Philadelphia: Westminster Press, 1946), pp. 121 ff.

[7] Isa. 1:16-17. [8] Hos. 6:6. [9] Mic. 6:6-8.

When we turn to the New Testament, we find that the first Christian martyr was charged with speaking ". . . words against this holy place, and the law . . ."; it was charged that Stephen had said ". . . that this Jesus of Nazareth shall destroy this place, and shall change the customs which Moses delivered unto us."[10] Stephen undoubtedly had been echoing the attitude of the prophets to the temple and the whole sacrificial cult.

For the apostle Paul, the whole sacrificial system was eliminated in the light of his experience with Jesus. In Romans he sublimates the whole idea when he says, "I beseech you therefore, brethren, by the mercies of God, to present your bodies a living sacrifice, holy, acceptable to God, which is your spiritual service."[11]

Without doubt we have, in the great, eighth-century prophets, an anticipation of that which came to full fruition in Jesus, Stephen, Paul, and the other New Testament writers. In these prophets we have the beginnings of an approach to the "religion of maturity" revealed in the New Testament. It is to be noted that this type of religion stresses the socially ethical aspects of life.

Priestly Religion

In order to make the emphasis which the prophetic tradition represented, it was often necessary to repudiate another type of religion, which is to be found in the Old Testament: the priestly. The prophets had to protest the cult when it became a substitute for ethical living. Admittedly, there was not a complete lack of ethical emphasis in priestly religion. Jesus quoted from the Book of Leviticus when he said ". . . thou shalt love thy neighbor as thyself . . ."[12] but the question is where the emphasis was placed.

[10] Acts 6:13-14. [11] Rom. 12:1. [12] Lev. 19:18.

It was the priest Amaziah who contrived to have the first of the literary prophets driven into exile,[13] and it was the high priest Caiaphas who led the opposition which finally nailed Jesus to the cross on Calvary.

The Reformation of the sixteenth century can be characterized as a break with this type of religion. The weaknesses of human nature have always tended in the direction of the development of this phenomenon, toward a priestly, cultic, and nonethical emphasis. It is always a reversion in the direction of the primitive as opposed to the "religion of maturity." Even in our own church of the Reformation, we sometimes hear the expression "parish priest" used in reference to the pastor of a congregation. Reference is sometimes made to the "priestly function" of the pastor. A pastor has the same priestly function as any other Christian, but none other. It has even been stated that when a pastor functions at the altar he is a "priest" and when he functions in the pulpit he is a "prophet." The New Testament itself repudiates this type of religion, and in our evangelical Lutheran tradition there is no room for it.

One of the most significant things about a priesthood is the idea that priesthood is a caste. This caste possesses certain extraordinary powers which make it possible to perform certain mediatorial acts other people cannot perform. The Levitical priesthood of the Old Testament is a well-known example. The priest was born into his status, and this status was determined by tribal or family considerations. After the days of Ezekiel, the sons of Zadok, by virtue of their descent, were accorded a special status in relation to other Levites. Sometimes such a status may be provided by ordination, consecration, or investiture. The emphasis here is not upon moral or spiritual considerations, or a personal prophetic call from God, but rather upon the sanctions of tradition. No

[13] Amos 7:10-17.

divine call was required or claimed by the priest. His status was legitimate by virtue of his birth or investiture.

Walter Rauschenbusch has said, "The priest is the religious professional. He performs religious functions which others are not allowed to perform. It is therefore to his interest to deny the right of free access to God, and to interpose himself and his ceremonial between the common man and God. . . . It is essential to the priestly interest to establish a monopoly of rights and functions for his group. He is all for authority, and in some form or other he is always a spokesman of that authority and shares its influence. Doctrine and history as he teaches it, establish a *jure divino* institution of his order, which is transmitted either by physical descent, . . . or by spiritual descent through some form of exclusive ordination, as in the Catholic priesthood. . . . He is the middleman of religion, and like other middlemen he is sincerely convinced that he is necessary for the good of humanity and that religion would perish without him. But underneath all is the selfish interest of his class, which exploits religion."[14]

Luther completely rejected the idea of a priestly caste, and in this fact alone there should be found a dynamic for a social ethical emphasis for the Lutheran. In the *Babylonian Captivity,* he said to all who would seek holy orders through ordination: "What then is there left to you that every layman does not have? Tonsure and vestments? A sorry priest, forsooth, who consists of tonsure and vestment! . . . Let every one, therefore, who knows himself to be a Christian be assured of this, and apply it to himself, that we are all priests, and there is no difference between us; that is to say, we have the same power in respect to the Word and all the sacraments. However, no one may make use of this power

[14] Walter Rauschenbusch, *A Theology for the Social Gospel* (New York: The Macmillan Company, 1917), pp. 274-75.

except by the consent of the community or by the call of a superior. For what is the common property of all, no individual may arrogate to himself, unless he be called. And therefore this sacrament of ordination, if it have any meaning at all, is nothing else than a certain rite whereby one is called to the ministry of the Church. Furthermore, the priesthood is properly nothing but the ministry of the Word. . . ."[15]

Again Luther says, "To ordain is not to consecrate. Therefore, if we know a pious man we single him out and through the power of the Word which we possess we give him authority to preach the Word and to administer the Sacraments. This is to ordain."[16]

For Luther, the ministry of the Word was a function entrusted to certain men. All implications of caste or magic were eliminated. He did not minimize the importance of this office, even though he completely rejected the idea it was a priesthood. Again he says, "To be sure, there have been many . . . who have praised this estate highly, though more because of the saying of mass than because of preaching. This praise and glorification grew to the point where the office and estate of the priesthood (that is, of the sacrificing of the mass) was placed above Mary and the angels, because the angels and Mary could not say mass and a priest could. A new priest and his first mass were glorious, and blessed was the woman who had borne a priest; though the office of preaching is the highest and chief of all, and it was not regarded so highly. In a word, a priest was a man who could say mass, even though he did not know a word to preach and was an unlearned ass."[17] Luther thought highly of the office of the ministry, but for him it was not a priesthood—it was not a caste, limited to a particular religion or social order.

[15] *Works of Martin Luther* (6 vols.; Philadelphia: Muhlenberg Press, 1915-43), II, 282-83. Hereafter referred to as *PE*.

[16] *Ibid.*, VI, 234. [17] *Ibid.*, IV, 143.

Luther arrived at his doctrine of the ministry through his study of the New Testament. There the ministers of the Word are called prophets, apostles, evangelists, pastors, presbyters, and bishops. Never once in the New Testament is a minister of the Word called a priest. The designation "priest" is an importation, either from the Old Testament or from pagan sources. Priests are mentioned in the New Testament. Perhaps the best known are Annas and Caiaphas. Paul, Peter, James, John, and the other apostles were not the successors of Annas and Caiaphas. These ministers of the Word belonged to another significant tradition—the prophetic.

In some countries in which the Lutheran church has been established, the language itself is a source of confusion with respect to the significance of the office of the ministry. For example, in Sweden a pastor is sometimes called *prest*. Luther's knowledge of history is rather remarkable at this point. In his treatise to Emser he said, "The word 'priest' has come from the Greek, in which *presbyteros* means what *senior* means in Latin, and elder in our own tongue."[18] Archbishop Yngve Brilioth has shown clearly that presbyters became pastors of local congregations very early in the history of the church. The word *prest* in the Swedish language does not mean "priest"; it is a contraction of the word presbyter.[19] The history of the development of ecclesiastical offices in the church proves that the early church recognized no priestly caste; all such manifestations are foreign importations, and did not originally belong to the genius of the Christian faith.

In connection with one of the crises in the history of the Lutheran church in America, in 1856, the Pittsburgh Synod

[18] *Ibid.*, III, 322.

[19] Yngve Brilioth, *Svensk Kyrkokunskap* (Stockholm: Svenska Kyrkans Diakonistyrelses Bokförlag), p. 114.

adopted a paper prepared by Dr. C. P. Krauth, Jr. This resolution states that "there is no priesthood on earth except that of all believers."[20] This is the only genuine Lutheran position and doctrine. There is a universal priesthood of believers, and we have a great and eternal high priest in the heavens, but there is no priestly caste on earth.

Another characteristic of priestly religion is that the priest depends primarily upon materialistic means in order to exercise his function. Priests were primarily ministers of sacrifice. They specialized in sacrificial ritual. Their instruction was intended primarily to teach the people about the acceptable and proper worship of God through ritual and ceremony. They were the cultic specialists. The use of proper vestments (which were often of regal magnificence), the observance of seasons, and the proper techniques of the cult ritual, were the primary matters which engaged the attention of the priest.

Professor Julius August Bewer characterized the difference between the prophet and the priest when he said that both "wanted to make the people acceptable to God. But . . . the priests believed that it could be accomplished by ritual holiness. In and through the cult they sought to educate the people in obedience to Yahweh. . . . A purely moral and spiritual religion was too high and exacting for the mass of the people."[21] Professor Bowman has said that "the difference between the prophet and the priest . . . was that which always is found to pertain between the man of vision and his fellow of practical sense or worldly prudence, between the statesman and the politician, the architect and the draftsman, the landscape artist and the gardener, the sculptor and the stone mason. The priest . . . wrote the prophets sympho-

[20] H. K. Carroll and Others, *The American Church History Series* (13 vols., New York: The Christian Literature Company, 1893-97), IV, 427.

[21] Julius August Bewer, *The Literature of the Old Testament* (New York: Columbia University Press 1922), pp. 266-67.

nies in a lower key where they could be appreciated by the so-called 'man in the street' and stepped down the required obedience to the divine will, which for the prophet involved personal sacrifice, to the level of the offering of the personally owned animal that had a monetary value rather than a moral one."[22]

This does not mean that there were no priests who had a Word of God for the people; Jeremiah and Ezekiel are examples to the contrary. But it does mean that a priest could function in his office without any developed sense of moral or spiritual values, and it does mean that we often find a tension between the prophetic and priestly type of religion as the prophets sought to stress moral and social values. The struggle between prophet and priest is also evident in the history of the church. The sacrifice of the Mass is characteristic of Romanism, and the chief function of the priest is to offer this sacrifice. The Lord's Supper is recognized as a sacrament among us, also, but there is a great difference between the presuppositions of the "sacrifice of the Mass" and our idea of "Communion, the Lord's Table," "the Sacrament of the Altar," "Abendmahl" or "Nattvard." The "sacrifice of the Mass" and the "Sacrament of the Altar" are not the same thing. In no sense is the pastor at the Communion service a sacrificing priest. The celebration of the Lord's Supper is not a Protestant version of the Roman Mass. It is something quite different.

In a priestly religion, salvation by the people was to be attained by the right performance of certain ceremonial rites. Interest in the cult does not necessarily mean salvation. Jesus spoke to the Samaritan woman about her salvation, and in doing so he was constrained to point to some of the unethical aspects of her life, from which he offered her salvation. This seems to have been rather painful for the

[22] Bowman, *op. cit.*, pp. 93-94.

Samaritan woman and she immediately tried to change the subject of conversation. She commenced to question Jesus about the cult and its practices. "Our fathers worshipped in this mountain; and ye say, that in Jerusalem is the place where men ought to worship"[23] was the statement by which she tried to avoid facing the real issues of life. She was interested in the cult and in worship, but this did not mean salvation. Worship, as a cultic practice, is not a kind of filling station at which people can tank up salvation. Worship is one of the highest expressions of the human spirit but we can go through the forms, and even enjoy it, without worship in spirit and truth.

Another characteristic of the priestly religion is that it tends to emphasize the institutions of religion. The priest concerned himself primarily with the "high place," or the temple. "Trust ye not in lying words, saying, The temple of Jehovah, the temple of Jehovah, the temple of Jehovah, are these"[24] is a passage in which Jeremiah echoes the typical cry of priestly religion.

Note that we are never told in the gospels that Jesus brought any sacrifices to be offered in the temple. A sacrifice was offered in connection with his presentation in the temple, but that was an act on the part of Joseph and Mary. It is also significant that usually, when Jesus visited the Temple, conflict developed for him. Jesus never emphasized the institutions of religion. Even the word "church" was used only twice by Jesus, according to the record in the gospels. The institutions of religion are important, and religion cannot dispense with them; but they are means to an end and never ends in themselves. It is noted to be that it was the synagogue and not the temple which supplied a pattern for the worship life of the early church. Temple worship ex-

[23] John 4:20.
[24] Jer. 7:4.

erted some influence on the worship of the synagogue, but the function of the priest and the sacrificial cult were eliminated.

The Jewish priesthood belongs to history, and the temple, with its smoking altars, has been destroyed; but the great prophets—and Jesus, who belongs in their line of succession—survive. The prophets of the Old Testament, Langland in England, and the Reformers in Germany offered the same complaints of their priests. "God's judgment of priests is perennial," says R. F. Horton.[25]

We have devoted so much space to the prophetic and priestly type of religion because the prophets so often had to struggle against the priestly type as they emphasized God's will for social righteousness. An emphasis on the institutional church, on theology, and on the cult may all be good, but it is also possible for such emphases to produce a climate where there will be little emphasis upon social responsibility. Theology may become a sponsor for a priestly type of religion where theology is simply an attempt on the part of the church to define its self-consciousness, and where it stresses the relationship to God in such a manner that the relationship to fellow men is minimized. Religion without a social ethics is something else than our Christian faith. The scriptures themselves emphasize the need to stress the ethical in the light of perversions of the Hebrew-Christian tradition. The Roman church has developed a program for social action in various countries, together with its particular type of religion, but we cannot forget the social situation in Catholic countries like South America, Portugal, and Spain. A priestly religion and a sense of social responsibility do not necessarily exist together, and where a social emphasis is found with a priestly religion the ethical consciousness does not come from this religion.

[25] Robert Forman Horton, *The New Century Bible* (Oxford), I, 29.

Revivalism

Another type of religion which needs an emphasis upon the social ethics of scripture is revivalism. This phenomenon has been a characteristic feature of American Christianity. Camp meetings and revivals were typical of a frontier religion with Charles G. Finney and Dwight L. Moody as its representative exponents. It must be admitted that revivalism has sometimes been connected with a concern for social ethics. Modern evangelists have been known to stress social action, and we are mindful that Walter Rauschenbusch could express his appreciation of the work of Dwight L. Moody.[26] Timothy L. Smith has advanced the thesis that there was a connection between social reform and revivalism which flourished about the middle of the last century.[27] However, the type of revivalism which Smith describes preceded the period when revivalism had hardened into a particular technique. Revivalism stresses individual reception of grace as against an institutional administration of grace. Revivalism emphasizes experience as the priestly religion stresses authority—the authority of the church or the hierarchy. It ought to be an axiom, but it is often overlooked, that if individual conversion is to be socially effective, such conversion will have to be to a religion with a social emphasis. Usually, revivalism has been extremely individualistic and has failed to come to grips with the problems of society in any constructive manner. An extreme example of such individualism is found in a sermon by W. H. H. Murray, when he says, "Separate yourself from all your kind, make of the world a solitude, depopulate the globe, and think of yourself as the only living soul upon which the attention of Heaven and Hell is fixed tonight. . . . Undue importance, as it appears to me, is attached to the

[26] Rauschenbusch, *A Theology for the Social Gospel,* p. 97.

[27] Timothy L. Smith, *Revivalism and Social Reform* (Nashville: Abingdon Press, 1957).

connection of Christians one with another, and to the good or bad effect such connection has upon individual growth."[28] The attitude is often expressed that if people will just experience conversion to the revivalists' particular brand of religiosity, all social problems automatically will be solved. There is often an attempt to escape from the harsh realities of life. If men can only get the experience which the evangelist seeks to produce, they will be vindicated in the New Age to come. There is rarely any sense of social responsibility, and all the convert can hope for is the end of this present evil age. We are not minimizing the significance of the Christian hope for the next life; there can be a great dynamic in this hope, but it must not be separated from a sense of responsibility for the world and its problems. A vindictive delight in the destruction of the world and our own glorification are hardly an aspect of the gospel of the Lord Jesus Christ.

The Social Gospel

One movement of an earlier generation, which had the merit of recognizing the need for a Christian social emphasis, was the so-called "social gospel" movement. The year 1957 was the fiftieth anniversary of the book *Christianity and the Social Crisis* by Walter Rauschenbusch. It established the author as the greatest interpreter of the "social gospel." Reinhold Niebuhr, in his Rauschenbusch Lectures of 1934, speaks of Rauschenbusch as "the real founder of social Christianity in this country," and "its most brilliant and generally satisfying exponent to this day."[29] Walter Rauschenbusch did more than any other man in America to bring

[28] Henry Farnham May, *Protestant Churches and Industrial America* (New York: Harper and Brothers, 1949), pp. 83-84.

[29] Reinhold Niebuhr, *An Interpretation of Christian Ethics* (New York: Harper and Brothers, 1935), preface.

to the church an emphasis on Christian social responsibility.

The disciple does not always have the background of the master, and he may overemphasize, out of context, certain aspects of the doctrine of the teacher. He may also not maintain the balance of the teacher in his perspective of all the facets of the Christian faith. This undoubtedly happened among many who got their inspiration from Rauschenbusch, and the "social gospel" movement laid itself open to the criticism that it was theologically shallow. It sometimes became all "social" with very little, if any, "gospel." Sometimes it missed the real meaning of the kingdom of God in relation to history. It sometimes tended to be humanistic and lacked an emphasis upon the supernatural. There was a tendency to exalt the imminence of God at the expense of his transcendence. The conception of human nature was sometimes romantic and unrealistic, and Pelagianism was not absent as man's work took the place of divine activity. The reaction came in various types of neo-orthodoxy, and the reaction in a man like Barth was so violent that the Christian faith was removed from any relevance and relation to the world, except as God's activity is arbitrary and fortuitous. Then came Bultmann and Tillich who said that, in the light of Barth's position, we shall have to "demythologize" and reinterpret the faith in terms of human experience. The two latter theologians at least have the merit of sensing the need for contact with life.

The "social gospel" movement never did reach down to the level of the average church members. They heard about it, but it was never taken very seriously. Judging from the literature which is coming from our presses, it may be that we are on the verge of witnessing a resurgence of a social emphasis in Christian circles; but if it does arrive, it will be with a quite different theological orientation than the older "social gospel."

The term "social gospel" is, itself, a rather unfortunate expression. There is only one gospel, and that gospel is for the individual and society as well. If the term simply emphasizes a neglected aspect of the Christian faith, it may well be retained and perhaps we do need the expression in order to call attention to an aspect of the gospel which has so often been neglected. However, the social gospel is not a different gospel from the gospel for the individual. The gospel is one and inseparable for the individual and for society. The individual and the social emphasis run side by side throughout scripture.

Quietism

The Lutheran church has often been accused of quietism. At the Stockholm conference on "Life and Work," in 1925, it appeared very clearly that two types of Protestantism were represented with respect to attitudes to social responsibility. The Lutheran type was individualistic and eschatological in its orientation, emphasizing the transcendent aspects of the kingdom of God and held a rather pessimistic attitude toward the world and the social process. This group had the merit of insisting that Christian activity not be separated from divine grace, but lacked social consciousness.

The Evangelical Academy Movement developed in Germany after the close of the Second World War and it is one of the most significant attempts in German Lutheranism to develop a Christian social ethical emphasis. Many of the leaders in the movement, and in related movements in Germany, stress the fact that they have a great deal to "live down" from past history, and they are well aware of an historical quietism. The need of a social emphasis is also manifesting itself in the church in Sweden by a few voices.[30]

[30] Anders Tauson-Hassler, *Kämpande Kyrka* (Stockholm: Svenska Kyrkans Diakonistyrelses Bokförlag, 1951).

A typical attack on Lutheran quietism is that by Harris Franklin Rall when he says, "One thing we cannot do and that is to assign to religion and the Church the spiritual life of man, with some attention to social benevolence, and leave all other interests to secular control. How fateful such a conclusion could be we see when we observe its later influence, especially as illustrated in Luther and the Lutheran Movement in Germany. Here Church and state were set side by side as coordinate divine institutions. The rulers of the state presumably were to obey God and the Christian was to obey the state in all matters that concerned government and the affairs of 'the world.' True, Luther stressed the religious significance of the daily vocation, but about the total social order within which the vocation was carried on, the Church had no word to speak. But in the meantime, while the Church concerned itself with the inner and individual life, the modern age brought far-reaching changes. Industry and the nation-state grew and became mighty. Over against them the Lutheran Church with its quietism, with its separate 'spiritual' sphere in which it preached the 'pure Word,' made no pretense of challenge to the growing paganism of the social order in the name of the God who was Lord of all life. . . . Now the last stage of totalitarian statism has made plain to us that its triumph would mean the destruction of the Christian religion. Unfortunately the elements of fascism were present in western lands even before the name was coined or its logical conclusions drawn. They appeared with those who claimed for state or business a control which recognized no authority of God, no relevancy of the way of Christ, and no right of the Church to speak in regard to the social-political order."[31]

There is a dualism in Luther's thinking about spiritual

[31] Harris Franklin Rall, *According to Paul* (New York: Charles Scribner's Sons, 1945), p. 217.

and temporal power and life which has deeply influenced Lutheranism. It may be the least satisfactory aspect of Luther's thought. However, his doctrine of the "two realms" is not a dualism which manifests a consistent parallelism but the relationships of the two realms is one of interpenetration, in Luther's thinking. The spiritual and the temporal, the religious and the secular, do not run in parallel lines which never meet. H. Richard Niebuhr says, "Luther's answer to the Christ-and-culture question was that of a dynamic, dialectical thinker. Its reproductions by many who called themselves his followers were static and undialectical. They substituted two parallel moralities for his closely related ethics. . . . It is a great error to confuse the parallelistic dualism of separated spiritual and temporal life with the interactionism of Luther's gospel of faith in Christ working by love in the world of culture."[32]

Luther's thinking in this matter may have been misunderstood because the followers of Luther did not have his presuppositions. A legalistic interpretation of Luther without Luther's axioms may have given Lutheranism a different attitude to ethics than the reformer intended. No one can read Luther's treatise, an *Open Letter to the Christian Nobility,* without recognizing that Luther did not divorce Christian ethics from their social implications. In his treatise "On Trading and Usury" Luther dealt with the economic problem in the name of his religion. His interpretation of the meaning of the Fourth Petition of the Lord's Prayer is also significant in this connection. In his Catechism of 1520 the Roman tradition was followed and daily bread was interpreted to mean "the Lord Jesus Christ, who feedeth and comforteth the soul." In the edition of his Catechism of 1529 Luther had abandoned this interpretation of daily bread

[32] Helmut Richard Niebuhr, *Christ and Culture* (New York: Harper and Brothers, 1951), p. 179.

and includes in it "Everything that is required to satisfy our bodily needs; such as food and raiment, house and home, fields and flocks, money and goods; pious parents, children and servants; godly and faithful rulers, good government; seasonable weather, peace and health; order and honor; true friends, good neighbors and the like." In this explanation Luther certainly connected the religious interest with the problems of society. This is the more remarkable in the light of the fact that he broke with Roman Catholic tradition and thus indicates that he had considered the matter, and thus deliberately reached the conclusion to connect the religious interest with the problems of society. Whatever blame may be attached to Luther for the quietism of Lutheranism, there are aspects of his thought which point in the other direction.

Not only in Lutheranism is there need for a social ethical emphasis. F. R. Barry has said, "So completely did (Calvinism) identify religion with the nonreligious activities of spirit that it has failed to control them effectively by spiritual and religious standards. . . . Calvinist religion identified itself so completely with worldly activities as to find in the end that the world is too strong for it."[33] Max Weber was undoubtedly right when he emphasized that there was a relationship between Calvinistic ethics and the development of capitalism. His thesis may have been too simple and there may have been other factors in the development of capitalism which were more important than Weber grants, but there can be no doubt that capitalism received a good deal of inspiration from Calvinistic ethics, with its emphasis upon thrift, fitness, and energy.[34]

The ethics of the Roman church inclines to capitulate to the mores of society when the interests of the institutional

[33] F. R. Barry, *Christianity and the New World* (New York: Harper and Brothers, 1931), p. 29.

[34] Talcott Parsons (trans.), Max Weber's *The Protestant Ethic and the Spirit of Capitalism* (New York: Charles Scribner's Sons, 1958).

church are safeguarded. A former pope could be indifferent enough to the social implications of the situation to sign a concordat with Hitler and other dictators. The ethics of Calvinism has inclined toward identification with the world. The ethics of Lutheranism has tended to withdraw from the social situation. All are in need of a renewed and increased emphasis on social ethics. In the meantime, civilization may lose its soul.

3

A THEOLOGICAL POSTULATE FOR SOCIAL RESPONSIBILITY

Various Approaches

Numerous theological approaches for social responsibility have been attempted. A biblical approach has been rather common and can never be ignored if the Bible is to be accepted as the rule of faith and practice. The Bible does emphasize social responsibility, and if the Bible is authoritative the matter is settled for the Christian.[1] The difficulty is this approach may develop into legalism when the nature of the Bible is not fully comprehended as a progressive revelation of God and his will. Very recently, biblical passages have been quoted as a justification for racial segregation.

The doctrine of justification by faith has also been used as a theological postulate for social responsibility. "In and through the process (of justification) arises the most wholesome motive for goodness in the future," says James A. Pike.[2]

[1] Abraham Cronbach, *The Bible and Our Social Outlook* (New York: The Riverdale Press, 1941); William Bennett Bizzell, *The Social Teachings of the Jewish Prophets* (New York: Riverdale Press, 1941); Charles Arthur Hawley, *The Teachings of the Prophets* (New York: Association Press, 1924); Charles Foster Kent, *The Social Teachings of the Prophets and Jesus* (New York: Charles Scribner's Sons, 1917); Walter Lee Lingle, *The Bible and Social Problems* (Union Theological Seminary, James Sprunt lectures; Westwood, N. J.: Fleming H. Revell Company, 1929); Walter Rauschenbusch, *The Social Principles of Jesus* (New York: Association Press, 1921); C. H. Dickinson, *The Social Aims of Jesus* (West Rindge, N.H.: Richard R. Smith, Inc., 1930); B. C. Plowright, *Rebel Religion* (Los Altos, California: Round Table Press, Inc., 1937).

[2] James A. Pike, *Doing the Truth* (Garden City, N.Y.: Doubleday and Company, 1955).

Albert Schweitzer has said that "Western theology is mainly concerned with the doctrine of the forgiveness of sins, and its task is to interpret the death of Jesus in such a way that men may find in it forgiveness ever available, ever renewed, for all the lapses of which they become guilty."[3] This doctrine is a very important doctrine and it is a specific article in the Apostles' Creed itself. Without forgiveness there is no reconciliation with God for man. We must not detract from the significance of this doctrine, but we ought to use it in the framework of the whole New Testament faith. The Second Article of the Creed is important but there is a First and a Third Article, as well. If we neglect to emphasize the First Article, it will be difficult to deal with the Third Article, because it is in God's creation that the life of sanctification is to be lived. Luther stressed the doctrine of justification as the pearl of great price, but Luther had a great variety of theological axioms which he took for granted and held in common even with his adversaries. When some of Luther's followers make use of his writings as a kind of legal code (while lacking the axioms which he held) they arrive at quite a different position from Luther and what he contemplated.

Another theological approach to social responsibility has been the doctrine of "vocation." We have already pointed out that this approach has not proved dynamic in the light of history. It is also significant that the idea of an "earthly calling" is found only once in the New Testament. In I Cor. 7:20 Paul says, "Let each man abide in that calling wherein he was called." Here the word undoubtedly is used to refer to man's station in life. This fact is significant for those who seek a theological nexus between religion and the problems of society in the doctrine of "vocation." Such an emphasis is

[3] E. N. Mozley, *The Theology of Albert Schweitzer for Christian Inquirers* (New York: The Macmillan Company, 1950), p. 94.

a rather modern innovation. In the New Testament the term is used in an almost exclusively religious sense, and has reference to the call of the Christian to share in the salvation which God offers in Christ.[4]

The Kingdom of God

There is a theological concept in the scriptures which inevitably leads to a sense of social responsibility. This concept is the "kingdom of God." When the meaning of the kingdom of God is grasped, religion immediately becomes social in its outlook because the kingdom of God is, in itself, a social concept. Many years ago I determined to find out what those who manifested a sense of social responsibility had, theologically, that was absent in those who failed to emphasize the social responsibility of the Christian. The answer was not difficult to find. Almost invariably a sense of social responsibility was connected with an insight into the meaning of the kingdom of God.

Toyohiko Kagawa, the famous Japanese Christian, says, "The kind of Christianity which makes me want to save myself alone is useless."[5] He had been a leader in the labor movement and in the co-operative movement in Japan. He initiated the Kingdom of God movement in his country. The kingdom of God became, for Kagawa, a dynamic for social action.

The New Testament exegesis of Walter Rauschenbusch is subject to revision in the light of modern New Testament scholarship but he, too, made the kingdom of God central in his thinking, and that insight is a permanent and vital contribution for all time. He says, "If theology is to offer an adequate doctrinal basis for the social gospel, it must not

[4] Rom. 11:29; Phil. 3:14; II Thess. 1:11; Eph. 1:18; II Tim. 1:9; II Pet. 1:10.

[5] Toyohiko Kagawa, *Meditations on the Cross* (Chicago: Willett Clark and Company, 1935), p. 37.

only make room for the doctrine of the Kingdom of God, but give it a central place."[6] The Brotherhood of the Kingdom was organized by Rauschenbusch at Rochester when he commenced to teach there, and this fellowship exerted a far-reaching influence.

Albert Schweitzer has sensed the meaning of the kingdom of God for the Christian faith. His activity has been confined largely to the remedial realm, but the motivation and inspiration of the meaning of the Kingdom of God is evident in his life work. He says that "whenever the idea of the Kingdom of God is no longer at the center of faith . . . (it) has led to far-reaching impoverishment."[7] Furthermore, he says, originally "Christianity had been the religion of faith in the Kingdom of God."[8] In the same vein he says, "Originally, the dominant thought of the Kingdom of God meant that believers shared with one another the blessings of a new creation. But (then) the experience of the individual (began to take) precedence of that of the community. Each separate believer . . . (came to be) concerned with his own redemption. He cares nothing for the future of mankind and of the world. There is something cold and unnatural about the naive egoism of such piety."[9] He also says that, "Only as it comes to be understood as something ethical and spiritual . . . can the Kingdom of God regain, in our faith, the force that it had for Jesus and the early Church. Christianity must have a firm hold of this, if it is to remain true to itself, as it was at the beginning—religion dominated by the Kingdom of God."[10] Again he says, in a classical passage, "Belief in the Kingdom of God makes the biggest demands of all the articles of the Christian faith. It means believing the

[6] Walter Rauschenbusch, *A Theology for the Social Gospel,* p. 131.
[7] Mozley, *op. cit.*, p. 91.
[8] *Ibid.*, p. 92.
[9] *Ibid.*, p. 90.
[10] *Ibid.*, p. 110.

seemingly impossible—the conquest of the spirit of the world by the Spirit of God. We look with confidence for the miracle to be wrought through the Spirit."[11]

One of the relatively few modern evangelists with a social message is E. Stanley Jones. His concern about the problems of the laboring man, racial equality, and war and peace, are evident in all his books. In all of his writings the dominant note is the kingdom of God. One of his books bears the title *Is the Kingdom of God Realism?* Here, too, an emphasis upon the kingdom of God and a social interest are inseparably united.

In 1925, the ecumenical conference on "Life and Work" convened in Stockholm. This conference devoted its attention to what its name designated; namely, life and work. It may have been a loss to the Christian cause that "Faith and Order" and "Life and Work" were united at the Oxford conference. Archbishop Nathan Soderblom was the leader at the Stockholm conference, and Soderblom was a theologian with a greater sense of social responsibility than is usually found among Swedish theologians. He published a volume on the conference, and he designated the outstanding question of the conference as having been the meaning of the kingdom of God.[12] The delegates could not come to grips with the problems of life and work without consideration of the meaning of the kingdom of God. This again illustrates how intimately the idea of the kingdom of God is connected with the social mission of the church.

The kingdom of God expresses the very essence of Christ's life purpose. It was the key phrase of Jesus' teaching and message. He made use of the phrase from the beginning to the end of his ministry. The Sermon on the Mount centers in this theme. Those who live in the light of the presence

[11] *Ibid.*, p. 116.

[12] Nathan Söderblom, in *Kristenhetens Möte i Stockholm* (Stockholm: Svenska Kyrkans Diakonistyrelses Bokförlag, 1926), p. 233 ff.

of the kingdom of God are following in the footsteps of Jesus and are dominated by the spirit which was in him. The kingdom of God was a central concept for Jesus, and to deny this would be the equivalent of denying that we have any reliable information about the mind which was in Christ Jesus.

The phrase is not so common in the epistles of the New Testament as it is in the Synoptic Gospels. However, Paul's letters were usually written in response to certain specific problems, and we cannot draw the conclusion from his letters that he minimized the preaching of the kingdom of God. To the elders of the church at Ephesus, Paul said that he had gone about "preaching the kingdom," according to his devoted friend, Luke.[13] Likewise, in the last glimpse which we get of the apostle in the Book of Acts, we are told that "he abode two whole years in his own hired dwelling, and received all that went in unto him, preaching the kingdom of God . . ."[14]

What, then, is the kingdom of God? Archbishop Soderblom has defined the concept of the kingdom in the following words: "The Kingdom of God is the sovereignty of God. The Kingdom of God means the realm where God rules—in the heart of man, in the social life of peoples, in greater and smaller organizations (*samfund*), in humanity and in existence in its entirety."[15] Walter Rauschenbusch says, "The Kingdom of God is humanity organized according to the will of God."[16] The horizons of Walter Rauschenbusch were so wide that one must be careful not to quote him out of context, but if we compare Soderblom's definition with this statement by Rauschenbusch we recognize quite a dif-

13 Acts 20:25.

14 Acts 28:30-31.

15 Nathan Söderblom, *Jesu Bergspredikan* (Stockholm: P. A. Norstedt & Söners Firlag, 1926), p. 2.

16 Rauschenbusch, *A Theology for the Social Gospel*, p. 142.

ferent orientation. Soderblom does not leave the social scene untouched by the kingdom of God, but he would undoubtedly never have said what Rauschenbusch did. It is extremely important to keep clearly in mind, as Soderblom did, that God's kingdom is God's activity.

God is the absolute sovereign in his creation and is active in history, accomplishing his good purposes. God is not geographically transcendent, in any faraway manner, waiting on some celestial throne to be discovered by man. He is living and active and makes himself known through his activity and sovereignty. The kingdom of God is the rule of God in the hearts and lives of men. The kingdom of God is always coming and pressing in upon the present. It is the very energy of God pressing in upon human affairs. It is the "eternal" in the midst of time, and it is both present and future. The powers of the kingdom of God were supremely present in the person of Jesus.

The Kingdom of God in the Book of Daniel

One of the most significant descriptions of the meaning of the kingdom of God is to be found in the Book of Daniel. It is fundamental for an understanding of the New Testament conception of the kingdom. Chapter VII of that book is one of the more important chapters of scripture. The Babylonian, the Median, the Persian, and the Greek kingdoms are represented by four beasts who "came up from the sea." Anyone familiar with the symbolism of Babylonian mythology, and that of Psalms 8, 74, 89, 93, 95, 96, 97, and 98, will recognize the source of the imagery which was used by the author of the Book of Daniel. There can be little doubt that the Babylonian myth of creation supplied much of the symbolism used in these Psalms as well as in the Book of Daniel. The Babylonian myth related how the world was created when Marduk, the chief Babylonian deity, slew Tiamat, the great sea monster, who represented the powers of Chaos. Tiamat, Rahab, Leviathan, and the monsters coming up out of the sea were opposed to the rule of God and represented the enemies of God. These monsters were attempting to undo the work of God's creation and reduce the world to chaos. They were set against God and his creative purposes.

However, these monsters are not outside the control of God. Although the heathen nations still roar, they will be subdued; for the "ancient of days did sit" upon his throne, and the monsters will have their dominion taken away. Set against the destructive beasts are the power and purpose of God, who will ultimately subdue all things to himself. Evil is arraigned before the heavenly court of God and judgment is passed upon the arrogant kingdoms of the world.

The figure of the Son of Man also enters the picture. The beasts represent kingdoms opposed to the rule of God. The Son of Man represents the people in whom the sovereignty of God is to be manifested, and through whom the rule of God on earth is to be revealed. Dominion is to be taken away from the beasts and given to the Son of Man. In the Book of Daniel, the Son of Man represents the faithful people of Israel, but any student of the gospels will recall that one of the favorite phrases with which Jesus identified himself was—the Son of Man. He was the representative of God who created the world, and he has a function to fulfill in the judgment and restoration of the world. He appears upon the stage of history, and he will defeat the powers of evil. Through the Son of Man, the kingdom of God comes; and God's sovereignty over his creation will be established. The coming of the Son of Man and the coming of the kingdom are identified.

The majestic symbolism of the Book of Daniel presents

God as Creator, Redeemer, Judge, and King. The God of Creation is none other than the God of Redemption and the two must be identified theologically. Creation and Redemption are not distinct and unrelated activities of God but are both manifestations of the same sovereignty of God. The New Testament is equally insistent upon maintaining this connection.[17] Theology ignores it at its peril. God has not abandoned his creation to those who are opposed to his will. He is active in his world and history, and his kingdom is a dynamic reality through which he is working out his purposes. The radiant and venerable Judge sits upon his throne and ultimate authority belongs to him. This is the meaning of the phrase, "The kingdom of God." God *is* Creator, Redeemer, Judge, and King. In this framework every doctrine of the Christian faith should be set. If we isolate any one of these aspects of the divine activity from the others, it will carry with it dire consequences for theology and the Christian life. The ethical teaching of Jesus is inextricably bound up with this view of God's kingdom. In the final analysis, God's will is sovereign over all men and the whole of creation; and the implications of this point of view, for social responsibility, are too apparent to need explication. We cannot understand the meaning of the kingdom of God and fail to see its implications for the social order. God is making something out of his creation.

The Kingdom as a Gift

It is God who exercises his sovereignty and, therefore, his kingdom is his gift. It is something "given." The sovereignty of God does not depend upon man's will or activity. At no place in the New Testament are we told to "build the kingdom." It is already established "from the foundations of the

[17] John 1:3; Col. 1:16.

world." We can "see . . . enter . . . proclaim" and "suffer" for it. But we cannot build it. The kingdom is something to be accepted, submitted to, and obeyed. The rulers of this world have their day, but the ultimate authority is God's. God is King; and Jesus, as the absolute revelation of God, exercises a kingly office.

Human Responsibility

If this be the nature of the kingdom, then what of human responsibility? And we *are* concerned about responsibility in this series of lectures.

Neither activism nor quietism is an answer to our question. The Christian will not become passive to responsibilities in the social order and simply wait for a celestial relief expedition. There are types of modern theology which leave the impression that the theologian is interested in the doctrine of creation and in the doctrine of the parousia, but expects nothing to happen between those poles. This attitude involves the thought that despair and defeatism are the only realistic attitudes with respect to the whole realm of history. Extra-canonical apocalytic supplies historical background for this attitude.

The Christian does have a responsibility for the character of society because he has been laid hold of by the powers of the kingdom, and those powers work in and through him. Paul realized it was God who was bringing in his kingdom, but that fact did not release Paul from a tremendous missionary task. Paul could say, "It is God who worketh in you both to will and to work," but he could also speak of his "labor" for the Lord.[18] The prophets of the Old Testament often spoke of the Exodus from Egypt as the work of God,[19] but

[18] Phil. 2:13, 16.
[19] Amos 9:7.

Moses was given a task to perform in connection with that deliverance. God performed his deliverance through the instrumentality of a man. A secular historian might write an account of the Exodus from the point of view of the leadership afforded by Moses, but the sacred historian sees, back of the human instrumentality, the movements of God in history. C. T. Craig has well said, "The message of the Kingdom (of God) does not deal with our social task but with God's saving act. This fact should never be made an excuse for quietism. If Jesus saw in his healing ministry 'signs' of the coming of the kingdom, we may interpret signal victories of social and economic justice in similar fashion. Though the perfected rule of God never comes completely into time, it is still always possible to attain a more Christian social order. The resistance of man's radical sinfulness should never plunge us into defeatism and despair. Though our faith is not *in* man we must retain hope *for* man. It is possible to taste here and now something of the powers of the age to come" (Heb. 6:5).[20] The kingdom is a gift, but the powers of the kingdom operate through human agents. The kingdom is the supreme gift of God, but by virtue of this, it also becomes for each of us, our supreme task. God establishes his kingdom, but in so doing he takes us into his service. Man's activity in the interest of the kingdom of God is God's activity in man. To wait for the coming of the kingdom in the spirit of quietism is not true to the genius and the dynamic power of the Christian faith. A gift is bestowed upon us, but that gift involves a call to a task in which God uses men as his instruments. This task is more than an effort to help men understand themselves and God's will for them as individuals. It involves the whole realm of history and society, and the transformation of human institutions for human betterment.

[20] Clarence Tucker Craig, "The Teaching of Jesus," in *The Interpreter's Bible* (12 vols.; Nashville: Abingdon-Cokesbury Press, 1952), VII, 153.

Freedom

The fact of human responsibility also poses the question about freedom. The highest type of freedom is Christian freedom. Christian freedom is not license. It is not liberty to sin and then trust in the goodness of God for forgiveness. The grace of God is no cloak for maliciousness. Christian liberty consists in the agreement of the human and the divine will. When man is laid hold of by the powers of the kingdom, there will be constraint but no restraint. Man is made free by being bound in the will of God. Paul was the bond servant of Jesus Christ, but at the same time he was free. Freedom exercised so as to violate the laws of health does not lead to real freedom. It leads, rather, to bondage under disease. In like manner, freedom does not consist in the ability to sin, but in finding oneself in harmony with God and his will. Little man cannot dethrone God or deprive him of his sovereignty. God's kingdom is not dependent upon man's consciousness of that kingdom. God rules, either in judgment or in mercy, and no man can escape the "hound of Heaven"; and the only real freedom there is must be found in harmony with his will. Every other relationship is bondage under sin.

The position taken above involves a paradox. Calvin tried to deal with the matter in a logical manner and arrived at his doctrine of double predestination. The most significant thing about the doctrine of double predestination is that it says there is no logical solution for the question of the relationship of divine sovereignty to human responsibility. From the point of view of the Christian faith, we are conscious of both divine sovereignty and human responsibility—and we must assert the reality of both. Here we leave the matter, and if life and experience are not logical it will have to be too bad for logic. Divine activity and sovereignty do not override human responsibility and freedom. It uses them to serve the divine will.

A Philosophy of History

Faith in the kingdom of God gives the Christian a vital philosophy of history. A philosophy of history involves an attitude to, and a determination of, the forces which fashion man's history, and a consideration of the means involved in securing the predetermined goals. The prophets and the apocalyptists both had their philosophy of history, but with a difference. H. H. Rowley says, "Whereas the prophets believed in the divine initiative and control in all history, the apocalyptists seem to reserve it for the great final act of history. I do not think this is quite fair to them (the apocalyptists), however. Their supreme interest is in the great final act of history, and they wish to set that act, in all its uniqueness, in sharp relief against all the history that has preceded it. I do not think they would have denied the hand of God in all history, for they certainly did not repudiate the teaching of the prophets. But they looked at all the course of human history merely from the human side, as the record of human lust for power and oppression and ruthlessness, until they came to the final denouement of history, which was regarded solely and uniquely as the act of God. (Here God) would Himself act in a way as solely his own as His act in creation had been. . . . Hence, for the apocalyptists to have emphasized the divine hand in all history would have obscured the uniqueness of this expected act of God."[21]

Rowley does offer a legitimate apologetic for some of the apocalyptic writers, but it is also true that, generally speak-

[21] H. H. Rowley, *The Relevance of Apocalyptic* (New York: Harper and Brothers, 1955), pp. 154-55.

ing, "the apocalyptic scheme was not a product of pure Hebrew thought, but an exotic growth. In fact, its dualism and transcendentalism were a radical departure from Hebrew religion."[22] Apocalypticism produced a prolific literature, but out of this great mass of literature only two books found their way into the canon of scripture—the Book of Daniel in the Old Testament, and the Book of Revelation in the New Testament. We have shown that there is an emphasis in both of these books on the activity of God in history, and this may be one of the chief reasons why these books found their place in the canon. The apocalyptic books which lacked this emphasis were excluded. The Hebrew-Christian tradition sees God not only above and at the end of history, but in the processes of history itself. Isaiah could speak of the Assyrian as the rod of God's anger and the staff in whose hand was God's indignation.[23] Any interpretation of history which excludes God from the processes of history does not have its origin in biblical faith. The realm of history is also the realm of social responsibility. Apocalypticism, with its dualism and transcendentalism, have been particularly influential in much modern theological thinking, and this has not been conducive to any emphatic social emphasis. Neo-orthodoxy is often at fault in failing to recognize this fact, and it has sometimes tended to make the devil the lord of history. We shall have to take the realm of history seriously as a stage for divine activity if we are adequately to sense our social responsibility. In the Book of Daniel, God not only manifests his sovereignty at the end of the age,[24] but the kings Nebuchadnezzar, Belshazzar, Darius, and Cyrus are also subject to the control of God. The power and the kingdom of God manifest themselves not only at the end

[22] Walter Rauschenbusch, *Christianizing the Social Order* (New York: The Macmillan Company, 1912), p. 56.
[23] Isa. 10:5.
[24] Dan. 2:34, 35, 44.

of the age or in the crises of history, they are always a present reality. To believe that God is in ultimate control of the forces of history is one of the most challenging articles of the Christian faith. We stand in need of an emphasis upon the relation of the kingdom of God to the historical process, and we can never be satisfied with a theology which attempts to explain away this connection. God is the Lord of history —not only at the end, but in the process itself. Our God is the God of religious experience; he is the God of eternity, but he is also the God of time and history.[25] This does not mean that every specific event of history is a product of God's will, because the fact of human sin can deflect the course of history from a full realization of God's good will. It does mean, however, what the author of the Book of Job has in mind when he says for the Lord:

> "Hitherto shalt thou come, but no further;
> And here shall thy proud waves be stayed."[26]

Hegel had his philosophy of history. He absolutized the state and made the state a kind of incarnation of the divine idea as it exists on earth. Karl Marx had his philosophy of history. For Marx, the economic productive forces make up the power which determines the course of history. The Greeks had their cycle theory of history, and Oswald Spengler has, in modern times, resurrected this theory. Fascism, free enterprise, and the "American way," all have their conscious or unconscious philosophies as to what determines the course of historical development. Against these philosophies of history stands the Christian faith, and it insists that the ultimate determining factor for human history is the kingdom of God. To believe this, means to believe in a moral determinism of history; for God is not only power,

[25] Isa. 40:12-31.
[26] Job 38:11.

he is also an ethical Being. One of the greatest advances in the history of religion occurred when men came to see God in terms of the ethical. History is not blind fate, but behind history is God and his kingdom. This is a faith on the basis of which we can face the human predicament of our time.

The Christian Hope

In some philosophies of history the idea of progress has played a significant role. Under the influence of the biological evolution theory, society has been thought of in terms of a gradual advance toward an ideal state. The idea played a very important part in liberal theology, and one of the sharpest criticisms by neo-orthodoxy has been aimed at the idea of progress. Much of this criticism has been justified, but there were some religious values in the concept which need to be re-emphasized lest the baby be thrown out with the wash water. The concept of progress did have the merit that it took the realm of history seriously.

Often there was a naive optimism associated with the idea of progress. Two world wars and a terrible depression in the economic area have tended to shake such optimism. The alternative, however, is not a pessimism which would forget a God who is living and active in the realm of human history. In his *Decline of the West,* Oswald Spengler says, "Time does not suffer itself to be halted; there is no question of prudent retreat or wise renunciation. Only dreamers believe there is a way out. Optimism is cowardice. We are born into this time and must bravely follow the path to the predestined end. There is no other way. Our duty is to hold on to the lost position—without hope, without rescue—like that Roman soldier whose bones, found in Pompey, showed that during the eruption of Vesuvius he died at his post because his superiors forgot to relieve him. That is greatness. That is what it means to be a thoroughbred. The honorable end is the one thing that cannot be taken from man."[27] Here is a philosophy of history without the idea of progress and without hope. Here is a philosophy without consciousness of God and in the spirit of the deepest pessimism. It foregoes its right to "wonder why" for do and die.

Instead of talking about progress, as Christians we can talk about hope. ". . . now abideth faith, hope, love, . . ."[28] says the apostle Paul. Faith and hope belong together. Hope is simply our faith projected into the future. We have hope because of our faith in God and what we know about him. Our hope is not a "fool's paradise" but is anchored in our knowledge of God and his kingdom. Hope is the expectation of the good. It is directed to something not yet realized. The Christian hope extends to the realm beyond history, but it also involves history. We are not beating the air as Christians when we find ourselves committed to a realization of the will of God on earth. We hope—and we believe—that more of the gracious and good will of God can be realized on earth and in the realm of history than is now prevalent. This hope is not an air castle, but a firm conviction. It is not based upon the development of means of mass destruction, but upon obedience to God and his will. It is a strange phenomenon that, at a time when some of the secular philosophies of history should be holding forth a hope for society, popular theological trends should be gripped by the spirit of despair for the social order. There is hope *for* history and *in* history, because God is a living and active God even in the realm of history. The apocalyptic hope of communism must be challenged by our Christian hope, or the appeal of our preaching and teaching is not going to be significantly vital. God's reign in his creation and history must not be abandoned

[27] Oswald Spengler, *Decline of the West* (2 vols.; New York: Alfred A. Knopf, Inc., 1945).

[28] I Cor. 13:13.

in theology. The meaning of God's kingdom for history requires a renewed emphasis in our day.

This position does not involve perfectionism. The Christian hope involves the whole doctrine of Christian eschatology, and the historical process itself does not contain the eschatological goal. However, the eschatological goal is always relevant for the historical situation. It always stands over against us, in judgment and as a guiding star. The North star was important for the sailor even though he never reached it. So the ideals of the kingdom of God are always relevant for the social order. They mark the direction in which our hope is to seek realization. Socially, our Christian hope is realized in the measure in which Christian ideals become increasingly possible.[29] James Orr said, long ago, that "Christianity, and more particularly the Christian idea of the Kingdom of God, furnish the only solid ground for (hope) for mankind."[30] The kingdom of God means hope for society.

The question is often asked: To what extent will the ideals of the kingdom of God be realized in the historical process? The answer is: we do not know. Furthermore, we have not been called to succeed; we have been called to be faithful. How much of his good will God will realize in history is within his good counsel. Our responsibility is to be faithful to our task. We cherish the hope that God—in us and through us—will realize more of his will on earth than is now the case.

Degrees of Sin and Guilt

If we are not to fall into the perils of perfectionism, this attitude involves degrees of guilt. One of the ways in which some forms of neo-orthodoxy have undermined a sense of

[29] Alfred N. Whitehead, *The Adventures of Ideas* (New York: The Macmillan Company).

[30] James Orr, *The Christian View of God and the World* (Grand Rapids, Mich.: Wm. B. Eerdmans Publishing Company, repr. 1947), p. 454.

social responsibility has been through a denial of the inequality of sins and guilt. Classical Christian theology has always recognized this distinction. Sins were classified as *graviora et leviora.* There is good New Testament authority for this position. Jesus said to Pilate, ". . . he that delivered me unto thee hath greater sin."[31] The word "greater" is a comparative. Matthew 11:24, Luke 12:48–49, and Matthew 12:29–34 are other classical examples of degrees of guilt.

One of the favorite passages for those who would deny the fact of degrees of sin and guilt is James 2:10, where the author says, "Whosoever shall keep the whole law, and yet stumble in one point, he is become guilty of all." This passage of scripture does not deny the fact of the degrees of sin and guilt, but refers rather to the essence of sin. One deliberate choice of sin indicates that the personality is evil and disposed to sin. If a man willfully transgresses one commandment, it shows that in principle he disregards all. Actual transgression of one commandment involves potential transgression of all the commandments.

George F. Thomas has made some significant remarks on this subject, among them: "There has been a strong tendency in orthodox Protestantism to reject the doctrine of the inequality of sin on the ground that it encourages man's pride and self-sufficiency. Most recently, Reinhold Niebuhr has asserted 'the equality of sin' while admitting the 'inequality of guilt.' According to his view, guilt 'represents the objective and historical consequences of sin,' and it is a plain fact that while men are equal in their sin, the consequences of their sin are very unequal. This position cannot be maintained. In the first place, there seems to be no biblical basis for it. For example, the statement of St. Paul, 'For there is no distinction; since all have sinned, and fall short of the glory of God,' is not to the point. It asserts that there is no

[31] John 19:11.

difference between men with respect to the presence of sin in their lives, but not that there is no difference between them with respect to the degree of sin; that is, it asserts the universality rather than the equality of sin. In the second place, the guilt of a person is more closely related to his sin than Niebuhr's view recognizes. If the guilt of two men is unequal, it can be only because their sins are unequal. For if sin is the ground of guilt, there must be degrees of sin to account for degrees of guilt. To say that the greater guilt assigned to a person is due simply to the fact that his acts have worse consequences for others, is to estimate guilt in too external and utilitarian fashion; and to transform guilt from a moral, into a legal, category. The conclusion follows that, if there is inequality of guilt, there must also be inequality of sin."[32]

This doctrine must never be used in the interest of self-righteousness, but it is a tremendously important aspect of Christian anthropology. Growth in sanctification and its possibility are recognized by this doctrine. If the Christian cannot be perfect in this life, and if there are no degrees of sin and guilt, the conclusion is inevitable that there can be no growth "unto the measure of the stature of the fulness of Christ: . . ."[33] In like manner, if we cannot expect a full realization of the ideals of the kingdom of God in history, we shall be reduced to a simple holding operation, unless there be inequality in sins and guilt. Our Christian hope involves that we can attain to more than we have. If we destroy this aspect of hope, the whole realm of social responsibility becomes meaningless. The attacks of some modern theologians upon the doctrine of degrees of sin and guilt are another example of the manner in which some types of contemporary theology whittle away at the ethical

[32] George F. Thomas, *Christian Ethics and Moral Philosophy* (New York: Charles Scribner's Sons, 1955), p. 184.

[33] Eph. 4:13.

contents of the Christian faith. The fifth petition of the Lord's Prayer will undoubtedly continue to be meaningful to the end of time, but this does not mean that we eliminate the categories of less and more. The black reality of human sin does not obscure the fact that there may be more or less of it.

The realm of history is His story, and His kingdom gives us our social responsibility. For the Christian faith, the kingdom of God is a present reality; and from the point of view of that reality we view all of life, individual as well as social. ". . . the kingdom of God is at hand: repent ye, and believe in the gospel"[34]—*this* gospel.

[34] Mark 1:15.

4

A NORM FOR CHRISTIAN SOCIAL RESPONSIBILITY

An examination of a goodly number of ethical treatises written during the last quarter of a century will give the impression that it is hopeless to attempt a systematic presentation of a Christian ethic. Neither reason, natural law, nor scripture provides us with principles so we can arrive at Christian duties and virtues which are normative.[1]

The position is sometimes maintained that the ultimate standard for the Christian life is the Christian himself. In the first place the statement is not true, because the ultimate standard is to be found in the will of God. In the second place, the statement says precisely nothing with respect to the concrete content of the Christian life.

The Need of Law and Moral Principle

We cannot allow ourselves to fall into such obscurantism that we deprive ourselves of any means of discriminating between what is good and what is evil. We must come to grips with the problem and determine the manner in which we, as Christians, are to resist and reform the corporate orders of existence. A statement of principle and policy is

[1] Emil Brunner, *The Divine Imperative* (Philadelphia: Westminster Press, 1947); Reinhold Niebuhr, *Moral Man and Immoral Society* (New York: Charles Scribner's Sons, 1952); Werner Elert, *The Christian Ethos* (Philadelphia: Muhlenberg Press, 1957).

imperative or we shall have an ethics without vitality. Whence, how, and with what content, are questions which ethics cannot ignore. Unless we give some kind of answer to the question "How is the Christian ethic to be made effective in society?" we shall not be meaningful in our sense of social responsibility. There are those who would say that the answer to our problem is that the Christian lives his life in the light of the constant presence of God. We cannot quarrel with such a statement, but we still need some way of describing what this means in concrete terms of action. Moral principles do have their function in ethical decisions and ethics cannot dispense with them and remain vital. Love is a motivating power for good but the good has to be discriminated. Moral principles and categories are an imperative for any vital ethics. Love must be related to the concrete social situation, and this cannot be done without some sense of moral principles. All law or principle—from the point of view of the New Testament—must be interpreted in the light of the ethics of love, but principles are an interpretation of the meaning of love. Law is an expression of moral principle, and Paul, the great apostle of justification by faith, could say, "Do we then make the law of none effect through faith? God forbid: nay, we establish the law."[2] The assumption of antinomians—that without moral principles love would discover what is moral in each concrete situation—is just not realism. What men have seen as the will of God, in their historical experience, we ignore at our peril. Moral principles do not give us detailed information with respect to duty in every situation, but they do suggest the right direction for our conduct. To ignore the experience of the race in this realm is as great a folly as to do so in any other realm. We are not hesitant to use the word "principle," because the word describes an attitude; and only through

[2] Rom. 3:31.

the recognition of moral principle can the contents of the Christian ethic be communicated. Moral principle also has its value in giving direction for social action. Perhaps, also, we ought to remind ourselves that the Christian man is not wholly Christian in his sanctification, and moral principle and law are bound to be significant for him in this respect also.

Description of the Ethical

How, then, shall we describe the principle which is normative for Christian social responsibility? The moral philosophers, from Plato onward, have recognized that "the good for man must reside in that which completely harmonizes and most nearly brings to full fruition all his powers, capacities, and endowments."[3] Smyth says, "that is moral which at any time tends to preserve the life of man in its largest capacity and efficiency."[4] Martensen defines the ethical ideal as "human personality conceived in its purity and perfection."[5] Undoubtedly, Albert Schweitzer had the same idea in mind when he wrote, "I see that evil is what annihilates, hampers, or hinders life. Goodness . . . is the saving or helping of life, the enabling of whatever life I can to attain its highest development."[6] Undoubtedly, too, Schweitzer includes more in the term "life" than do most ethical thinkers, but he would doubtless include the definitions given above in his definition of the term. The fourth Gospel quotes Jesus himself as saying, ". . . I came that they may have life, and may have it abundantly."[7]

[3] Frank Russell Barry, *Christianity and the New World* (New York: Harper and Brothers, 1931), p. 141.

[4] Newman Smyth, *Christian Ethics* (New York: Charles Scribner's Sons, 1903), p. 86.

[5] C. Spence (trans. and ed.), D. Martensen's *Christian Ethics* (Edinburgh: T & T Clark, 1873), p. 3.

[6] As quoted in now defunct magazine *Christendom,* I(2), 230.

[7] John 10:10.

The Law of God

The law of God is a description, in concrete terms, of the will of God. God reveals himself and his will, and man describes his experience of revelation in the form of law or principle. The law and its relation to Christian living have been subject to a great deal of debate in theological circles during the last quarter of a century. The so-called third use of the law, which has reference to the relation of the Christian to the law, has sometimes been denied, sometimes minimized, and sometimes included in the first use of the law, which has to do with civic righteousness. A certain antinomianism in modern theology is apparent, also, in this attitude and attacks the very foundations of Christian ethics. The Christian faith is something more than a "consolation for the misery of sin"—to use Harnack's phrase. The law of God, as a description of his will, is significant for the Christian. The Lutheran Confessions emphasize this when they say the law is one and the same, to wit: "the unchangeable will of God, whether it be set forth before the penitent or the impenitent, the regenerate or the unregenerate . . . we reject and condemn, as pernicious and contrary to Christian discipline and true godliness, the erroneous doctrine that the law in the manner and treasure indicated above is not to be urged upon Christians and true believers but only upon unbelievers, non-Christians, and the unrepentant."[8] It is also significant that the keeping of the law should be described in this article as one of "the fruits of the Spirit." In like manner, Luther says, "But the spirit, which is divine grace, gives strength and power to the heart, yea, creates a new man, who grows to love God's commandments and does with joy all that he ought to do. . . . By this . . . grace a man does what the law commands and satisfies it."[9]

[8] Theodore G. Tappert (trans.), "Formula of Concord, Article VI," *The Book of Concord* (Philadelphia: Muhlenberg Press, 1959), pp. 563-68.
[9] *PE,* III, 354-55.

Therefore a concrete place must be given to the law as an expression of God's will for his people.

An antinomianism which would "make void the law through faith," as someone has said, does not belong to the classical Christian tradition. Some forms of Gnosticism would have been hospitable to it. As antinomianism can manifest itself in connection with an emphasis upon faith, so it can also manifest itself in connection with an emphasis upon agape, or love. The antinomian divorces religion from morality and morality from religion. Christianity has always had to be on guard against this tendency. There is an echo of the spirit of antinomianism in the words of the New Testament, "All things are lawful for me; . . ." and in the words "Meats for the belly, and the belly for meats: . . ." in I Cor. 6:12–13. The Nicolaitans[10] apparently were a party which converted the liberty of the gospel into license for the flesh. At the time of the Reformation, the tendency found a champion in the person of Johann Agricola. He taught that a man is justified if he believes the promises of the gospel, no matter how impure his life may be. The believer is above the law. He suggested that all who had anything to do with Moses should go to the devil, and that Moses be hanged.[11] Antinomianism is a tendency to be guarded against. Among its several uses, the law also has a didactic function even for the Christian. Torah and nomos, the Old and the New Testament designations for the term "law," are not exactly synonymous, but they do have this in common: that both describe and clarify man's responsibility before God. Torah involves the whole content of the revelation and purpose of God, and thus also emphasizes man's responsibility. Nomos often has the sense of a collection of principles or a legislative code which describes man's responsibility before

[10] Rev. 2:6.
[11] Wittenberg Disputation, 1537.

God. The moral laws of the Bible are men's interpretation of the will of God in concrete terms, and they must not be ignored or their significance minimized. Paul, long ago, saw that the law is impotent as a way of reconciliation with God, but he still revered the "giving of the law" as a heritage of his race which he cherished[12] along with "the worship, and the promises" that belonged to the Israelites

The Decalogue often has been spoken of as a summary of the law. Such a statement is inadequate; at least until the Decalogue is interpreted in the light and in the spirit of the New Testament. The Decalogue has exerted a tremendous influence upon religious and moral life, but we must not forget how the prophets went beyond the minimal demands of the Decalogue and pleaded for justice and mercy.[13] Justice and mercy are also significant principles for the Christian life. We are not suggesting that the revelation of God has come to man in the form of ideas and codes and principles, but we insist that the revelation of God has, and will, issue in a recognition of moral principles when it is interpreted by man.

The vitality of this position is emphasized when we remind ourselves of the parallels to the legislation of the Decalogue which are to be found outside of the Hebrew tradition. The Code of Hammurabi and the Decalogue do have their similarities, and if we should be disposed to deny historical contacts, the psychological and experiential factors still remain. Historical experience played its part in the formulation of these "principles," and it is to be noted that, in the Book of Exodus, the same chapter states that God wrote the Decalogue and that Moses wrote it.[14] Apparently, to say that God wrote the Ten Commandments and to say that Moses wrote them was to say the same thing. That the

12 Rom. 9:4-5.
13 Hos. 6:6; Amos 5:24.
14 Exod. 34:1, 28.

historical situation had something to do with the giving of the law points to what theology has called "natural law."

Natural Law

Modern theologians have been afraid of the concept of "natural law." They have felt that to recognize the concept would be to place something above God which would challenge his sovereignty. However, natural law is not something determinative for God. It is the regular and constant order by which God rules the universe and which his wisdom presents to the sense and reason of men. The laws of nature and natural instinct, in our modern vocabularies, are not the equivalent of *lex natura*. Natural law is a description of the activity of God in his world. By virtue of its existence, all men can distinguish between right and wrong—and do so, in a greater or lesser degree. Dr. Dodd says, "The implication is that there is in (all men) a capacity for sound moral judgment, a communis sensus which will lead them to recognize as good that which the revealed Law of God declares to be good."[15] The conception of the law of nature finds one of its clearest expressions in Romans 1:19 ff. and 2:14 ff. Anders Nygren deals with this section of Romans in an interesting manner.[16] He tries to make it mean something other than what it says. Karl Barth likewise ignores the implications in these passages. Luther was not averse to recognizing the existence of a natural law. He says, "so we read Moses, not because he concerns us or that we must obey him, but because he rightly corresponds with natural law."[17] Again he says, "I keep the law of Moses, not because Moses

[15] C. H. Dodd, "Natural Law in the Bible," *Theology*, May and June, 1946, p. 6.

[16] Carl C. Rasmussen (trans.), Anders Nygren's *Commentary on Romans* (Philadelphia: Muhlenberg Press, 1949).

[17] *D. Martin Luthers Werke*. Kritische Gesamtausgabe (Weimar, 1883-) XXIV, 14. Hereafter referred to as *WA*.

has commanded it, but because it is planted in my nature and Moses rightly corresponds with nature."[18] God's moral order is imprinted in the very nature of our own beings and in the very nature of the universe in which we live. God himself is active in this moral order. Jesus emphasized that an institution like marriage was not due to Jewish law or any special kind of revelation, but was based upon an "order of creation." As male and female, God created man.

Because of modern developments, the phrase "natural law" may have to be discarded. However, there is a truth and an insight involved in this concept which must be revived if our social task is going to be meaningful. Justice is no mere creation of man; it is based upon the holy will of God. Only on the basis of what is involved in the concept of natural law can we find a basis of cooperation for the Christian and the non-Christian. Only on the basis of some such common agreement among men can the Christian speak to the social problems and needs of the world with any degree of hope. Emil Brunner has said that "the opposition to the law of nature has not only prepared the way for the totalitarian state but made it possible."[19] The idea for which this term has stood is necessary and relevant for all time. There may be times when we cannot appeal for a redress of social evils on the basis of the Christian gospel, but we can always make that appeal on the basis of law; and here we often discover a common ground for men of varying theological attitudes, or even agnostics. Robert E. Fitch has said that Charles Darwin was uncertain "about God and immortality" but he recognized "the Moral Law, a universal standard of right and wrong that was built into the structure of nature and of human nature. Like the law of gravitation it was operative everywhere, at all times, among all people. . . . It

[18] *WA*, p. 10.

[19] Emil Brunner, *Justice and the Social Order* (New York: Harper and Brothers, 1945), pp. 82-89.

was not something abstract and remote; and it could be found in the home. . . . He was sure that he could find it in evolution. When it came to the critical question of what really sets off man from the animals, he recorded his agreement with those writers 'who maintain that of all the differences between man and the lower animals, the moral sense or conscience is by far the most important. . . . It is summed up in that short but imperious *ought,* so full of high significance. It is the most noble of all the attributes of man.' And then he went on to quote Immanuel Kant on the categorical imperative."[20]

When the modern fashion of theology has passed away, it is probable that the valid insights involved in the doctrine of natural law will again find a significant place in theology. The doctrine has been misused in many ways. It has been applied to areas where it has no relevance as, for example, the use Romanists have made of it in connection with their attitude toward birth control. However, the law of God must never be thought of as arbitrary or separate from the nature of creation. There are moral principles which men find and do not make. The nature of the law must be connected with the nature of reality itself or it will lose its relevance. Benjamin Franklin said that "sin is not hurtful because it is forbidden, but it is forbidden because it is hurtful," and so connected the moral law with reality itself. The prophet Jeremiah could say to his people, "Thine own wickedness shall correct thee, . . ."[21] Hosea said to his people, "It is thy destruction, O Israel, that thou art against me, against thy help."[22] In a similar spirit Amos addressed his people, saying, "Seek Jehovah, and ye shall live; . . . Seek good, and not evil, that ye may live; and so Jehovah, the God of hosts,

[20] Robert E. Fitch writing in the *New Republic* (Washington, D. C.), February 9, 1959.
[21] Jer. 2:19.
[22] Hos. 13:9.

will be with you, as ye say."[23] The prophets saw the moral law in the order of creation itself. Sin disintegrates and destroys and a society of none but the wicked would soon destroy itself. The moral law is to be found in the nature of reality itself, and the operation of this law is the activity of God himself in his creation.

The Imitation of Christ

The doctrine of the "imitation of Christ" has fared no better in the hands of some modern theologians than the law. The Christian is called to grow to "the measure of the stature of the fulness of Christ: . . ."[24] The same epistle says, "Be ye . . . imitators of God, . . ."[25] On behalf of God, the Old Testament says to the people of God, ". . . Ye shall therefore be holy, for I am holy"[26] and the New Testament says, "Ye therefore shall be perfect, as your heavenly Father is perfect."[27]

This doctrine, too, has fallen into eclipse in the hands of some modern transcendentalists. The Imago Dei doctrine is related to this matter as it connects man with God as his child, and with Christ as the image of God.[28] It sees in man something more than a brute, or a drop in the vast ocean of nature. This doctrine also sees in man something more than sin. Christianity has never asserted that the essence of human nature is sin. In describing sin, classical dogmatics has always spoken of it as "non essentiale sed accidentale." We must, therefore, distinguish between sin and the sinner. Paul speaks of sin "which dwelleth in me,"[29] and thus makes a

[23] Amos 5:6, 14.
[24] Eph. 4:13.
[25] Eph. 5:1.
[26] Lev. 11:45.
[27] Matt. 5:48.
[28] Col. 1:15.
[29] Rom. 7:20.

clear distinction between sin and the sinner. Furthermore, the doctrine of the sinlessness of Christ would lose all meaning if human nature and sin were to be identified. We must maintain the distinction between Creator and creature, but the doctrine of the Imago Dei still belongs to the Christian tradition. Anders Nygren finds the doctrine difficult to incorporate in his theory. He quotes with approval a statement by E. Lehmann which ascribes the origin of the doctrine to Greek influence, and that is supposed to invalidate it.[30] If we abandon the Imago Dei doctrine, it will be impossible to talk about the "imitation of Christ." Somehow, man's morality and ethics are related to the nature of God. The essence of the moral is a unity for both God and man.

However, as soon as we ask ourselves the question "What do we mean by the imitation of Christ?" we realize that we have a problem on our hands. Jesus lived the life of a celibate; he never assumed the obligations of husband or father. He showed little interest in art, science, or philosophy. The historical Jesus never saw a modern factory and never faced the ethical and moral problems which the modern machine age has created. How, then, can an individual who lived almost two thousand years ago, in faraway Palestine, have anything to say to the twentieth century situation?

Likewise, we are faced with a problem when we look upon the impact of Christianity upon personality in history. The Christian life has unfolded itself in a great variety of forms. There is the hermit, the monk, the crusader, and the social reformer. They all claim to be inspired by Jesus in their particular mode of life and attitude. Furthermore, the Christian life unfolds itself in connection with education, patriotism, economic effort, art, science, and various other fields of interest.

In the midst of all this diversity, what can it mean to imi-

[30] Nygren, *Commentary on Romans*, pp. 188-89.

tate Christ or to order our lives in imitation of his life? Underneath all the diversities referred to above we can detect a unique, distinctive quality. There is a sense of the reality of God pressing in upon human life and exerting its influence upon it. Jesus never gave his followers a code of laws as regulative for conduct, and he never outlined any kind of social program. He did give us a spirit which we are to apply to our changing situations. This spirit is applicable to all times, all problems, all conditions. To follow Christ means to translate his spirit into action in our own circumstances. Christian ethics will, therefore, never become obsolete. Christians are called not to an outer imitation of Christ, but to obedience to Jesus' spirit of love. Jesus Christ is our model in disposition, in relation to God and to man. The imitation of Christ offers no ready-made solutions in our ethical decisions, but it does offer us a quality of character in the light of which solutions and a direction are to be found. He who is our Prophet and our Example is also the source of creative power. We would remind ourselves of the words of Luther when he says: "non imitatio facit filios, sed filiatio fecit imitatores."[31]

Legalism

I hasten to add that any norm for Christian social responsibility will not be some form of legalism. Neither a recognition of the significance of law nor an emphasis upon the imitation of Christ need lead to any type of legalism. Legalism has many dangers connected with it. The way of salvation for the legalist is often not by grace, but by law, obedience, and reward. Where grace is allowed to enter, it frequently becomes a concession to human weakness; or it comes as a supplement to man's striving, rather than as some-

[31] *WA*, II, 518.

thing fundamental for all Christian life. The whole idea of merit has to be ruled out for the Christian. Unquestionably, everything that we are or have belongs to God, and there certainly can be no merit in giving God what is already his possession.

The legalist also tends to be bound by a set of detailed and definite rules of conduct. Society is never static and we have no rules by which we can determine a solution for every concrete situation which arises. Love, justice, and mercy are not legalistic rules to be obeyed, but involve a spirit which is always relevant to the social situation. The legalist, in his devotion to the letter of the law, will often violate the very spirit of the law.[32]

The difficulties involved in attempting to use the scripture as a legal code are well illustrated by the difficulties which the church has experienced in dealing with the matter of divorce. The General Council of the Evangelical Lutheran Church in North America took the position that "Violations of the marriage covenant completely disrupting it, are: (a) Adultery, Matt. 5:32; 19:5, 6. (b) Malicious desertion, I Cor. 7:15. While the language of the passages in Matthew seem to restrict divorce to but one ground, 'adultery,' St. Paul in I Cor. 7:15, shows that desertion is the essential principle of adultery."[33] Most of the Lutheran groups in America have, for a considerable period of time, followed this legalistic interpretation and have recognized adultery and malicious desertion as legitimate grounds for divorce. Matthew 5:32 says, "I say to you that everyone who divorces his wife, except on the ground of unchastity, makes her an adultress: and whoever marries a divorced woman commits adultery." Only adultery is recognized in this passage as a

[32] Matt. 23:23.

[33] S. E. Ochsenford, *Documentary History of the General Council of the Evangelical Lutheran Church in North America* (Philadelphia: General Council Publishing House, 1912), p. 391.

legitimate ground for divorce. There are many difficulties involved in the use of this passage as a legitimate ground for divorce. The meaning of fornication and unchastity has to be considered. In the same chapter in which this passage occurs, Jesus says, ". . . I say to you that every one who looks at a woman lustfully has already committed adultery with her in his heart."[34] The question must be asked whether or not that kind of adultery is a legitimate basis for divorce, if the passage in question is to be interpreted in a legalistic sense. It is also to be noted that the exception is not given in the parallel passages in Mark and Luke. In the latter two Gospels, divorce is not legitimatized by Jesus on any grounds. The ideal that there shall be no divorce is emphatically stated. In the light of this circumstance, most modern Bible scholars hold that the exception in Matthew did not belong to the original tradition but was an attempt by the early church to legislate for difficult cases. Furthermore, if the passage in Matthew is a law, it applies only to men. Women are not given the right to divorce their husbands even on the ground of unchastity. Another complication arises when we consider that churches which have recognized adultery as a legitimate ground for divorce have often permitted the remarriage of the innocent party. No such justification can be drawn from this passage. Who or what is going to determine who the innocent party may be? The inconsistencies involved in a legalistic use of Matthew are further revealed when we find that "malicious desertion" has been recognized as a legitimate ground for divorce. In the first place, I Cor. 7:15 does not say that "malicious desertion" is a legitimate ground for divorce and, in the second place, if Matthew recognizes only one ground for divorce we cannot add another from Paul. The impossibility of a legalistic approach to this matter is clear.

[34] Matt. 5:28, R.S.V.

If a legalistic approach to this problem must be rejected, we still must answer the question as to how the church should deal with divorce. The problem well illustrates the nature of the norm of Christian social responsibility.

The ideal emphasized in the New Testament is that marriage should terminate only with death. The Christian ideal is not consonant with divorce on any grounds. Divorce is always a violation of the Christian ideal. Sin is the cause of divorce under any and all circumstances. The church must always hold high the ideal. However, because of sin in the world, divorce does occur. When it does take place, the church must face that sin in exactly the manner it deals with all sin. Here, too, the church must exercise its disciplinary powers, but always in the interest of the temporal and spiritual welfare of all concerned.

Legalism also has sometimes manifested itself in ridiculous forms. On the basis of Mark 9:43 ff., men have been known to cut off their limbs as a means of conquering some form of sin. But the severing of a limb from the body does not remove sin from the soul. On the basis of the words of the apostle Paul, it has been insisted that women wear some kind of covering on the head in the church building.[35] Again, sermons have been preached on the sinfulness of women bobbing their hair.[36] I Timothy 2:11 and 12 have been used as an argument against the propriety of women voting in the assemblies of the church.

We arrive at the same attitude to legalism when we recognize that there are certain social relationships not compatible with the Spirit of Christ, and for which no prohibitions can be found in the Bible. The Bible does not expressly prohibit slavery. Someone has said that the words of emancipation trembled on the lips of Paul when he wrote his letter to

[35] I Cor. 11:5.
[36] I Cor. 11:15.

Philemon on behalf of the runaway slave, Onesimus; but slavery is not expressly prohibited. The Spirit of Christ, however, cannot tolerate any form of slavery. The case relative to war is in the same category. War is not expressly prohibited, but there is something about the spirit of Christianity which is recognized to be incompatible with war, and which makes Christians uncomfortable with the involvements of war. Proof-texts cannot justify either slavery or war, and they will not abolish them. The Bible is not a book of law for the Christian, and moral laws are always subordinate to the spirit of love.

The Sacredness of Personality

Christian social responsibility requires of us that we try to find some fundamental principle which may be used to determine the direction social living ought to take. We need a standard by which to judge social phenomena. We offer no apologetics for this statement, for we have good precedents in the biblical emphasis on law, justice, mercy, and love. We must seek what is essential for a Christian social order. Biblical religion has given us such a principle in its recognition of the sacredness of human personality. This means that, in the realm of social relations, human personality is the highest value we know. The welfare of men and women, boys and girls, is the supreme goal of all social endeavor. Men must never be used as means for other ends but, in the realm of social relations, must always be considered as ends in themselves. Human values are the supreme test in the realm of social living. Human personality is unique. It is sacred in the sense of being set apart. It is sacred in the sense of the original meaning of the word holy. Sin does not alter this fact in any way. This, of course, means that we can speak of the value of human personality, and here again we stand in opposition to Anders Nygren, who will know nothing about the value of man.[37] Jesus did ask his disciples, "Are not ye of much more value than they?"[38] On another occasion, Jesus said, "For what will it profit a man, if he gains the whole world and forfeits his life?"[39] Apparently a human being had some value in the sight of Jesus. We can be sure that the father in the parable of the Prodigal Son valued his son. To imply that God loves what is of no value is a peculiar way of thinking. God is a poor Creator and we reflect on his creative work if what he has created is of no value. The same Bible which speaks about man as a sinner speaks of man as "a little lower than the angels . . ."[40] Man is a sinner, but he is also the crown of God's creation.

Instead of the term "sacredness of personality," we might speak in terms of love for our fellow man; but the former expression is broader than the word "love." To be devoted to the principle of the sacredness of human personality involves love of fellow man, but a sense of social responsibility also includes the patterns and the forms of society and when we deal with this aspect of our subject the word "love" is not applicable. We can hardly speak about loving monogamy as a pattern for marriage. It is true that the fundamental Christian virtue is love, but when we consider our social responsibility we are also interested in the social context in which love functions and therefore the term "sacredness of personality" is to be preferred as a norm for Christian social responsibility. The term points to a social context, to a relative scale of values and describes the meaning of love for the social order.

This norm is not something which we arbitrarily choose. It

[37] Anders Nygren, *Den Kristna Kärlekstanken* (Stockholm: Victor Petersons, 1930), p. 33.

[38] Matt. 6:26.

[39] Matt. 16:26, R.S.V.

[40] Ps. 8:5, A.V.

is given to us by the revelation of God as He has unfolded His nature and purpose in human history. Just to seek to be humane will never prove to be a very significant dynamic in human affairs. The question must be asked as to why we should be humane. It is not primarily our fellow man and his need which call forth our sense of social responsibility, because most of the people about whom we ought to be concerned as Christians we have not even seen. Human personality is sacred to the Christian, not because of anything inherent in man apart from God, but because God has placed such value upon human personality. William Paton stressed this point when he said, "If this humble and obscure man is in reality one whom God has made, whom He made in love, so that he shall never know peace except in loving God in return; if this man is one to whom God speaks; if this man is the object of a divine solicitude so great that the Word became flesh for his salvation, the Son of God died for him —if this be true, then this humble and obscure man has a link with eternity, with the creative love that made the world. He cannot then be rightly treated as a cog in a machine, or as sample of a racial bloodstream, or one of the individual atoms that make up a nation."[41]

This norm was enunciated by the prophets of the Old Testament. They condemned cruelty in wars of conquest, they denounced the cruelties of slavery, they took the part of the oppressed against the privileged classes, and they denounced the evils of child labor. If cheap labor and larger profits are more important than human rights and values, there is no meaning in the condemnation of slavery or of child labor. If the possession of added territory is more important than human rights, condemning wars of conquest and the dispossession of the poor have no meaning. The

[41] William Paton, *The Church and the New Order* (New York: The Macmillan Company, 1941), p. 150.

fundamental principle underlying all the social attitudes of the great prophets calls human rights and welfare primary.

We find the same emphasis in the teaching of Jesus. For him, even the obligations to the sacred ceremonials of religion had to yield before this principle. He defended the action of his disciples when they were accused of violating the law of the Sabbath because they were eating grain which had been plucked on that day. For Jesus, the satisfaction of human need was more important than ceremonial purity.[42] He interpreted the Sabbath commandment in the light of this principle when he said, ". . . The sabbath was made for man, and not man for the sabbath: . . ."[43] From the point of view of our Christian social responsibility, we may apply the words which Jesus spoke about the Sabbath to every area of life. We say that the state was made for man and not man for the state. Industry is made for man and not man for industry. The economic order exists for man and not man for the economic order. Likewise, the farm organization and the labor union exist for man and not man for these organizations. There is a potential social revolution latent in this principle in every area of social life.

The most Christian social order would be a society in which the highest possible development of human personality would be the primary consideration. The Christian may be critical of specific programs and techniques which government may develop as it tries to meet human need, but the enlightened Christian can never speak in derogatory terms of the "welfare" state. Ideally, the whole Christian social outlook is directed toward the welfare of people.

This fundamental principle of Christian social ethics is no idle utopian dream. It is practical, and has been basic—consciously or unconsciously—for every advance that has

[42] Mark 2:23.
[43] Mark 2:27.

been made down through the history of human civilization.

A denial of this principle was once written into the constitution of one of our states, where we read that, "The right of property is before and higher than any constitutional sanction, and the right of the owner of a slave to such slave and its increase is the same and as inviolable as the right of the owner of any property whatsoever."[44] Few will deny that the emancipation of the slave was an advance in civilization. Under any circumstances it was the Christian thing to do. That emancipation was a recognition of and application of this principle. The person who understands the meaning of the doctrine of the sacredness of personality will see it in operation in the movement to abolish slavery.

Grievous sins have been committed against children. Child labor, by which we understand the work of children under conditions which interfere with their physical, mental and spiritual growth, is being progressively eliminated. As this sordid story in the history of the human race is relegated to history, we see another direct application of the principle of the sacredness of personality.

The emancipation of woman also is due to a recognition of the validity of this principle. In many lands and climes woman is, and has been, a piece of property, owned and disposed of at the will of her husband like any other property. As recently as the twentieth century, the Nineteenth Amendment to the Constitution of our country became law and granted women the franchise. The emancipation of woman from her inferior position is a significant application of the norm of the sacredness of human personality.

Our American public school system is one of the fine things of which we Americans can boast. We today take it as a matter of course, but it was not always so. Governor

[44] Kirby Page, *Individualism and Socialism* (New York: Farrar and Rinehart, 1933), p. 36.

Berkely of the colony of Virginia, at the end of the seventeenth century, said, "I thank God we have no free schools or printing; and I hope we shall not have these hundred years. For learning has brought disobedience and heresy and sects into the world; and printing has divulged them and libels against the government. God keep us from both."[45] In connection with the struggles of Horace Mann for popular education, he said, "I believe that this amazing dereliction from duty, especially in our own country, originates more in the false notion which men entertain respecting the nature of their right to property, than in anything else. . . . The rich man who has no children declares that the exaction of a contribution from him to educate the children of his neighbor is an invasion of his rights of property."[46] In this statement by Horace Mann we see the struggle between an application of the principle of the sacredness of personality and property rights. But who will deny that the ascendancy and victory of the application of the principle of the sacredness of personality was a step in the right direction?

In the realm of government, democracy is the closest approach to an application of the principle of the sacredness of personality. Democracy and Christianity are not to be equated, and Christianity has existed where democracy has not been known. However, democracy means that every man has a vote, and equality before the law. Wealth does not vote in a democracy. It is people who vote. Human values are placed above property values, and so again the principle is being applied. There have been trends toward democracy outside the Hebrew-Christian tradition, but I think it can be said, without contradiction, that the most dynamic force in history toward democracy has been that tradition.

[45] *Ibid.*, p. 37.
[46] *Ibid.*, pp. 39-40.

At any rate, the closest approach to an application of our norm to the realm of government is democracy.

Partisan Identification

A word must be spoken against the tendency to find a Christian norm in partisan allegiance. The Christian is involved in politics, and the political realm must not be abandoned by the Christian to the non-Christian. We are concerned that politics be governed by Christian principle and that politicians function as Christians. We are also concerned that every Christian assess his political functions in the light of the Christian ideal. The Christian should not forget his faith when he votes. However, we cannot identify Christianity with any political party or with any pressure group. The Christian, of necessity, will exercise his political functions within the framework of political partisanship, but his primary allegiance is to Christ, not the party.

The church cannot ally itself with any political party but should define its own position on social matters and then let parties assume their attitude to that position. We ought to support or condemn a politician not because he is a member of a certain party, but because of his attitude to what we consider valid for us as Christians. The church can appeal for support for programs and measures only because it considers them to be right and because they are Christian, or more Christian, than other alternatives. Identification of the church with political parties is a dangerous matter. In the first place, there is so much sin in all parties that such identification becomes a denial of the faith. Christ stands in judgment over all political parties. In the second place, parties often change their complexion in the light of historical developments. There was a time Republicans were called "Red Republicans."

The Christian is involved in politics, and he certainly should not remain aloof from the political arena; but the Christian faith, rather than party allegiance, should be the determining factor. In this political realm, also, the principle of the sacredness of personality becomes a significant guide for determining our allegiance. If anyone doubts the vitality of the principle of the sacredness of personality, let him give it a sincere trial in the political realm and he will soon discover its relevance.

5

THE CHURCH AND SOCIAL RESPONSIBILITY

The Doctrine of the Church

The word "church" has many meanings and is used in many senses—both historically and in the contemporary scene. We use it to designate a particular denomination, such as the United Lutheran Church. It is frequently used to signify the church building at a certain address. Sometimes it stands for a particular corporate congregation as a legal entity.

It is significant for us to note the meaning of the term as it is used in the New Testament. The word translated "church" means "called out," and refers to the assembly of Christians who have been called out from the world. One of the earliest manifestations of the development of a "church" is found in the activity of the prophet Isaiah. He speaks of himself as a teacher, and he had gathered about himself a group of disciples whom he considers to be a gift of God. He instructed them and sent them out to preach and teach.[1] Here was a group of disciples who had a unique position in the nation and were "called out" and separated from the nation for a particular purpose. If not the earliest, it is one of the earliest "churches" in history.

In the New Testament, the word "church" is sometimes used to designate a local situation. Paul uses it in this sense

[1] Isa. 8:16-22.

when he says, ". . . salute the church that is in their house."[2] He also uses the expression, "to the church in thy house."[3] Paul also could speak about "the church of the Thessalonians" in addressing them. Paul calls these local groups of Christians "the church" and the church in all its essential fulness was there. The means of grace create the church when they are received in faith, for the forgiveness of sins and life in the Spirit.

That there are assemblies of Christians who have been "called out," scattered throughout the world, is also a fact. There is a sense in which all Christians constitute the church and in this sense the word is used in Matthew 16:18. The church is not a political unit nor an ecclesiastical organization, in the New Testament sense of the word. In this doctrine of the church as well as with respect to sacerdotalism, Luther completely broke with Rome and the Middle Ages. For Lutheranism, the church is the communion of saints, in which the Word of God is taught in its purity and the sacraments are administered in accordance with the institution of Christ.[4] An empirical organization is necessary, but it is only by a figure of speech that we can speak of this outward organization as the church.

Luther says that "the Church is called the assembly of all the believers in Christ upon earth . . . just as we pray in the Creed: 'I believe in the Holy Ghost, a communion of saints.' This community or assembly consists of all those who live in true faith, hope and love; so that the essence, life and nature of the Church is not a bodily assembly, but an assembly of hearts in one faith. . . . Thus, though they be a thousand miles apart in body, yet they are called an assembly in spirit because each one preaches, believes, hopes, loves, and lives like the other. . . . That means in reality a

[2] Rom. 16:5.
[3] Philemon 1:2.
[4] Tappert, *op. cit.*, "The Augsburg Confession, Article VII," p. 32.

spiritual unity, because of which men are called a communion of saints. . . . The Church is made separate from all temporal communities, as not being anything external. And this blind Romanist makes it an external community. . . . The Church is not at Rome, nor is it bound to Rome or any other place, but it is where there is faith in the heart. . . . Therefore whoever maintains that an external assembly or an outward unity makes a Church, sets forth arbitrarily what is merely his own opinion. . . . The conclusion is inevitable, that just as being in the Roman unity does not make one a Christian, so being outside of that unity does not make one . . . unchristian. . . . Therefore all those who make the Christian communion a material and outward thing, like other communities, are in reality Jews. . . . A man is not reckoned a member of the Church according to his body, but according to his soul, nay, according to his faith. . . . The Church is a spiritual community, which can be classed with a temporal community as little as spirits with bodies, or faith with temporal possessions. . . . Whosoever would not go astray should, therefore, hold fast to this, that the Church is a spiritual assembly of souls in one faith, and that no one is reckoned a Christian for his body's sake; in order that he may know that the true, real, right, essential Church is a spiritual thing, and not anything external or outward, by whatever name it may be called." The kind of unity of which Luther continues to speak in this connection "is of itself sufficient to make a Church, and without it no unity, be it of place, of time, of person, of work, or of whatever else, makes a Church."[5]

Relation of the Church to the Kingdom of God

In considering the relation of the church to our subject, it is necessary to keep clearly in mind what we mean by the

[5] *PE*, p. 332 ff.

term "church." We must not make of the church what it is not by its nature. The doctrine of the church is important and we would not minimize it, but it is significant that, as far as we know, Jesus used the term only twice.[6] The second of these two passages may reflect an historical background a good deal later than the earthly life of Jesus. There is a theological theory abroad in the world today which would make of the church itself the very essence of Christianity. The church is a part of God's kingdom but *only* a part. The church is also God's instrument through which God is working to accomplish his good will. The church is instrumental to the fulfillment of God's purpose. It is not the goal of that purpose, at least it is not considered so on this side of the parousia.

There are those who claim that Christ and his church are one. Bishop Aulen says, "Christ and the Church belong together. They constitute an inseparable unity. The Church has its existence in and through Christ. But neither does Christ exist apart from his Church."[7] ("Men icke heller Kristus existerar utan sin kyrka.") That this statement is not a word casually spoken is evident from the fact that Aulen quotes from Nygren as being in agreement with him. He quotes the latter as saying, "When the church is designated as the body of Christ and Christ as the head of the church, it does not mean that one part is given to Christ and another to the church, but rather to emphasize their inseparable togetherness and unity. Christ is not simply the head, but precisely the head for his church. And the church is not simply the body, apart from the head, but precisely the body of Christ. The body of Christ is Christ himself. The church is Christ, who after his resurrection is present among us and meets us here on earth."[8] It should be added

[6] Matt. 16:18; 18:17.
[7] Gustaf Aulen, *Den Allmanliga Kristna Tron* (4th ed.; Stockholm: Svenska Kyrkans Diakonistyrelses Bokförlag, 1943), p. 362.
[8] *Ibid.*, p. 362.

that Aulen has modified his position in a later edition of his work, but the earlier edition does exemplify a certain mind-set which is significant.

This atitude amounts to virtually a divinization of the church. It is practically idolatry, because it exalts the relative to the place of the absolute. This is precisely another form of one of the fundamental errors of Catholicism. We are not particularly concerned to assert that Catholicism practices idolatry, but rather that it *is* idolatry in that it makes what is relative, absolute. Paul makes clear distinction between Christ and his people. They are one with him in the work and in the trials to which he has called them, but his people are not identical with him.[9] The church itself stands under judgment and in need of constant renewal and transformation. Furthermore, to make use of the figure of the church as the body of Christ in such a literalistic manner as Aulen and Nygren have done is just poor exegesis. The church is not Christ, but it is his servant.

The Church of Rome

Any student of church history is aware that the Church of Rome has had a certain social consciousness. The ultimate goals of the church may be subject to severe criticism, and the social impact of the Church of Rome in Spain, Portugal, South America, and Poland, not to mention other Roman Catholic countries, leaves much to be desired. However, during the Middle Ages the church did recognize a certain responsibility for the character of society. It did exert an influence upon group life socially, economically, and nationally. The ideal had been a church-state. The pope had tried to control temporal as well as spiritual affairs. Every area of interest for man was part of a larger unity. Education, art,

[9] I Cor. 15:23.

and science were all viewed in the light of the theological framework of the church. The church influenced the economic order when it forbade the taking of interest and when it encouraged the development of the guilds for the welfare and protection of the workers.

Social interest on the part of the Church of Rome needs no theoretical justification for Catholics. Two of the best known modern papal encyclicals emphasize this. In 1891, Leo XIII issued his famous encyclical Rerum Novarum, on the condition of Labor. Forty years later, Pius XI issued his encyclical Quadregesimo Anno, on reconstructing the social order, in commemoration of Rerum Novarum. Joseph Husslein, in his systematic interpretation of these two encyclicals, says that his work "presents . . . a survey of the social doctrine of the Church as taught by her highest representatives. It is in a sense, a Christian Sociology, as set forth by the Sovereign Pontiffs."[10] The Catholic church in our own country has often manifested an enlightened social consciousness. Pope Benedict XV, in a letter addressed to the Bishop of Bergamo states: "Let no member of the clergy imagine that . . . social activity is outside his priestly ministry on the ground that it lies in the economic sphere. It is precisely in this sphere that the salvation of souls is in peril. Hence, it is Our desire that priests regard it as one of their obligations to devote themselves as far as possible to social theory and action, by study, observation, and work, and that they support in all ways those who in this sphere exercise a wholesome influence for the good of Catholics."[11] Pius XI says, "No easy task is here imposed upon the clergy, wherefor all candidates for the sacred priesthood must be adequately prepared to meet it by intense study of social matters."[12]

[10] Joseph Casper Husslein, *The Christian Social Manifesto* (Milwaukee: Bruce Publishing Company, 1931), p. 328.
[11] *Ibid.*, p. 254.
[12] *Ibid.*, p. 236.

The activities of the National Catholic Welfare Conference in the United States are well known. Note that this conference functions under the direction of the bishops of the church and is no mere addendum to the ecclesiastical machinery. Examples can be given of programs which have been developed which have served the genuine welfare of people.

In 1925, the pope issued an encyclical, Anno Santo, in which he established a new festival for the church year, a festival of Christ, the King. In this encyclical it is stated expressly that the Roman church is the kingdom of God on earth. This was no new doctrine in the Roman church. Very early in the history of the church the idea of "the kingdom" began to be displaced by the idea of "the church." "Augustine completed this process in his De Civitate Dei. The millenium began when the church was founded. This practically substituted the actual, not the Ideal Church for the Kingdom of God. The beloved ideal of Jesus became a vague phrase which kept intruding from the New Testament. Like Cinderella in the kitchen, it saw the other great dogmas furbished up for the ball, but no prince of theology restored it to its rightful place. The Reformation, too, brought no (renascence) of the doctrine of the Kingdom; it had only eschatological value, or was defined in blurred phrases borrowed from the Church."[13] Theology was now concerned "and by its theoretical discussions did its best to stimulate sacramental actions and priestly importance. Thus the religious energy and enthusiasm which might have saved mankind from its great sins, were used up in hearing and endowing masses, or in maintaining competitive church organizations, while mankind is still stuck in the mud. There are nations in which the ethical condition of the masses is the

[13] Walter Rauschenbusch, *A Theology for the Social Gospel* (New York: The Macmillan Company, 1917), pp. 132-33.

odd reverse of the frequency of the masses in the churches."[14]

When the doctrine of the church became a substitute for the doctrine of the kingdom, we witness a fall of Christianity. When the church arrogates to itself and to sinful men the prerogatives that belong to the kingdom of God, we have reached a state of idolatry. The temporal power of the church must not be substituted for the kingdom of God. Furthermore, we are unalterably opposed to the proposition that the church should be established as a temporal power. We insist upon the separation of church and state, from both the point of view of the New Testament and our democratic institutions. We are not willing that an ecclesiastical hierarchy, as such, shall exercise temporal power. To be sure, such separation of church and state is functional, and both of these orders have their origin in God's will and ought to function in accordance with his will. It will always be the function of the church to leaven thought and action for its members for the affairs of the state, and if the church fails at this point the state will become a law unto itself and religion will become irrelevant for the social sphere. However, this is something entirely different than to vest the church with temporal power and make it the administrator of programs. The temporal power of the church during the Middle Ages and in more modern times does not inspire us with any degree of enthusiasm to vest the church with temporal power. Temporal power for the church has usually been an evil, not only in connection with Romanism but, also, wherever it has existed. In emphasizing the social relevance of Christianity, we are not proposing a church-state ideal; nor the situation in Calvin's Geneva experiment, in which he tried to make the invisible sovereignty of God as tangible and visible as the Medieval church had been. We are not advocating the type of sovereignty involved in the

[14] *Ibid.*, p. 134.

various historical attempts to establish theocracies. We are rejecting all attempts to place temporal power in the hands of the church. The church has only one sword and that sword is "the sword of the Spirit, which is the word of God: . . ."[15] Through witnessing to that word the church makes its primary social impact.

The identification of the church and the kingdom appears in Luther, also, and it is not surprising that he was unable to divest himself completely of his medieval background. When, in his Catechism, he interprets the Second Petition of the Lord's Prayer, he certainly does not identify the church with the kingdom; but in his "Answer to the Celebrated Romanist at Leipzig" he makes this mistake. He has spoken of the unity of the church as being not an external unity and then, by way of substantiation, he quotes the words of Christ to Pilate when Christ said, "My kingdom is not of this world." Then Luther adds, "This is indeed a clear passage, in which the Church is made separate from all temporal communities, as not being anything external."[16] That Luther, in this connection, confused the kingdom and the church is evident in that he fails to make a distinction between the two.

Bishop Aulen makes the same mistake. He says, "Just as impossible as it is to think about the church apart from Christ, it is to think about Christ—the Lord—apart from his area of sovereignty, or apart from the communion which belongs to him. Where Christ is, there is the church. The sentence can also be turned around: where the church is, there is Christ. . . . Christ has taken form in his church. . . . The church is, under earthly circumstances, the living and continuously active form for the revelation of Christ."[17] He also says, "The church can be described as the kingdom of

[15] Eph. 6:17.
[16] *PE*, I, 349.
[17] Aulen, *op. cit.*, p. 362.

Christ, regnum Christi, as it exists under earthly conditions."[18] There is also a tendency in Aulen's work to identify the empirical organization with the church.[19] As he looks over this Romanizing precipice, he finds it difficult to maintain his balance and says, "But it means that faith does not lose the insight as to what it is that makes the church a church."[20] I am not disposed to attribute to the "regnum Christi" some of the things that I know from the history of the church.

To make the kingdom synonymous with the church is to make the church what it is not. If we substitute the word "church" wherever "kingdom" occurs in the Gospels, we soon discover it is impossible to identify the church with the kingdom.[21] The situation becomes just as absurd if we substitute the word "kingdom" where the word "church" occurs.[22] The church is important and it is a means (and an indispensable means) by which God advances the goals of the kingdom, but it does not have the central place that the kingdom of God had in the thinking of Jesus. We must not minimize the significance of the church, but we must set our doctrine of the church in the framework of the doctrine of the kingdom. Without the doctrine of the kingdom of God we may have systems of redemption and humanistic ethical systems, but we shall find it difficult to establish any organic relationship between them and the social order.

In a great many treatises on dogmatic theology, the kingdom of God is scarcely mentioned. A cursory look at the indices to the works on systematic theology will reveal this. Often when the phrase is used the author reveals his lack of understanding of the meaning of the kingdom of God. Often

[18] *Ibid.*, p. 361.
[19] *Ibid.*, p. 367 ff.
[20] *Ibid.*, p. 369.
[21] *See* Matt. 3:2; Mark 1:15; Matt. 5:3; and Luke 12:32.
[22] *See* Matt. 18:17.

the kingdom is identified with the church and this is, perhaps, the most common mistake. Walter Rauschenbusch enumerates a list of consequences which follow any loss of emphasis upon the kingdom of God. He says "the church then moves up into the position of the supreme good. The conscience of the church is then often muzzled, for the kingdom is the test and corrective of the influence of the church. Without a consciousness of the kingdom the church may become a reactionary social force, as it is the kingdom that contains the revolutionary force of Christianity. Movements for social justice are left without a religious backing when the kingdom idea is lost. Secular life is often belittled as compared with services rendered in and through the church. The church without the idea of the kingdom tends to breed priests and theologians while it is the vision of the kingdom which breeds prophets. Without the kingdom there may be an emphasis on worship in the church without righteousness."[23]

Even so early in the church's history as the time of formulation of the ecumenical creeds, the kingdom of God was relegated to a position subordinate to the church's. The Nicene Creed says of Jesus Christ that his "kingdom shall have no end." Note the eschatological emphasis in this one instance where the kingdom is mentioned. The significance of the kingdom for the social order can be gathered only by implication. Likewise, most of the hymnals of the church have had very little to say about the kingdom. The new Service Book and Hymnal of the Lutheran Church in America has the merit of having one section of hymns devoted to the kingdom of God, even though it contains only eight hymns. There are also a number of prayers in this book which deal with the kingdom and the social concerns of the Christian and the church. One deserves to be quoted in full

[23] Rauschenbusch, *Theology . . . Social Gospel,* pp. 133 ff.

because it is something rather new in the history of Lutheranism. It reads:

> "O Lord, who hast set before us a great hope that thy kingdom shall come on earth, and hast taught us to pray for its coming: Make us ever ready to thank thee for the signs of its dawning, and to pray and work for the perfect day when thy will shall be done, on earth as it is in heaven; who livest and reigneth with the Father and the Holy Ghost, one God, world without end. *Amen.*"[24]

The church and the kingdom are not identical concepts or realities. It is the primary function of the church to witness, by Word and by life, to the presence of the kingdom.[25] Even the sacraments, from Luther's point of view, are related to the Word. He says the scripture does not say "A righteous man shall live by the sacraments, but 'by his faith'; for it is not the sacraments, but faith in the sacraments, that gives life and righteousness." He further says that "a man can become righteous by faith without bodily reception of the sacraments, so long as he does not despise them; but without faith no sacrament is of any use, nay, it is altogether deadly and pernicious. . . . Now, as we plainly see, God deals with us in no other way than by His holy Word and the sacraments, which are like signs or seals of His Word."[26] For Luther, the Word was central, even in the worship service of the church. He says, "The principal part is to preach and teach God's Word." The fundamental task of the church is to witness through the Word to the world. And even the sacraments are like signs and seals of this Word. As a witness, the church will become the "salt of the earth" and the "light of the world."[27] However, it must bear witness to something

[24] *Service Book and Hymnal* (Minneapolis, etc.: Augsburg Publishing House, etc., 1958), p. 227.

[25] Acts 1:8. [26] *PE,* III, 19 ff.

[27] Matt. 5:13, 14.

beyond itself. We cannot measure the success of the church in terms of membership statistics. The kingdom imposes on the church a task of social responsibility, and if the church fails to witness to the state, with respect to its ethics and morals, who shall perform the task? The mission of the church is to witness to the Word of God, and wherever and whenever moral issues are at stake it must speak even to the state. The church has the Word, and this Word is relevant to the affairs of that "order of creation" which we designate the state.

Relation of Church and State

That matters of state are definitely matters which concern the church, has been abundantly demonstrated in our generation. The rise of various forms of fascism and communism in the modern world have impressed upon the church the fact that it cannot ignore the form the state assumes. Both of these movements are secular forms of religion. They demand wholehearted obedience to authority. They offer a gospel of salvation for the individual and for society; they worship their heroes as Saviors; they have their authoritative writings, dogmas, and some measure of cult; they elicit devotion and self-sacrifice; there is an intense partisanship and missionary zeal; there are martyrs, holy wars, and vivid apocalyptic hopes. These are the marks of religions which seek the allegiance of mankind. They are ways of life; and unless the Christian faith meets them with its faith as a way of life, the challenge will not be met at all. People are asking what relevancy the Christian faith has for life, and unless we give an answer the church will be ignored.

As we look at history we find four different relationships manifested with respect to the relation of the church to the state. The state, at times, has been hostile to the church.

Before the days of Constantine, the state often persecuted the church; and this has also been true at other times as well as in modern times. At other times, the state has dominated the church. The Old Byzantine Empire, czarist Russia, and some Protestant countries of Europe are examples. The absurdity of this relationship is illustrated by the principle *cuius regio eius religio,* under which the inhabitants of the Rhenish Palatinate had to change their religion four times in sixty years. Vital religion cannot flourish where people are forced to adopt the religion of the monarch.

A third relationship has existed under which the church has dominated the state. This has been an ideal striven for by the Church of Rome, and at times it has been attained. We have already rejected this attitude as an ideal to be striven for. A fourth relationship has maintained the separation and independence of church and state. This is the ideal for which the constitution of our land stands, and which was inherent in the principles of the Reformation of the sixteenth century.

The words of Jesus, ". . . Render therefore unto Caesar the things that are Caesar's; and unto God the things that are God's,"[28] have often been quoted as a proof-text in support of the doctrine of the separation of church and state. The passage does imply the existence of two separate realms, but it has often been forced to carry more meaning than it did on the lips of Jesus.

At the time of Jesus there were at least three attitudes to Rome on the part of Jews. One party was revolutionary and ready to raise the banner of revolt if favorable circumstances presented themselves. A second party was complacent and well satisfied with the situation as it was. A third group felt uncomfortable under Roman domination, but chose peace by submission. Jesus took the part of the third group,

[28] Matt. 22:21.

and what he meant by the statement quoted above was that the Jews should pay their taxes to Caesar as long as God could be worshiped and served by them. Jesus realized that revolution against Rome would be fatal and futile. He also realized that because Jerusalem would not consider "the things that make for peace," but would keep on looking for a chance to revolt, it would be destroyed.[29] Jesus never said —and never implied—that the church has nothing to do with the social order or with the state. Such an implication cannot be drawn from his words, in the interest of a quietistic type of piety.

The state is a political unit. It is the political unit which makes and enforces law. As we have defined the church above, in its true essence the church is not a political unit. If these definitions of the church and state are maintained, church and state are separate by their very nature. On the basis of these definitions, we say not only that church and state ought to be separate, we say they *are* separate. There are two different realms: the one church, the other state. The state and the church have two different functions and these functions must not be confused. The doctrine of the separation of church and state is based upon a recognition of separate functions for church and state.

This does not mean the church is not concerned with the problems of society or the state. Members of the church function in the state, and it is incumbent upon them to strive to function, in this capacity, as Christians. Furthermore, the church must interpret the will of God to the state. The church has an obligation, in the name of God, to speak to the state, for the state is also God's order. In addition, it is the duty of the church to enlighten the conscience of its membership so the will of God may be accomplished in the social realm. There are two realms, and church and state have

[29] Luke 19:41-42, R.S.V.

separate functions, but these realms are not parallel lines which never meet. They constantly cross each other and, while it is the province of the state to wield temporal power, it is the province of the church to speak to the state, in the name of God, with respect to his will.

We are not interested in developing a theocracy, in gaining temporal power for the church, in permitting the state to use the church as a tool, or in having the church function as a political unit. We are concerned that the church act as a leaven for human thought and action so the spirit of the Christian faith may permeate the social order. When we speak of Christianizing the state, we do not mean writing the name of God or Christ into the constitution of the land. What we do want is an incorporation of the spirit of our faith in our laws, in our political life, and in our social programs. We want to apply the norm of the last lecture in all the various relationships of life, individually and socially. This is the meaning of Christian social responsibility.

Class Structure and the Church

If the church is to bear the kind of witness suggested above, it will mean broadening the meaning of the term "evangelism." Evangelism will not be simply a preaching mission on a revivalistic note. Christians must be made to understand that evangelism involves the impact of Christian ideas and ideals on every aspect of man's daily living. The labor union or the farm organization may be the stage for an effective evangelism in the measure in which Christian ideals are presented and put into action. If this is to be done, it will be imperative for the church to be cognizant of, and sympathetic to, the needs of all classes of men. It is at this point that preaching and teaching must be made relevant, if they are to have an appeal to man.

One of the great problems which the church faces, in this connection, is one which goes way back to the beginnings of the industrial era. It is a problem particularly for the Protestant church. The church has tended to be dominated by a bourgeois psychology, and this has alienated—to a large extent—whole classes of people.

This problem is not confined to America; it is discovered on the continent of Europe and in the Scandinavian countries. In one of Europe's theological schools, a survey recently was made of the occupational backgrounds of the students' families. Of the 344 questioned, only nine came from industrial workers' families. Eleven came from farms, 120 from employers' or managers' families, and 103 came from families of a professional nature. In another school it was found that out of a group of 173 students, only two came from homes where the father was an industrial worker and only five came from farms. If the overwhelming number of leaders in the church come from the bourgeois segment of society, it is a very serious matter and should lead to earnest self-examination on the part of the church. Various movements of a Christian character in postwar Germany indicate how keenly some of the leadership in the church feels this problem. I refer to such movements as the Kirchentag, the Evangelical Academy, and the "Evangelische Männerarbeit der Evangelischen Kirche in Deutschland."

In America we do not like to talk about classes in society, but the fact remains that they do exist. Sociologists recognize three classes, with various subdivisions. The upper class involves about three per cent of the population, the middle class includes about forty per cent, and the lower class about fifty-seven per cent.[30] It is not difficult to determine which class is dominant in the church when we notice the locations

[30] Joseph Alan Kahl, *The American Class Structure* (New York: Rinehart and Company, Inc., 1957).

which our Protestant churches choose when they move from the inner city areas. As far back as 1884 the *Andover Review* stated that it is "by no means altogether a result of evil that the churches stand for what is respectable and even refined, nor within proper limits, that certain lines of social cleavage appear in the group of people in denominations and in the several churches. Let the fact be recognized, then, that as the church has the better classes of society, it will be disliked by the worse classes who are yet outside."[31]

Kahl, in his study of the class structure of our country, says, "Even churches—institutions supposedly rejoicing in the common brotherhood of a common Father, are class typed. In most American towns the people of higher status belong to those Protestant denominations that feature services of quiet dignity and restrained emotion . . . The common men are more often seen . . . where the services are more vigorous, or in Catholic churches, (reflecting their origins from southern or eastern Europe). Those lower-class individuals who go to church at all are most likely to join revivalistic and fundamentalist sects. Some authors believe that the higher status groups are expressing, in ritual and dogma, attitudes of conformity and support for the good life within the current social system; whereas the religions of the lower status people are offering a palliative for failure in this life through salvation in the next."[32]

Class distinctions have reference to a cultural type. Class is, among other things, a matter of psychology and a sense of belonging. The middle class, which is so characteristic of large sections of the church, has an easily recognizable set of attitudes. The middle-class person usually lives in a suburb, in a home which he owns, though there may be a mortgage on the house. His pleasures usually revolve around material

[31] Henry Farnham May, *Protestant Churches and Industrial America* (New York: Harper and Brothers, 1949), pp. 120-21.
[32] *Ibid.*, pp. 149-50.

things and comforts. He has a certain sense of security and tries to provide for his retirement and the education of his children. He is individualistic in his economic theories. He hates bureaucracy and regimentation. Social welfare must never be allowed to restrict his economic theories and liberties. He believes that laissez faire made America great. He is suspicious of, and sometimes negative, in his attitude to labor unions. Labor leaders and their motives are suspect. He believes in honesty, thrift, efficiency, and hard work. He is usually affiliated with a church; and even though the faith of the church does not affect him very seriously, he believes in insurance even if he should never cash in on it. In business relationships, he is hardheaded but usually willing to contribute to charitable and community causes. He believes in his class and is confident that it is the depository of the national ideal. In the measure that his Christian faith touches his economic theories, it issues in an emphasis upon stewardship, vocation, and charity. However, the social patterns in which those virtues are to manifest themselves give him very little concern. Reflecting this view of life, his political theories tend to be conservative as he seeks to maintain the status quo in the situation and environment of which he is a part.

Middle-class people may be so isolated from the underprivileged groups of society that they fail to understand the problems and the needs of these groups, and therefore lack a sense of social responsibility to them. It should be pointed out, also, that general denominational statistics do not reveal the class structure of the church, because it is on the level of the individual church that the stratification appears most clearly. If the church is to take its social responsibility seriously, it will be up to the local congregation to create an atmosphere where all classes feel welcome and at home. The laboring man has often been alienated—from the church and the formal expression of the Christian faith in the church—because the church has lost touch with and lacks sympathetic understanding of his problems.

A Social Creed

Throughout its existence, the Federal Council of the Churches of Christ in America manifested a great deal of interest in the social aspects of the Christian faith. Early in the century, a social creed was adopted; and it was revised from time to time as new social problems developed. With few exceptions the social creed confines itself to the enunciation of principles. It is a remarkable document and indicates clearly what a Christian social order implies. This creed is still a significant expression of a sense of social responsibility.

It says the churches should stand for:

1. Practical application of the Christian principle of social well-being to the acquisition and use of wealth; subordination of speculation and the profit motive to the creative and cooperative spirit.

2. Social planning and control of the credit and monetary systems and the economic processes for the common good.

3. The right of all to the opportunity of self-maintenance; a wider and fairer distribution of wealth; a living wage, as a minimum, and above this a just share for the worker in the product of industry and agriculture.

4. Safeguarding of all workers, urban and rural, against harmful conditions of labor and occupational injury and disease.

5. Social insurance against sickness, accident, want in old age, and unemployment.

6. Reduction of hours of labor as the general productivity of industry increases; release from employment at least one day in seven, with a shorter working week in prospect.

7. Such special regulation of the conditions of work of women as shall safeguard their welfare and that of the family and the community.

8. The right of employes and employers alike to organize for collective bargaining and social action; protection of both in the exercise of this right; the obligation of both to work for the public good; encouragement of co-operatives and other organizations among farmers and other groups.

9. Abolition of child labor; adequate provision for the protection, education, spiritual nurture, and wholesome recreation of every child.

10. Protection of the family by the single standard of purity; educational preparation for marriage, home-making, and parenthood.

11. Economic justice for the farmer in legislation, financing of agriculture, transportation, and the price of farm products as compared with the cost of machinery and other commodities which he must buy.

12. Extension of the primary cultural opportunities and social services now enjoyed by the urban populations, to the farm family.

13. Protection of the individual and society from the social, economic, and moral waste of any traffic in intoxicants and habit-forming drugs.

14. Application of the Christian principle of redemption to treatment of offenders; reform of penal and correctional methods and institutions, and criminal court procedure.

15. Justice, opportunity, and equal rights for all; mutual good will and cooperation among racial, economic, and religious groups.

16. Repudiation of war, drastic reduction of armaments, participation in international agencies for the peaceable settlement of all controversies; the building of a co-operative world order.

17. Recognition and maintenance of the rights and responsibilities of free speech, free assembly, and a free press; the encouragement of free communication of mind with mind as essential to the discovery of truth.[33]

This consensus on the social responsibility of the church is one of the most significant documents on the subject in the history of the American church; and it is still, after almost three decades, a vital guide for social action. Note that this creed advocated, in principle, many of the goals which have been realized through legislation, and advocated them long before legislation was enacted. A practical course on social ethics might be given with this creed as an outline. The creed illustrates what it means to apply Christianity to the social order. It points to the kind of a world which would be possible if the Christian faith were seriously applied to the problems of society.

[33] Herman C. Weber (ed.), *Yearbook of American Churches,* "A Record of Religious Activities in the United States for the Year 1932," Issued under the auspices of the Federal Council of the Churches of Christ in America (1933 ed., Los Altos, California: Round Table Press, Inc., 1916-), pp. 319-20.

Appendix A
AUGUSTANA SOCIAL STATEMENTS

Church and State:

1952 Opposition to appointing a Vatican ambassador
1957 Privacy of confession
1958 Christians active in politics
1960 Catholic as president

Economic Affairs, Labor:

1939 Oxford conference—worth of labor
1952 Social Security Act to include ministers
1954 Ministry to industrial workers
1958 Labor corruption, danger of bias

Gambling:

1938 Opposition to gambling, church raffles

Human Relations:

1948 Prejudice rejected, equal rights urged
1956 Non-violence commended, Supreme Court upheld
1958 Previous stance affirmed

International Affairs, War, Peace, Draft:

1939 War is power of sin, not justified

1941 Conscientious Objector status sought for Augustana members
1942 To work toward just and lasting peace
1946 To choose life, not revenge, after war
1947 To fight Marxist Communist propaganda
1948 To work for international organization
1948 Concern over Universal Military Training
1952 To defeat Universal Military Training
1954 McCarthyism attacked
1956 Opposition to arms race
1957 Opposition to military bases, etc.
1957 To end nuclear testing

Leisure:

1950 Dancing allowed at college
1954 National Lutheran Council asked to promote wholesome radio and TV
1960 Films
1960 Sabbath

Marriage and Family:

1939 Birth control
1957 Opposition to pre-nuptial agreement

Temperance:

1938 Opposition to alcohol, liquor traffic

Appendix B
CHRONOLOGY OF ALVIN DANIEL MATTSON

1895	Born November 24 in Bloomington, Illinois. Son of Pastor J. A. Mattson and Anna C. nee Carlson. J. A. came from Värmland, Sweden, in 1869, attended Gustavus Adolphus College and Augustana Seminary, was ordained at St. Peter, Minnesota, in 1894, and served parishes in a number of states and Canada.
1913	Graduated from Manson, Iowa, High School.
1916	Augustana College B.A.
1918	Married Freda A. Anderson of Manson, Iowa, on May 23.
1919	Augustana Seminary graduation. Ordained in Lindsborg, Kansas.
1919-20	First parish in Avoca, Minnesota.
1921-24	Second parish, St. James, Minnesota. Dr. L. H. Beck accepted a call to a neighboring parish, influenced Mattson to attend Yale Divinity School.

1923 S.T.M. granted from Augustana Seminary: "The Tools of Christianity."

1924-26 Third call, to East and West Sveadahl, Minnesota.

1926-28 Served West Haven and Ansonia, Connecticut, parishes in order to attend Yale Divinity School.

1926-28 Graduate work at Yale Divinity School.

1928 S.T.D. granted from Augustana Seminary: "Knowledge, Emotion, and the Will in Religious Experience."

1928-29 Taught at Upsala College, New Jersey, and served college church.

1929-31 Professor of Christianity, Augustana College.

1931-65 Professor of Sociology and Ethics, Augustana Seminary, which merged into the Lutheran School of Theology at Chicago. The seminary did not move to Chicago until 1967.

1934 Addressed the American Lutheran Conference: "The Kingdom of God and Society." Conference voted to establish a Commission on Social Relations, of which Mattson was a member.

Mattson granted tenure at Augustana Seminary, installed as permanent professor, November 11. Address: "The Kingdom of God."

1935 Mattson considered a call to Wilmar, Minnesota.

1936 Trip with W. Uphaus and others to investigate the sharecropper situation in the South.

Vocal support of Franklin Roosevelt.

Augustana's preliminary Commission on Morals and Social Problems approved at convention.

1937 Trip with Uphaus to the West.

1938 Publication of *Christian Ethics*, revised 1947.

First trip to Russia with Jerome Davis.

1939 Considered call to Gethsemane Lutheran Church, Seattle, Washington.

1939-48 Served on board of the Augustana Book Concern, president of board for three years.

1941 Published *Polity of the Augustana Lutheran Synod*, revised in 1952 and titled *Polity of the Augustana Lutheran Church*.

Considered position in Minneapolis, Minnesota.

1941-46 Consultant on rural parishes for the Augustana Synod.

1944 Published *Mid-West Rural Churches of the Lutheran Augustana Synod*, revised in 1946 and titled *Town and Country Churches*.

1945 Published *The Meaning of Baptism for a Lutheran*, still available from Fortress Press, Philadelphia.

1948 Chairman of Quad-City campaign for Henry Wallace, introducing Wallace at Wharton Field House in Moline, Illinois.

Considered running as a Democrat for U.S. Congress.

1950 Consultant, Religious Affairs (labor), West Germany.

1957 Second trip to Russia with Jerome Davis, with group from Promoting an Enduring Peace.

Publication of *Christian Social Consciousness*.

1960 Joined other Lutherans in public endorsement of John F. Kennedy.

Supported the union at John Deere.

Gave Knubel-Miller lectures, *The Social Responsibility of Christians*.

1962 Supported Larry Halvorson, who was arrested for demonstrating for integration in Georgia.

Honored by AFL-CIO.

1965 Appointed to Social Trends Committee of the National Lutheran Council.

Retired, presented with letters of appreciation from students, former students, colleagues, and faculty members.

1966 Honored by Lutheran School of Theology at Chicago, testimonial given by U.S. Senator Paul H. Douglas.

Aided Douglas in his final senatorial campaign.

1970 Died on October 19 in Bemidji, Minnesota. Buried on October 23, Riverside Cemetery, Moline, Illinois. Memorial service (following burial) at St. John's Lutheran Church, Rock Island, Illinois.

Appendix C

FAMILY TREES

Lutheran Church in America

and

The American Lutheran Church

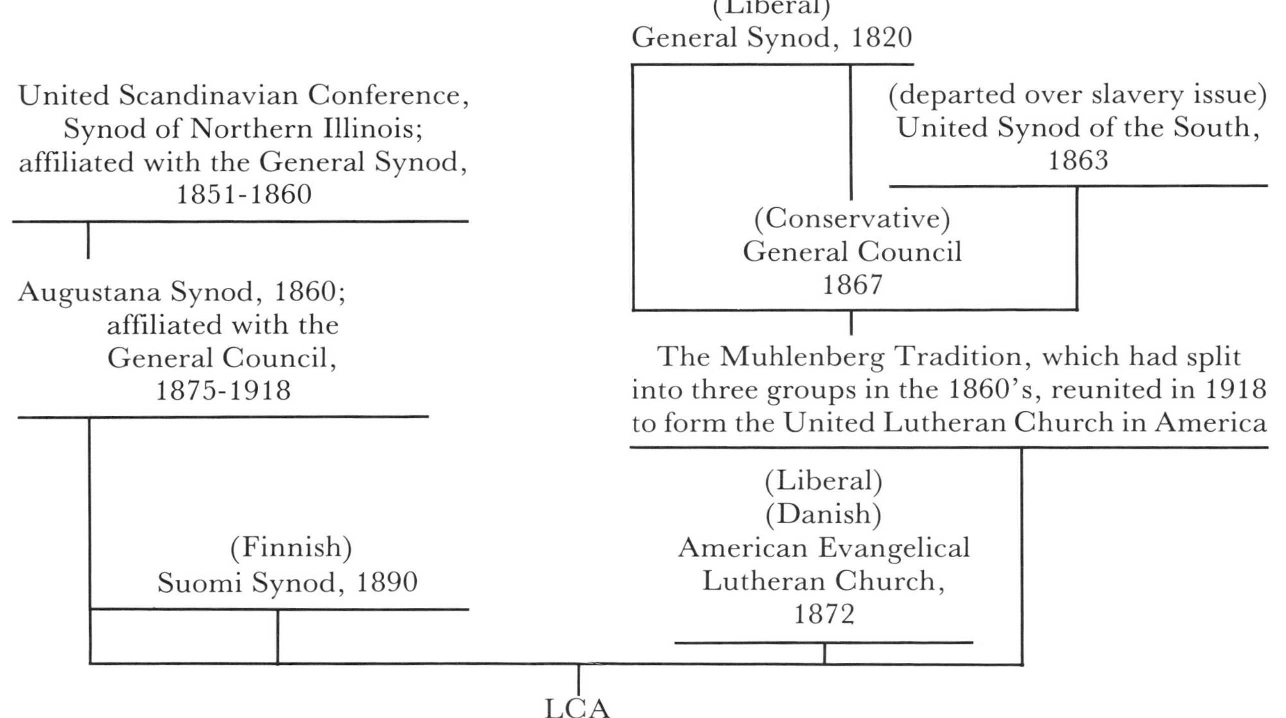
LUTHERAN CHURCH IN AMERICA, 1962
(Liberal)
General Synod, 1820
United Scandinavian Conference, Synod of Northern Illinois; affiliated with the General Synod, 1851-1860
(departed over slavery issue)
United Synod of the South, 1863
(Conservative)
General Council
1867
Augustana Synod, 1860; affiliated with the General Council, 1875-1918
The Muhlenberg Tradition, which had split into three groups in the 1860's, reunited in 1918 to form the United Lutheran Church in America
(Liberal)
(Danish)
American Evangelical Lutheran Church, 1872
(Finnish)
Suomi Synod, 1890
LCA

THE AMERICAN LUTHERAN CHURCH, 1960

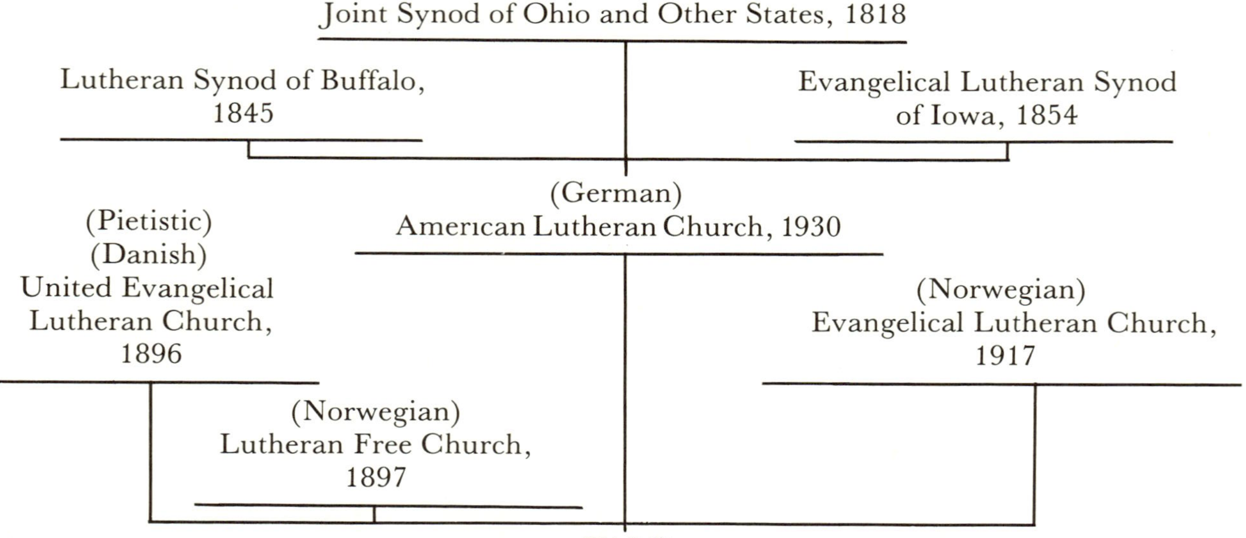

The National Lutheran Council included all the groups on the previous pages, as constituted, 1918-1966. The Lutheran Council/USA was formed in 1966 to include the Lutheran Church-Missouri Synod.

The American Lutheran Conference, 1930-1954, included the groups on the previous pages but excluded the ULCA as a way of moderating between the conservative LCMS and the liberal ULCA. Suomi did not participate in the American Lutheran Conference.

NOTES

Preface

1. Emil Fischer, ''Some Values of the Social Gospel,'' *Lutheran Church Quarterly*, III (1930), p. 129.

2. The term ''Social Gospel'' had a late origin and did not occur in most of the writings of those known as early leaders, such as Richard Ely and Washington Gladden. A community established in Georgia by George D. Herron published a journal in 1898 named *The Social Gospel*. The term was not generally used until fifteen years later, but the magazine popularized the name. When Rauschenbusch used Social Gospel in the title of his 1917 Taylor lectures at Yale, the term became permanent. Ronald Cedric White, *The Social Gospel: Religion and Reform in Changing America* (Philadelphia, 1976), p. 176. C. Howard Hopkins, *The Rise of the Social Gospel in American Protestantism* (New Haven, 1940), pp. 196f. Hereafter cited as: Hopkins, *The Social Gospel*.
Joseph Sitler, ''Social Gospel,'' *Lutheran Encyclopedia*, III (Minneapolis, 1965), pp. 219f. John Daniels, ''Social Gospel,'' *Lutheran Cyclopedia*, (St. Louis, 1975), p. 722.

3. Alvin Daniel Mattson, ''The Kingdom of God and Society,'' *Lutheran Companion*, XLII (1934), p. 1478.

4. Alvin Daniel Mattson, *The Social Responsibility of Christians* (Philadelphia, 1960), pp. 107-109. Hereafter cited as: Mattson, *Social Responsibility*.

5. Interview with Karl E. Mattson, July 25, 1963. Cited in Lloyd Svendsbye, ''The History of a Developing Social Responsibility among Lutherans in America,'' (Unpublished doctoral dissertation, Union Theological Seminary, 1966), p. 290. Hereafter cited as: Svendsbye, ''Social Responsibility.'' Biographical summaries of all Augustana Seminary graduates are given in Conrad Bergendoff, *The Augustana Ministerium* 1850-1962 (Rock Island, 1980). Hereafter cited as: Bergendoff, *Ministerium*.

6. Harold H. Lentz, ''History of the Social Gospel in the General Synod of the Lutheran Church in America, 1867-1918.'' (Unpublished doctoral dissertation, Yale University, 1943). Hereafter cited as: Lentz, ''General Synod.'' Note the Lutheran church geneology in Appendix C.

Part I: Mattson's Career and Theology

1. Archives of the Lutheran Church in America, Lutheran School of Theology and Ruth Mattson Taylor.

2. Karl E. Mattson, "The Theological Pilgrimage," *The Seminary Review* (1964), p. 30. Hereafter cited as: K. Mattson, "Pilgrimage."

Mattson was a prankster. When he was in high school, he led a cow up to the second floor of a school one Halloween night. The cow would not budge the next day and had to be removed by a crane through a window. Phone interview with Lydia Mattson Wanland, January 5, 1982.

3. K. Mattson, "Pilgrimage," p. 30.

4. Conrad Bergendoff, "Augustana—A People in Transition," *The Swedish Immigrant Community in Transition*, ed. J. I. Dowie and E. M. Espelie (Rock Island, 1963), pp. 201-202.

5. Byron Ralph Swanson, "Conrad Bergendoff: The Making of an Ecumenist," (Unpublished doctoral dissertation, Princeton Theological Seminary, 1970), pp. 139f. Hereafter cited as: Swanson, "Bergendoff."

6. G. Everett Arden, *The School of the Prophets: The Background and History of Augustana Theological Seminary, 1860-1960* (Rock Island, 1960), pp. 32f. Hereafter cited as: Arden, *Prophets*.

7. Karl E. Mattson, "The Theology of the Augustana Lutheran Church," *Centennial Essays*, ed. Emmer Engberg, Conrad Bergendoff, Edgar Carlson (Rock Island, 1960), p. 47.

8. Interview with Glenn C. Stone, August 8, 1979.

9. Alvin Daniel Mattson, "The Theological Currents in Augustana History," source and date unknown. Mattson Correspondence Files. Hereafter cited as: Mattson, "Currents."

10. Mattson took over Lindberg's polity course, rewrote the textbook, and introduced Augustana's new social statements through the textbook. Alvin Daniel Mattson, *Polity of the Augustana Lutheran Church* (Rock Island, 1941).

11. *Ibid.*, p. 210. The attacks on Söderblom worked against the Missouri Synod rather than Hult. Augustana was still within the sphere of Missouri's confessional stance, but Augustana leaders resented being chastised for welcoming Söderblom when he visited America. Later, Missouri president Frederick Pfotenhauer publicly attacked Augustana Synod president G. A. Brandelle for joining the American Lutheran Conference. This attack and Bergendoff's influence made Augustana open to merger with the ULCA. Swanson, "Bergendoff," pp. 108, 208; G. Everett Arden, *Augustana Heritage: A History of the Augustana Lutheran Church* (Rock Island, 1963), p. 296. Hereafter cited as Arden, *Heritage*.

12. Swanson, "Bergendoff," p. 211.

13. Mattson, "Currents," p. 15.

14. *Ibid.*

15. *Ibid.*

16. C. A. Wendell, *The Larger Vision, A Study of the Evolution Theory in its Relation to the Christian Faith* (Minneapolis, 1923); C. J. Södergren, *Fundamentalists and Modernists* (Rock Island, 1925); and Arden, *Heritage*, pp. 286f.

17. Arden, *Heritage*, p. 285. Mattson exposed his students to the theory of evolution through lectures by Fritiof Fryxell, an Augustana geology professor.

18. C. J. Södergren, *Is the Bible Alive?* and *Is Jesus God?* (Rock Island, n.d.).

19. Arden, *Heritage*, p. 286.

20. E. Clifford Nelson, *Lutheranism in North America, 1914-1970* (Minneapolis, 1972), p. 180. Hereafter cited as: Nelson, *Lutheranism.*

21. C. J. Södergren, "The Church and the Social Problem," *Augustana Quarterly*, IV (1925), p. 143.

22. *Ibid.*, p. 147. Södergren was the first Augustana leader to (1) reject Fundamentalism as un-Lutheran; (2) advocate a Christian response (other than Inner Mission) to social problems; and (3) propose a more inclusive style of Lutheran fellowship.

23. Alvin Daniel, Junior, died in 1971. Ruth Elaine (Taylor) lives in South Portland, Maine.

24. K. Mattson, "Pilgrimage," p. 31.

25. Mattson, "Currents," p. 13.

26. Mattson, "Pilgrimage," pp. 31ff.

27. Alvin Daniel Mattson, "Objects and Opportunities of the Luther League," *Lutheran Companion*, XXIX (1921), p. 552.

28. Alvin Daniel Mattson, "What Kind of Theology Should We Promulgate?" *Lutheran Companion*, XXXII (1924), p. 57.

30. *Ibid.* Mattson's courses at Yale Divinity School were: Philosophy of Religion, Systematic Theology, Modern Theological Seminar, all taught by Douglas Macintosh; Psychology of Religion, by Luther A. Weigle; and Pauline Epistles, Synoptic Gospels, by Benjamin W. Bacon. Detra J. MacDougall (YDS registrar) to Gregory L. Jackson, n.d.

31. Leigh D. Jordahl, "American Lutheranism: Ethos, Style, and Polity," *The Lutheran Church in North American Life*, ed. John E. Groh, Robert H. Smith (St. Louis, 1979), pp. 47f.

32. Richard D. Weigle, *The Glory Days* (New York, 1976), p. 69.

33. Roland Bainton, *Yale and the Ministry* (New Haven, 1957), p. 263. Hereafter cited as: Bainton, *Yale.*

34. Some of the letters were routine requests for information about a prospective student. Weigle also wrote to encourage Mattson not to quit his seminary post. Luther A. Weigle to A. D. Mattson, March 9, 1936. Mattson Correspondence Files.

35. Earl Mattson finished at Yale in 1934 and was ordained in 1935 in the Augustana Synod. Karl E. Mattson was ordained in 1930, earned an S.T.M. degree from Union Theological Seminary, served Bethesda in New Haven from 1939-1945, was elected president of the New England Conference of the Augustana Synod in 1945, and became dean of Augustana Seminary in 1948. Bergendoff, *Ministerium*, pp. 125, 138.

36. Vergilius Ferm, *The Crisis in American Theology* (New York, 1927), p. viii.

37. Bainton, *Yale*, p. 227. Mattson's dissertation cannot be located.

38. Bainton, *Yale*, p. 229.

39. Svendsbye, "Social Responsibility," pp. 83, 101.

40. Douglas C. Macintosh, *Social Religion* (New York, 1939).

41. Alvin Daniel Mattson, *Christian Ethics* (Rock Island, 1938), p. 62. Hereafter cited as: Mattson, *Ethics*.

42. Glenn C. Stone to Gregory L. Jackson, April 12, 1979. Arden lists economic, social and religious factors for people leaving Sweden, but does not mention the draft, *Heritage*, pp. 12ff, pp. 11-66.

43. Conrad Bergendoff to Gregory L. Jackson, March 6, 1979.

44. Robert Calhoun to Gregory L. Jackson, January 12, 1979.

45. Charles Reynolds Brown, *The Social Message of the Modern Pulpit* (New York, 1912).

46. "Scholarship and the Ministry," *Christian Century*, LIV (1937), p. 737.

47. Robert Calhoun to Gregory L. Jackson, January 12, 1979.

48. Roland Bainton to Gregory L. Jackson, February 10, 1979.

49. "Yale Drops Professor Jerome Davis," *Christian Century*, LIII (1936), pp. 1445f. "The Jerome Davis Case," *Christian Century*, LIII (1936), p. 1680. *Christian Century* concluded that Davis was too controversial and that the charge "unscholarly" was trumped up to justify the purge. "Yale on Trial," *New Republic*, LXXXIX (1936), was a special edition. However, Bainton himself voted against tenure, on scholarly grounds.

50. Willard Uphaus to A. D. Mattson. Mattson Correspondence Files. The turmoil is explained below on p. 47.

51. Willard Uphaus, *Commitment* (New York, 1963), p. 73.

52. "Dr. Weigle, Dean of Yale Divinity School, made the observation that a man of 33 years old should begin his lifelong task." K. Mattson, "Pilgrimage," p. 32.

53. Swanson, "Bergendoff," p. 331.

54. Stephenson, *Religious Aspects*, p. 342.

55. Arden, *Heritage*, p. 284.

56. L. H. Beck, a non-conformist in the synod, might have helped in his way. Luther Weigle had no authority in the synod, but he encouraged Mattson.

57. George Stephenson to A. D. Mattson, February 28, 1931. Mattson Correspondence Files.

58. C. A. Wendell to A. D. Mattson, March 6, 1931. Mattson Correspondence Files.

59. C. J. Södergren to A. D. Mattson, March 2, 1931, Mattson Correspondence Files.

60. *Ibid.*

61. *Ibid.*

62. George Stephenson to A. D. Mattson, February 28, 1931. Mattson Correspondence Files.

63. Vergilius Ferm to A. D. Mattson, November 14, 1934. Mattson Correspondence Files. Rauschenbusch, *Social Gospel*, p. 137. See below, pp. 51-52.

64. C. J. Södergren to A. D. Mattson, December 19, 1935. Mattson Correspondence Files.

65. C. J. Södergren to A. D. Mattson, March 20, 1934. Mattson Correspondence Files.

66. A. D. Mattson to Vergilius Ferm, December 1, 1934. Mattson Correspondence Files.

67. Mattson Correspondence Files.

68. Luther A. Weigle to A. D. Mattson, March 9, 1936. Mattson Correspondence Files. L. H. Beck to A. D. Mattson, March 15, 1936. Mattson Correspondence Files.

69. P. O. Bersell to A. D. Mattson, April 20, 1965. Retirement Letters.

70. Augustana Synod Convention Minutes, 1948.

71. C. J. Södergren to A. D. Mattson, March 3, 1931. Mattson Correspondence Files.

72. Mattson, *Ethics*, p. 15.

73. Carl Manfred to Gregory L. Jackson, February 9, 1979.

74. Arden, *Prophets*, p. 221; Swanson, "Bergendoff;" and Alvin Daniel Mattson, *Christian Social Consciousness* (Rock Island, 1953), pp. 100, 152. Hereafter cited as: Mattson, *Social Consciousness*. Söderblom won the Nobel Peace Prize in 1930.

75. Anders B. Hanson, letter published in *Concordia*, October 1, 1966. *Concordia* was published by the seminarians at Augustana.

76. Nels F. S. Ferre to A. D. Mattson, July 20, 1940. Mattson Correspondence Files.

77 .Conrad E. Lindberg, *Syllabus of Lutheran Church Polity* (Rock Island, 1927).

78. The lectures were given at various Lutheran seminaries across the United States. Alvin Daniel Mattson, *The Social Responsibility of Christians* (Philadelphia, 1960). Hereafter cited as: Mattson, *Social Responsibility*.

79. All of Mattson's books were published by the Augustana Book Concern in Rock Island, Illinois (owned by the Augustana Synod), with the exception of the Knubel-Miller Lectures, *Social Responsibility*, published by the ULCA.

80. Mattson, *Social Responsibility*, pp. 71f.

81. Mattson, *Ethics*, p. 90. Marxist ethical debate in Eastern Europe turned on this issue.

82. Mattson, *Social Consciousness*, p. 70.

83. *Ibid.*, p. 74.

84. *Ibid.*

85. Mattson, *Ethics*, p. 87.

86. *Ibid.*, p. 117.

87. *Ibid.*, p. 2.

88. *Ibid.*, p. 127.

89. Weigle was a Kant scholar. Weigle, *Glory Days*, pp. 18f.

90. Rauschenbusch, *Social Gospel*, pp. 274f.

91. Alvin Daniel Mattson, "Priest or Prophet?" *Lutheran Companion*, XLIV (1936), p. 746.

92. E. E. Ryden, Jr. to Gregory L. Jackson, May 19, 1979.

93. Mattson, *Social Consciousness*, p. 76. Rauschenbusch, *Social Gospel*, pp. 274ff.

94. *Ibid.*, p. 78.

95. *Ibid.*, p. 82.

96. Archives of the Lutheran Church of America. Lutheran School of Theology at Chicago.

97. Alvin Daniel Mattson, "The Kingdom of God," *Lutheran Companion*, XLII (1934), p. 1478.

98. Mattson, *Social Responsibility*, p. 46.

99. *Ibid.*, pp. 46f. Rauschenbusch, *Social Gospel*, p. 131.

100. Mattson, *Social Consciousness*, pp. 106f.

101. *Ibid.*, pp. 96ff.

102. *Ibid.*, p. 103.

103. *Ibid.*, p. 105.

104. *Ibid.*, p. 103.

105. Harm to others was the basis for the first Augustana commission statement on gambling.

106. Philip S. Watson, "Luther and Sanctification," *Concordia Theological Monthly*, XXX (1959), pp. 243-259.

107. John P. Milton. Mattson Correspondence Files.

108. Watson, "Luther and Sanctification."

109. Mattson, *Ethics*, p. 155.

110. *Ibid.*

111. *Ibid.*

112. *Ibid.*, p. 157.

113. Mattson, *Social Consciousness*, p. 76.

114. Rauschenbusch, *Social Order*, p. 93.

115. Mattson, *Ethics*, p. 175.

116. *Ibid.*, p. 176.

117. *Ibid.*, p. 180.

118. *Ibid.*, p. 181. Seminary professor S. Sibelius had grave doubts about the conference; Arden, *Heritage*, pp. 304f; Mattson, *Social Consciousness*, pp. 100, 152f.

119. Mattson, *Social Consciousness*, pp. 106f.

120. *Ibid.*, p. 107.

121. *Ibid.*

122. *Ibid.*, p. 109.

123. *Ibid.*

124. *Ibid.*, p. 114.

125. *Ibid.*, pp. 116f.

126. *Ibid.*, pp. 118f.

127. *Ibid.*, p. 126.

128. *Ibid.*, p. 187.

129. Mattson, *Social Responsibility*, p. 37. H. Reinhold Niebuhr, *An Interpretation of Christian Ethics* (New York, 1935), preface.

130. Mattson, *Social Responsibility*, p. 20. Mattson, *Social Consciousness*, p. 16.

131. Mattson, *Social Responsibility*, p. 15.

132. Mattson, *Ethics*, p. 50.

133. *Ibid.*, pp. 50f.

134. *Ibid.*, p. 53.

135. Mattson, *Social Responsibility*, p. 159.

136. Mattson, *Social Consciousness*, p. 165.

137. Mattson, *Ethics*, p. 314.

138. Rauschenbusch also made many laudatory references to cooperatives in his works.

139. He knew Douglas as a professor at the University of Chicago, corresponding with him at that time. Mattson Correspondence Files. Mattson was known at the University of Chicago (where Douglas taught) as the only Lutheran who knew what was happening in the world. Glenn C. Stone to Gregory L. Jackson, August 8, 1979.

140. Mattson Correspondence Files.

141. Harold Metcalf, "At Rock Island," (letter to the editor), *Christian Century*, LIII (1936), p. 1724.

142. Carl Lund-Quist to A. D. Mattson, December 1, 1938. Mattson Correspondence Files. Karl John Mattson (the son of Karl E. Mattson) to Gregory L. Jackson, April 3, 1979.

143. Myron Lindblom to A. D. Mattson, September 11, 1941. Mattson Correspondence Files.

144. Malvin Lundeen to A. D. Mattson, May 19, 1944. Mattson Correspondence Files.

145. Oscar Benson to A. D. Mattson, February 18, 1948. Mattson Correspondence Files. Benson was later the president of the Augustana Synod.

146. P. O. Bersell to Ivar Johnson, December 11, 1947. Mattson Correspondence Files.

147. A. D. Mattson to R. Leekley, March 8, 1948. Mattson Correspondence Files.

148. Henry Timbrook to A. D. Mattson, June 1, 1960. Mattson Correspondence Files.

149. Malvin Lundeen to A. D. Mattson, November 14, 1960. Mattson Correspondence Files.

150. A. D. Mattson to Malvin Lundeen, November 19, 1960. Mattson Correspondence Files.

151. Eric J. Gustavson, "Alvin Daniel Mattson, A Tribute," *The Seminary Review*, XVI (1964), pp. 28f.

152. Theodore Swanson to Gregory L. Jackson, April 22, 1979. Granger Westberg to Gregory L. Jackson, March 5, 1979.

153. Mattson, *Social Consciousness*, p. 257.

154. *Ibid.*, p. 255.

155. Karl John Mattson to Gregory L. Jackson, April 3, 1979.

156. Henry Arp to A. D. Mattson, November 11, 1936. Mattson Correspondence Files.

157. Filed under C. J. Esbjörn, Mattson Correspondence Files, 1936. Esbjörn was a leading Augustana layman, according to Arden, *Heritage*, p. 223.

158. P. O. Bersell to Rock Island couple, carbon, April 1, 1948. Mattson Correspondence Files.

159. A. D. Mattson to P. O. Bersell, January 14, 1948. Mattson Correspondence Files.

160. P. O. Bersell to A. D. Mattson, January 15, 1948. Mattson Correspondence Files.

161. A. D. Mattson to P. O. Bersell, January 17, 1948. Mattson Correspondence Files.

162. Newspaper clipping, November 6, 1960. Mattson Correspondence Files.

163. Malvin Lundeen to A. D. Mattson, November 7, 1960. Mattson Correspondence Files.

164. Malvin Lundeen, "The Church and Political Endorsements," *Lutheran Companion*, CVI (1960), p. 3. Hereafter cited as: Lundeen, "Church."

165. *Ibid.*

166. *Social Pronouncements of the Augustana Lutheran Church 1937-1962* (New York, n.d.), p. 10. Hereafter cited as: *Pronouncements*.

167. Lundeen, "Church."

168. Mattson's letter to the editor, *Lutheran Companion*. Mattson Correspondence Files.

169. Clipping in Mattson Correspondence Files. Ahlen was a friend of Mattson. At the time, most Lutherans felt that the Republican Party and Lutheran orthodoxy were synonymous. A. C. M. Ahlen to Gregory L. Jackson, April 5, 1979.

170. Norman A. Hjelm to A. D. Mattson, November 8, 1960. This was the only friendly letter in the Kennedy file of the Mattson Correspondence Files.

171. Svendsbye, "Social Responsibility."

172. Mattson, *Social Responsibility*, p. 217.

173. *Ibid.*, p. 214.

174. S. E. Engstrom to A. D. Mattson, February 10, 1943. Mattson Correspondence Files.

175. Alvin Daniel Mattson, *Mid-West Rural Churches of the Lutheran Augustana Synod* (Rock Island, 1944). Hereafter cited as: Mattson, *Rural Churches*.

176. A. D. Mattson to S. E. Engstrom, February 16, 1951. Mattson Correspondence Files.

177. S. E. Engstrom to A. D. Mattson, January 31, 1952. Mattson Correspondence Files.

178. Mattson, *Ethics*, p. 331.

179. *Ibid.*

180. *Ibid.*, p. 333.

181. Jerome Davis to A. D. Mattson, March 9, 1956. Mattson Correspondence Files.

182. Mattson Correspondence Files.

183. Archives of the Lutheran Church in America. Lutheran School of Theology at Chicago.

184. Pastor Allen C. Nelson. *Ibid.* The hymn quoted, written by F. M. North, was a favorite of the Social Gospel movement. *Lutheran Book of Worship* (Philadelphia, 1978), hymn #429.

185. *Witness From Beyond*, ed. Ruth Mattson Taylor (New York, 1975). The book has been widely publicized and is almost universally known among Mattson's former students. Olof Olsson (1848-1900) resigned as professor at Augustana after being attacked for publishing an untraditional view of the afterlife, after his wife died in 1887. However, he served as college president, 1891-1900. Bergendoff, *Augustana: A Profession of Faith: A History of Augustana College, 1860-1935* (Rock Island, 1979), p. 83.

186. *Ibid.*, p. 10.

187. Richard Baltzell to A. D. Mattson, November 11, 1955. Mattson Correspondence Files.

Part II: Mattson's Influence and Future Implications for Lutherans

1. H. Conrad Hoyer to Gregory L. Jackson, February 2, 1979.
2. Wilton E. Bergstrand to Gregory L. Jackson, March 6, 1979.
3. *Ibid.*
4. Arthur O. Arnold to Gregory L. Jackson, February 5, 1979.
5. Lawrence H. Holt to Gregory L. Jackson, February 5, 1979.
6. J. Erik Holmer to Gregory L. Jackson, n.d.
7. Carl L. Manfred to Gregory L. Jackson, February 9, 1979.

8. Richard Olson to Gregory L. Jackson, March 22, 1979.

9. E. Theodore Bachmann to Gregory L. Jackson, February 7, 1979. One of Bachmann's best students was Robert J. Marshall, later the LCA president.

10. Frederick Wentz, "Parachutes Among the Pyramids," *The Lutheran*, XVII (1979), pp. 12-14.

11. Mattson Correspondence Files.

12. Mattson, *Social Consciousness*, p. 12.

13. Charles V. Bergstrom to Gregory L. Jackson, February 14, 1979.

14. Robert Lowell Anderson, "The Awakening Social Consciousness of the Lutheran Church in America Since World War I with Special Reference to the Augustana Synod," (Unpublished master's thesis, Union Theological Seminary, 1959), p. 122. Hereafter cited as: Anderson, "Awakening."

15. Charles V. Bergstrom to Gregory L. Jackson, February 14, 1979.

16. James David Ford to Gregory L. Jackson, February 27, 1981.

17. Anderson, "Awakening," pp. 147f.

18. Bernard Spong to Gregory L. Jackson, April 8, 1979.

19. F. Jan Bengston to Gregory L. Jackson, n.d.

20. Arthur M. Holmer to Gregory L. Jackson, February 2, 1979.

21. Note the comments about Nasstrom and Mattson by Louis Almen, below. LC/USA was an agency which united certain efforts of the LCA, ALC, and Missouri Synods.

22. John A. Nasstrom to Gregory L. Jackson, March 30, 1979.

23. Carl W. Segerhammar to Gregory L. Jackson, February 21, 1979. John A. Nasstrom to Gregory L. Jackson, March 30, 1979.

24. Glenn C. Stone to Gregory L. Jackson, February 19, 1979.

25. Edgar M. Carlson to Gregory L. Jackson, February 19, 1979.

26. N. Everett Hedeen to Gregory L. Jackson, n.d.

27. Dick Fallow to Gregory L. Jackson, February 8, 1979.

28. Cecil Quails to Gregory L. Jackson, May 9, 1979.

29. Theodore N. Swanson to Gregory L. Jackson, April 22, 1979.

30. Charles De Vries, *Inside Rural America: A Lutheran View* (Chicago, 1962), p. 9.

31. *Ibid.*, p. 10.

32. G. Adolph Johns to A. D. Mattson, April 29, 1979. Mattson Correspondence Files.

33. Eric Wahlstrom to Gregory L. Jackson, February 19, 1979.

34. Eric J. Gustavson to A. D. Mattson, August 4, 1937. Mattson Correspondence Files. Gustavson spoke at Mattson's retirement dinner and published the Mattson bibliography.

35. Richard A. Olson to Gregory L. Jackson, April 9, 1979.

36. Gerald Nelson to A. D. Mattson, April 20, 1965. Retirement Letters.

37. "A Time for Burning," Lutheran Film Associates, 1966.

38. L. William Youngdahl to A. D. Mattson, April 22, 1965. Retirement Letters.

39. Reuben Swanson to A. D. Mattson, April 14, 1965. Retirement Letters.

40. Reuben Swanson to Gregory L. Jackson, March 5, 1979.

41. Paul V. Bergren to Gregory L. Jackson, March 6, 1979.

42. *Lutheran Book of Worship* (Philadelphia, 1978), hymn #429. Frank M. North, the author of the hymn, was also the author of the Methodist Social Creed, which was adapted for the Federal Council of Churches' Social Creed.

43. Constantine Trued, who has retired from Immanuel, said that Mattson exerted a profound influence on his ministry. Interview, May 20, 1980.

44. Glenn C. Stone, editor of *Lutheran Forum*, grew up at Salem.

45. Philip A. Johnson, *Call Me Neighbor, Call Me Friend* (New York, 1965).

46. Norman Nelson to Gregory L. Jackson, April 28, 1979.

47. Karl J. Mattson to Gregory L. Jackson, April 3, 1979.

48. Mattson Correspondence Files.

49. Interview with Arthur O. Arnold, 1979.

50. Arthur M. Holmer to Gregory L. Jackson, February 2, 1979. Joel Lundeen to Gregory L. Jackson, February 8, 1979.

51. Louis T. Almen to Gregory L. Jackson, March 22, 1979.

52. David Vikner to Gregory L. Jackson, April 16, 1979.

53. David Vikner, "Mission Is...Not" (Philadelphia, 1979). The same statement was printed in the LCA's *World Encounter* magazine, Spring, 1979.

54. H. Conrad Hoyer to Gregory L. Jackson, February 2, 1979.

55. A.G. Fjellman to Gregory L. Jackson, March 1, 1979.

56. A. G. Fjellman to A. D. Mattson, April 15, 1965. Retirement Letters.

57. Raymond J. Lingwall to A. D. Mattson, April 20, 1965. Retirement Letters.

58. Eric H. Wahlstrom to Gregory L. Jackson, February 19, 1979.

59. Some of Augustana's Social Statements, under Mattson, as listed in Appendix A of this book, were written as far back as 1938.

60. Harold Haas to Gregory L. Jackson, February 21, 1979. Harold Haas served as Executive Director of Tressler-Lutheran Service Associates, Camp Hill, PA.

61. Interview with Glenn C. Stone, August 8, 1979.

62. Louis T. Almen, "A Tribute," *LCA Partners*, 11 (1980), p. 7. Jacqueline Boynton, "Lettuce, Grapes, and Justice," *The Lutheran*, XVIII (1980), pp. 4-6.

63. A. D. Mattson to Vergilius Ferm, December 1, 1934. Mattson Correspondence Files.